Cultural Change and Everyday Life

Also by David Chaney:

Fictions of Collective Life
The Cultural Turn
Lifestyles

Cultural Change and Everyday Life

David Chaney

palgrave

First published 2002 by
PALGRAVE
Houndmills, Basingstoke, Hampshire RG21 6XS and
175 Fifth Avenue, New York, N.Y. 10010
Companies and representatives throughout the world

PALGRAVE is the new global academic imprint of
St. Martin's Press LLC Scholarly and Reference Division and
Palgrave Publishers Ltd (formerly Macmillan Press Ltd).

ISBN 0–333–76143–X hardcover
ISBN 0–333–76144–8 paperback

This book is printed on paper suitable for recycling and
made from fully managed and sustained forest sources.

A catalogue record for this book is available
from the British Library

Library of Congress Cataloging-in-Publication Data
Chaney, David, 1942–
    Cultural change and everyday life / David Chaney.
        p. cm.
    Includes bibliographical references and index.
    ISBN 0–333–76143–X (cloth)
    1. Social change. 2. Civilization, Modern–20th century. 3. Culture–Philosophy.
    I. Title.

HM831 .C43 2002
303.4–dc21   2001059201

10   9   8   7   6   5   4   3   2   1
11   10   09   08   07   06   05   04   03   02

Printed and bound in Great Britain by
Creative Print and Design (Wales), Ebbw Vale

Contents

Preface and Acknowledgements

In writing about cultural change and everyday life it has become apparent to me that the most significant feature of change in later modernity has been the diminution in the constraints and controls that typically structure ordinary life. As an example of the sort of thing I am thinking of, I can point to the now general indifference towards the moral conventions that ordained that heterosexual relationships should only be enjoyed by married couples. Not only are parents increasingly tolerant of their children's open sexual activity, couples can also live together without any sense of shame whether or not they become parents. This is not to say that marriage is discredited, as probably most couples aspire to be married and people are still congratulated when a marriage is announced; it is just that marriage is no longer felt to be necessary and a lack of married status no longer needs to be explained or apologised for or hidden.

Such a relaxation in moral controls might at first seem to be an indication that we as ordinary people have become freer. One immediate problem is, though, that freedom can be understood in at least two ways – negatively and positively. The negative understanding of freedom is that a moral order has been undermined so that individuals feel lost and alienated, unable to relate to each other except through competition. In contrast, the positive understanding of freedom is that individuals become more able to express themselves without the conventions or orthodoxies of repressive institutions. I will set out in the following chapters why I in fact do not believe that individuals in the less constrained social worlds of contemporary experience straightforwardly have more freedom in either of these senses.

What I am saying then is that although certain aspects of moral, social and political order have been relaxed, they have changed character rather than disappeared. More colourfully, the fabric of control and order in which everyday life is wrapped is changing its pattern. In particular, this means that how we understand everyday life is changing and the culture that gives our lives character and value is also changing. This book is about some of the trends in the emerging patterns of change. One of the key devices that I use to illuminate change is the idea that in order to understand a topic we have to be able to grasp it, or we could say picture it or represent it. I begin by arguing that everyday life in the modern era has been difficult to represent because it has appeared irrational in certain fundamental respects. Although the everyday has become a more explicit topic in later modernity, these new ways of representing it in practice have been important aspects of new strategies of control. Those who would resist control and maintain a struggle to achieve an advance in positive freedoms have in various ways often attempted to preserve or treat positively the irrationality of the everyday.

The book can then be read as a celebration of irrationality as a bulwark against the rationalising impetus that I take to be a defining feature of the progress of modernisation. This may well seem a shocking proposal. So ingrained is a commitment to rationality as the keystone of emancipation bequeathed to us by the Enlightenment that to turn away from it perhaps inevitably feels like an endorsement of superstition, prejudice and a reactionary refusal to explore human potential. What have been called the forces of conservatism have indeed used these irrational outlooks as ways of preserving privileges and fostering hatred and conflict between different social fractions. I can have nothing to do with such bigotry.

And yet a rationality that can spend time and money researching how better to make a chemical mixture that when dropped as a bomb will cling to the skin for as long as possible causing maximum damage; a rationality that takes it as a normal for someone seeking high political office in an 'advanced' democracy to be associated with skilful marketing of products to less sophisticated Third World societies knowing that they will cause lingering painful illnesses and death to large numbers of people; and a rationality that employs expertise to develop the production of raw materials in ways that have long-term destructive implications but maximise profits in the short term – these cannot be indices of progress and enlightenment. Not least because such a use of expertise more or less explicitly articulates taken-for-granted distinctions between them (to whom things can be done) and us who enjoy the privileges of mutual consideration.

Of course it can be argued that we need rationality to see the irrationalities of such policies, values and the deployment of expertise. But it seems equally clear that we cannot trust intellectuals and experts alone to act as guardians of the enlightened deployment of the skills of their peers; not least because they are almost certainly compromised in the labyrinths of the management of knowledge. In these circumstances we need to be able to step outside the presuppositions of rational discourse. We have to find other ways of being in the world that can nurture a sympathetic regard and respect for that which is unique in every living being and the most ordinary of situations. Rather than neglect the everyday as humdrum banality, I hope the discussion in this book will contribute to further consideration of how the everyday can act as a space for these other ways of being.

In writing this book I have as always enjoyed the company and support of friends and colleagues at the University of Durham. The work would not have been possible without the intellectual climate we all share; in particular a respect for independent thought, although sadly that is now being curtailed by an increasing concern by governmental interests with the management of creative work. I have also benefited from presenting ideas in papers to seminars and conferences both nationally and internationally. I am grateful to colleagues for receiving work-in-progress with respect and consideration and for the encouragement to continue. I am particularly grateful to my editor, Catherine Gray, who has put an enormous amount of work into both encouraging me to always aim for the best book possible and really helping me to bring out ideas that were initially even more imperfectly grasped. I am very conscious that in addition to the friends who are also colleagues I have enjoyed a great deal of love and support from a wider circle of friends. Although I do not think a list of names is appropriate I would like to say how much I have enjoyed their company and consideration. I have been particularly lucky in my everyday life while working on the book to have enjoyed the love and constant stimulation of Sophie, Rose, Jamie and Owen.

1

Introduction: Culture and Modern Life

Representing Everyday Life

In a newspaper article John Berger writes of paintings in the genre of still life by observing that this theme 'is a sedentary art, connected with the activity of keeping house.... Still lifes tell about how certain things have come together and, despite their evident ephemerality, will stay together. They are images of residence in every sense of the term' (2000, p. 12). The observation seems prescriptive rather than descriptive, but is even so relevant to studies of everyday life because still life is the genre in the 'high arts' that most directly concentrates on features of the everyday (Bryson 1990).[1] Berger's comments suggest that beneath the chance of mundane juxtaposition there might (or ought to) be an implicit order – a way of being together that he calls residence. Thus he goes on to write of two painters of still lifes that their art asks of each object: 'how is it there?' (ibid.). The question suggests a troubling difficulty for all attempts to represent everyday life – which is how we (that is both those who attempt to paint and those looking at paintings or any other mode of representation) know what this implicit order might or should be.

My book is about recent changes in popular experience. I begin from the questions of how we can get to know the character of any order to everyday life and appropriately represent what may be orderly or disorderly from different perspectives. Only then might we be able to trace the significance of change. In writing about the relationship of cultural change to everyday life, I am asking how the forms of order or residence in everyday life are changing as part of the development and elaboration of a culture of mass entertainment. The question is more difficult than it might seem because although the everyday is ordinary, in the modern era cultural change has made it uncertain and unreliable and harder to represent. It may seem silly to be puzzled by how to represent the everyday because it is so obvious, but it is like the old proverb about not being able to see the wood for the trees. We can all see the trees that immediately surround us but it hard to get a grip on the wood of which they are a part. I think this is why when sociologists have tried to write about everyday life their starting point has typically been a version of 'how is it possible?' So sociological

1

concern with everyday life has also asked about the possibility of an order containing the random flux of multitudinous happenings and doings.

It seems that in order to 'know' everyday life we have to be able to represent it; and our representations incline us towards certain sorts of knowledge. It may be that the forms of representation we are expected to use convey a sense of order that is possibly deliberately misleading, and thus actual experience of everyday life will be more open-ended and unpredictable than the imagery allows. Berger's use of a metaphor of neighbourliness to conjure the sort of order he is trying to describe is an example of persuasive language. Neighbours are more than people who are temporarily adjacent as in the case of people who are members of a bus queue. Being a neighbour or even more being a good neighbour implies a degree of moral obligation in everyday life. Being neighbourly may be displayed in a number of ways of course, but a good example is welcoming a newcomer to the locality with some food, preferably home cooked. There are, however, rights and responsibilities that flow from a commitment to neighbourliness which may become intrusive or even oppressive, although often thought preferable to an alternative of competitive individualism which some fear has become more likely in metropolitan life. Our language of representation and the sort of order we presume or try to find will shape our understanding of the character of everyday experience which straddles boundaries between public and private worlds.

I will not try to produce an overview of all the variety at different social levels and circumstances of what constitutes everyday life. Studies such as that by Bennett and his co-authors can provide fascinating insights into the social organisation of what they call 'everyday cultures' (Bennett et al. 1999), and mean by this patterns of taste amongst ordinary Australians; but they are, as they acknowledge, constrained by their methodology to a general overview. Publications such as *Social Trends* give even more fleeting glimpses (*Social Trends* 2000). Thus instead of such a survey I will point to forms of neighbourliness to illustrate how they relate individuals both to each other and to the more abstract collectivities of mass society. It is in this sense that I am concerned with how we represent and understand changing forms of the everyday. A pessimistic interpretation of change would suggest that Berger's intrinsic order has been swept away by tidal forces of mass culture which have robbed locality of any distinctiveness. While I recognise these tendencies I do not believe this is overwhelmingly true, and in the following chapters I will develop a different perspective. Neither, though, am I inclined to accept the alternative extreme position that everyday life has remained much the same beneath the froth of new forms of entertainment and leisure.

I am therefore concerned with the interpretation of change in the forms of order that structure and give meaning in the circumstances of daily interaction. I take it to be uncontroversial to assert that forms of order or neighbourliness are essential to the comfortable management of everyday life, and can then be called resources for practical actions; but they are also, like the welcoming pie in the earlier paragraph, ways of trying to symbolise or represent or dramatise the often disorderly experience of sociable life. A more complex way of putting this point that is important in ways that will become clearer as we progress is that *the social and cultural forms which make sense of everyday life do so practically for their inhabitants and as representations to be observed, enjoyed and interpreted as cultural performances.*

I fear that the term 'representation' may be becoming too 'baggy' or loose here, so I feel I need to backtrack a little to make clearer how representation is being used in this study. Sociologists tend to look for what they call a 'sociological perspective' in the work of students and colleagues. The use of this perspective is therefore a sort of craft skill, but it would be widely if ruefully recognised that in practice a definition of the ingredients of the skill is hard to find (Giddens 1982; Bauman 1990). It seems to me that one way of rendering this outlook is to describe it as an ingrained scepticism.[2] The consequence is that sociologists prefer to query the appearance of a situation or a person rather than treat it as self-evident. Thus to ask what that appearance masks, or how is the appearance put together or sustained, or what sort of interests are involved in making that appearance credible. The purpose of a sociological account is therefore to attempt to show that any social arrangement has not been arrived at 'naturally' in the sense of being an inevitable development (or even the consequence of biological or genetic inheritance), but has rather been produced probably in ways the actors concerned did not fully appreciate.

In previous publications I have suggested that the appearance or self-evident givenness of the social world can be helpfully understood as forms of fictional or dramatic production (1993). Although the development in recent years of cultural studies has not in general pursued this metaphor, it has encouraged a concern with the appearance of social life but now as a mode of representation (Tudor 1999). The metaphor of representation doubtless owes more to a filmic than a theatrical analogy, but it is more important to note that it also stems from the power of a concept of discourse which itself derives from certain theories of language. In brief, the founding outlook here is that the way something is (or in effect appears) is determined by how it is talked about (or conceived) – in effect how it is represented. Examples of how this representational outlook works can easily be found. For example (and these instances have been taken virtually at random from current publishers' catalogues), studies of how sport (Brookes 2001), race (Ferguson 1998) and masculinity (Spicer 2001) have been constructed as topics in cultural discourse all use a notion of representation to capture their analytic strategy (see also Hall 1997 for representation in cultural studies and Potter 1996 for issues in the representation of social reality).

It is not just that representation has become important as an analytic device, it is also generally held that it has become more important with the development of modernity. Reasons for this view will be set out more fully in the rest of the book, particularly the second chapter, so that for now I hope it is sufficient to point to two reasons. These are: a rise in the power and range of culture industries selling simulations (see for example Baudrillard 1983); and a feeling that the intensity of metropolitan life has put overwhelming emphasis on appearance (e.g. Simmel 1950). It should also be noted that an emphasis upon representation makes the identity of a person or an institution necessarily provisional; so that it follows that there will be political battles over how sexual, gendered and ethnic identities for example have been and are being constructed. Given the thrust of the basic perspective, it is unsurprising that studies of representation in general see themselves as 'deconstructing' (that is laying bare the artifice of) social phenomena.

Although I am not offering a conventional study in deconstruction, I begin with a notion of the representation of the everyday because I do feel that the normality of the everyday has masked that which is culturally problematic. Although the everyday is generally the bedrock of social reality, what can be taken for granted, I shall argue that in the development of modernity the possibility that Berger's intrinsic order in the everyday was no longer possible emerged. As this possibility raised questions about the practice of representation and any relationship between representation and experience that were/are deeply unsettling, the topic of the everyday was neglected. In essence because to raise questions about knowledge of the everyday threw any ability to know about or interpret social life into question. More recently, in later modernity the theme of the everyday has become considerably more prominent. But this does not mean that questions about who is representing for whom and why and how have been resolved. Issues about the legitimacy of representation remain crucial, and indeed I shall argue that how to articulate and represent the everyday is the main issue in the politics of culture. On the one hand between those who seek new modes of rationalisation to impose new forms of social order; and on the other hand those who seek to escape control by insisting on a lack of order in the everyday.[3] Therefore, I take the accomplishment of the everyday to be contentious in contemporary society for: ordinary people; and those who seek to represent social life in cultural imagery such as novels and paintings; and those who would seek to comment on how to interpret social life. These are three distinct 'projects' but it is crucial to my overall study to insist that in their common concern a fundamental aspect of cultural change is being revealed.

Cultural Change

I suggest that uncertainties about how everyday life is changing are related to developments in a culture of mass entertainment and therefore distinctive to the modern era. This is not to say that everyday life only came into existence in the modern era, but rather that the category of everyday life only becomes problematic then. Another way of putting this is to say that everyday life as a topic for social theory and as a theme for cultural representation was constituted in the modern era.[4] Crook (1998) has suggested that the discovery of the topic of the everyday for social thought was based in the radical interventions of the 1960s, and this perhaps supports my further argument that the topic and the ways it is envisaged and represented in commentaries and dramas has, and will continue to, become more significant in the cultural changes of later modernity. It is consistent with the increasing prominence of everyday life as a topic that it has come to feature more in the titles of recently published books, particularly in cultural studies (see for example Mackay 1997, Miller and McHoul 1998, Moores 2000, Silverstone 1994 and Storey 1999, although everyday life is usually not examined very critically in these studies).

It is important for my overall interpretation of change that why and how everyday life is becoming more significant should be understood and appreciated in relation to two processes I call radical democratisation and cultural fragmentation. I use radical in relation to democratisation to both indicate how forms of populism have become dominant in public discourse and to alert readers to the ironic possibility that this has not entailed any substantial popular emancipation.[5] Similarly, by using fragmentation in relation to culture I do not mean to imply that culture is becoming less important, quite the reverse, but rather that the authority of culture is increasingly dissipated and discredited.[6] Both of these processes have to be seen as aspects of a broader process of informalisation. This broader informalisation is then a blurring of many of the authority structures dominant in earlier phases of modernity. In terms of these processes the everyday is coming to dominate cultural discourse but is not thereby more 'transparent'.

Although I shall be specifically concerned with what I have called neighbourliness or the forms of residence of contemporary everyday life, more generally, I intend the book to introduce its readers to the sociology of cultural change in Britain at the end of the twentieth century. Although I use British experience as my primary point of reference, much of what I say will be relevant to all those societies we loosely lump together as 'post-industrial'. It is important to emphasise that I am concerned with the *sociology* of cultural change rather than attempting to describe the varieties of change in exhaustive detail. By the sociology I mean a way in which cultural change can be understood or interpreted through the forms of interpersonal interaction. More particularly, a sociological account is concerned with how cultural change is to be understood in the things people do and how the activities are organised and how those doings and forms of organisation are represented.

At the time of writing the air is full of worried speculation about the implications of new technologies that are creating virtual environments and relationships for new forms of commerce and entertainment (see for example Downey and McGuigan 1999, and van Dijk 1999, itself part of a tradition of futurology that has run through the modern era). My book is not a contribution to this tradition in the sense of adding to the speculation, but rather a more general interpretation of the meanings of change in late modern society that will provide some clues on how to understand ongoing cultural innovations. I believe that in doing this I am writing an innovative study of popular culture. Innovative in that it is concerned with the representations of popular experience in both staged and unstaged performances rather than just the features of those sorts of cultural productions oriented to popular or demotic tastes. There is an obvious affinity between the everyday and the popular such that one might believe the terms to be synonymous; and indeed some studies have been written as though popular culture is self-evidently the 'stuff' of everyday life (e.g. Cullen 1996). A further layer of obfuscation has been generated by those contributors to public discourse, principally but not exclusively politicians, who have claimed to be speaking from the everyday (or the real world) and to thereby claim to be more 'realistic' or commonsensical.[7]

The affinity between the everyday and the popular is that they both concern the lives of ordinary people. But popular culture is not necessarily a representation of popular experience. In fact very often popular culture has sought to provide entertainments that have been extra-ordinary, such as the feats of jugglers or magicians, the heightened emotions of the melodramatic stage, and the intensity of spectacular presentations in popular cinema. Of course these entertainments have been built into and become part of everyday life, but that does not mean that everyday concerns and values can be straightforwardly inferred from the dramatic narratives of cultural industries. If, as I shall argue, the topic of the everyday and the idioms of everyday experience have come to dominate popular culture in the later years of the modern era, then this poses further intriguing questions about why this is happening and the meaning of these representations.

A second reason why I am reluctant to equate the popular and the everyday too glibly is because I believe that popular cultural dramas and narratives interpenetrate other modes of representation in the everyday such as the social practices of shopping, eating and loving.[8] All together they provide forms of order and residence or visions of neighbourliness but these are understood differently from different social perspectives, not least from differences deriving from the by no means synonymous perspectives of men and women. Forms of neighbourliness are therefore means of social order as well as mediums of conflict, obfuscation and misrepresentation. In the imperfectly grasped practices of real life we are concerned with how the everyday gets invoked or staged or performed; the possibility of moral order does not imply an untroubled consensus or that meaning is confined to the self-evident. Thus the problematic uncertainty of the everyday is as much an issue in the practical representations of popular reality for ordinary people as well as in academic discourse.

What is Culture?

Everybody born in the twentieth century has been only too well aware of how new cultural industries such as television and tourism have generated unprecedented form of cultural change. For example, three instances of the distinctiveness of the changing cultural environment are: first, the cultural homogeneity of conventional experience has been broken up as Britain has become more multicultural. In part generated by waves of immigration, there has been a proliferation of indices of cultural diversity throughout the urban environment. If one adds to this the experiences of cultural diversity facilitated by mass tourism and regularly watched as part of a televisual diet, then familiarity with cultural variety has become standard rather than exceptional. Secondly, the means of entertainment for ordinary people have been vastly expanded by, amongst others, the development of television as a mass cultural form and the transformation of popular music using new means of recording and a proliferation of new styles of performance. Thirdly, an expansion in leisure time has not only changed the structure and rhythms of daily time but has also been associated with a new range of consumer goods and services facilitating leisure opportunities.

These types of change are very familiar, so that in referring to them it seems that I can use notions of culture unproblematically with the implication that what it is that is changing can be taken for granted.[9] Although I will continually point to different modes of change in order to explore their significance, I will in practice, as with the common sense of the everyday, need to begin with and keep returning to questions about the practice of representation. Culture is not a neutral or self-evident term but one that has been developed through an enormous overlapping literature of theoretical reflection, descriptive survey and ethnographic report. Culture has therefore been constituted in social theory, but it has also 'leaked out' beyond academic discourse to be used as a resource for making sense of perceived differences in ways of life and processes of change.

Culture has clearly been one of the basic bedrock concepts of social thought in the modern era. It has not only become a ubiquitous feature of social analysis; it has also spread beyond the sphere of professional concern to become a standard element in social commentary. As might be expected, such a widely used concept has acquired a variety of meanings, for example the commonly cited distinction between culture as artistic heritage either of a region or people or even humanity in general, and culture as a form of life with distinctive customs and values which is characteristic of a social group (Jenks 1993). Rather than try and prescribe a meaning for culture I will suggest three reasons for its significance in social thought. The first is that the concept claims an organisation to social life, which is more fundamental than the arrangements and contracts of voluntary agreement. Culture tells us that there is a distinctive way of doing things – painting a picture, making and eating a meal, and your expectations of children – which will be characteristic of a social group. As I suggested earlier, these distinctive forms of life are usually imbued with moral force, often as traditions, and they constitute a central element in group identity. These ways of doing things will therefore persist through generations; they will generally hold without discussion or question, and they display a level of group life that precedes individual experience.

Secondly, the idea of culture is significant because it is profoundly effective. Culture cannot fail to make sense of the variety of social life. Puzzled by an individual's behaviour we can relate it to their cultural background, and when seeking to illustrate cultural difference we can point to the distinctive features of representative individuals. Culture shows us that there is a level of collective existence and that it can be used to explain everyday experience (for example Hofstede 2000). Thirdly, culture has been significant because it offers a mode of explanation that potentially has infinite scope. What I mean by this is that if we can use a notion of culture to explain individual behaviour then not only is all behaviour, at least in principle, potentially explicable – another way of putting this is to say that everything is meaningful – but also the explanations need not be available to every member of society or indeed any of them. It becomes possible to offer an explanation as an outsider that 'transcends' native understandings. Such explanations are, however, clearly vulnerable to being criticised for being a mode of imperialism (see for example Clifford and Marcus 1986 and Atkinson 1990; on some of the advantages as well as difficulties of incorporating native understandings see Hertz 1997). The idea of culture therefore creates a level of discursive interpretation that is peculiarly the province of intellectuals and is capable of infinite intellectual elaboration and complexity.[10]

In combination, these reasons for the significance of culture all suggest the appropriateness of the concept for the modern era. When trade, colonisation and unprecedented migrations of peoples, both ordinary and elites, combined to make the normality of any locality extremely relative, then cultural difference became a necessary motif of ordering relations between groups. What this means in practice is that notions of culture – distinctiveness and difference – have been inextricably involved in structures of power both as legitimations of oppression and as resources for resistance (Hall and du Gay 1996; see also in relation to consumer culture Hearn and Roseneil 1999).

We can see this, for example, in the interrelationships between culture and nationhood. What I mean by the latter term is a compilation of (a) expressions of national identity (b) nationalism and (c) the possibility of national existence as a level of collective identity. For all these uses of a rhetoric of nation, the idea of a distinctive culture has been a necessary resource – a conceptual springboard for the imagination of national community (Cohen 1994; Cubitt 1998; Eley and Suny 1996; Hobsbawm 1990; and see also Smith 1998). A distinctive culture has not only meant heritage sites, heroes and their statues and national festivals but has also involved characteristic ways of life, thus in a sense inventing the everyday as a corollary of the invention of culture. It is also relevant to note that nationalist movements have been and are usually inspired by intellectual elites who have been active in discovering, inventing and articulating national cultural forms (see for example Handler 1988; Löfgren 1991; Macdonald 1993; Normand 2000).

If we recognise that the consciousness of culture is in effect an ideological intervention, so that there are necessarily a multiplicity of discursive and contested uses of culture, then culture becomes a resource in the production of social knowledge. I have already indicated that I think there are important continuities between forms of representation used in the fine arts, social theory, the dramas of popular entertainment and the practices of everyday life. In all these different ways of representing social experience we are struggling for viable forms of interpretation. But that does not mean that we know in advance, or can know independently, what it is that is being interpreted. The social determinist tradition, represented most fully in the varieties of Marxism, holds that culture stands for and is (ultimately) determined by the material production of social life, that is by independently knowable reality. The alternative to be explored in this book is that cultural forms as modes of institutionalised 'knowledge' are material practices that constitute, in part, the distinctiveness of local social experience.

The point I am making here reiterates that made previously, that ways of representing and knowing lived experience are the means through which that experience becomes 'doable' – or, more technically, cultural forms are reflexive in the practice of everyday life; that is: 'the methods people use to go about their ordinary affairs ... are identical to the methods they use that make those affairs *intelligible* and *accountable*'

(Miller and McHoul 1998, p. 20, emphasis in original). I will bring out in the following chapters why I believe that in the context of the social formation of late-modern Britain this intimate interdependence can be seen to be the basis for a process of cultural fragmentation; but first it is necessary to link these general notions of culture to the spheres of everyday life.

Everyday Life

In this introduction I will make some brief remarks on everyday life and develop the account more fully in the next two chapters. I assume everyday life to be the forms of life we routinely consider unremarkable and thus take for granted. The reality of habitual experience is provided in the routines or rhythms of occupations, relationships and residences. More generally there are frameworks of space and time that organise what is done when, with whom and where. Although across the varied circumstances of socially and culturally stratified Britain the details of what passes for everyday life will differ, there will be common expectations of 'a normality'.[11] Thus the normal is what can be relied upon or accomplished without a great deal of specific attention. It may well be thought of as dull and unexciting – even oppressive in the predictability of its routines – but it does not need to be specifically addressed as a source of problems or anxiety. Like walking down stairs, it can be 'done' routinely and only becomes strange or difficult if thought about too explicitly. And precisely because it is normal we will tend to assume that it is appropriate or even desirable. Breaking local expectations is usually seen to be distasteful and frequently provocative (and thus often exploited by self-conscious cultural radicals such as the young or artistic).[12]

The normal can therefore be described as what gives our lives order and stability – if considered we might think that it is the basis of meaningful experience. Particularly if we allow a further connotation in that the everyday is frequently considered to be natural or unaffected or artless. This is brought out well in the efforts of writers such as Ernest Hemingway or Raymond Carver to use everyday language and speech to tell their stories. Of course this simplicity – displayed in a lack of ornamentation or rhetorical flourish – masks the difficulty of achieving the effect, but it does convey a powerful facticity, almost inevitability, that has a convincing authenticity.[13] The idea that there is such a normality can be assumed to be a cultural universal (although obviously not what it is in specific settings). I believe, however, that in significant ways everyday life has come to consciousness in modernity (Featherstone has suggested in contrast to the prior ideal of a heroic life, 1992), in large part because there has been a general acceptance of the democratic imperative, that is that the people, or the popular will, should form the guiding spirit of public discourse.

And yet the neighbourliness of the everyday is as I have said not self-evident, so that the everyday and the popular have puzzlingly been both transparently present and troublingly opaque. The reason is that although the everyday is unremarkably present it is not a set of activities or even a structure of routines, but a way of investing those things with personal meaning.[14] Social theorists and the producers of cultural performances have found it difficult to adequately represent these meanings, and this might mean either that there have been deficiencies in their representational vocabularies or that there is some profound irrationality in modern experience which makes it resistant to interpretation.[15] In a subsequent chapter I will explain more clearly how the disorder, or what I will call the irrationality of everyday life, can be seen as the hidden topic of modernity. I will also develop an argument that says the neglect points to a fundamental incapacity to acknowledge the implications of popular democracy – because as I will argue everyday life has been generated in the cultural changes of modernity as inherent in the freedoms generated.

To describe everyday life as what makes experience meaningful and informs of notions what is desirable and valuable may seem to give it an undue importance. It is privileging the profane rather than the sacred – as I noted earlier Bryson (1990) accepts the still life as a minor genre both because of its subject matter and its association with female concerns. But the values of everyday life cannot be left out of more self-conscious considerations of social purpose and communal values. In an innovative instance of an earlier concern with making connections between the culture of the people and the rhythms of everyday life, Raymond Williams some years ago influentially insisted that culture is ordinary – it is how actors routinely make sense of their lives through forms of staging and performance (for Williams on culture see 1981; also Geertz 1975). As an intellectual challenge to ideologies and discursive traditions that had reserved culture as a privileged resource for social and intellectual elites, the move accomplished a lot in opening up neglected aspects of the formation of modernity (a great deal has now been published on this 'opening up' and the consequential development of cultural studies, see Chaney 1994, Chs. 1 and 2). I have already, however, set out some arguments why I do not believe it is appropriate to uncritically elide together the everyday and the popular.

My approach is therefore to see cultural change as both something accomplished and made manifest in the routines of ordinary (and extra-ordinary, see Chapter 8) experience, *and* how those routines are mediated (one could also say represented or articulated) in public discourses (including being fictionalised or staged). A consequence of the 'doubled' character of cultural change is that an exhaustive list or even quantification of lifestyle changes is necessary but not sufficient. Such an empirical account will give you a snapshot of change in action but not an interpretation of its significance. In order to do the latter one needs to be concerned with the form as well as the content of change. Quite what I mean by form and how it is important in the interdependence of cultural change and everyday life will be made clearer through the rest of the book. For now I hope it is sufficient to say that form here includes the structures of change in which I will include the implied members of the community or culture, their sense (concepts of identity) of themselves, and characteristic discourses and representations as well as their actions, habits and accomplishments.

I hope I can at this point then summarise the main themes in my narrative:

- First, I shall be concerned to show that everyday life became a theme in modernity, although it has resisted adequate representation for reasons I shall discuss in the following chapter. My account of these difficulties is abbreviated because my book is primarily concerned with developments in later modernity. I do though, in the third chapter, discuss the main traditions in the representation of everyday life in social theory. I have devoted a chapter to these traditions both because I am a social theorist and, more importantly, because I shall try to show that the 'non-rationality' of everyday life that social theory in general and sociology in particular has found so difficult to accommodate is central to later developments in representations of everyday life.
- This then brings me on to the second main theme of the book. This is that in contrast to its earlier neglect everyday life has become the dominant theme and idiom of cultural life in later modernity. In the remaining chapters I shall try to show both some of the forms of the shift in representation, as well as presenting reasons for the change and, in greater detail, consider the social and cultural implications of change. A central motif in the account will be an argument that many of the contemporary forms of representation of the everyday constitute ambiguously successful attempts to contain or commandeer the non-rationality of the everyday.

The Impact of Change

I am writing this book because I believe accounts of cultural change in modern societies have been concentrated to too great an extent on the features of the culture that have changed to the relative neglect of the implications of those changes for ordinary experience. I suppose it would be bizarre if studies of cultural change did not focus on different sorts of change, but the social consequences of those changes are not inevitable. This should not need saying, as for those writing in the human studies[16] it is a fundamental creed that technologies do not by themselves determine how they are to be used in different social settings (e.g. Flichy 1995; Silverstone and Hirsch 1992; Winston 1998). Rather, it has been accepted that the meaning of the technology is shaped by the context of competing expectations, interests and powers. It should also then follow that the ways in which the cultural forms of technological innovation are embedded in everyday life are equally 'constituted' in the context of competing and overlapping expectations, interests and powers.

In order to illustrate what I mean by popular expectations (and to show how they are simultaneously interpretations of social forms) I shall briefly list what I believe to be common expectations about what is important in everyday life. These are not meant to be exhaustive nor are they put in any order of importance, so that they will apply unevenly across a population while being widely shared.

- It is normal to seek to 'have a good time' which usually consists of being able to relax, not feel unduly constrained by either formal or informal conventions, have a laugh, be slightly (or considerably) self-indulgent and to be comfortable with one's companions.
- It is also normal to invest a great deal of emotional and practical energies in family relationships, so that the accumulation of new family generations is highly desirable, and in particular that children are treated as a form of sacred trust whose innocence must be protected and nurtured while simultaneously groomed as incipient social adults whose successes bring prestige to the family.
- Another common expectation is an assumption that the world, physically, culturally, historically, is available to be consumed and that the various ways of doing this are rewarding and life-enhancing.
- An obligation that is also an expectation that others will share is a responsibility to be as attractive as possible. This is not a set of universal values but is differentiated by lifestyles and thus local fashions, except that body maintenance, control and grooming are increasingly becoming unquestioned goods.
- This leads on to a further expectation of a desire to avoid pollution from contaminating noise, ugly sights, disease and the connotations of incompetence attached to the damaged. More positively, this expectation is associated with a search for stress-free environments, practical creativity and the connotations of nature and the natural.
- Finally, a further expectation about important concerns in everyday life is a responsibility to achieve some security both in personal terms and for significant others, particularly family members. Again there is another side to this value in that to be insecure whether emotionally, financially, in relations or practical matters is a source of great anxiety for the actors themselves or their significant others, generating a range of therapeutic services and interventions.

Some of these expectations will be rejected as inappropriate by particular groups, for others some will be inaccessible constituting forms of social exclusion, but in general they can be recognised as unproblematic ways of making sense of activities and relationships. My argument is that in the second half of the twentieth century these expectations increasingly have been articulated (and thus constituted) through what Dorothy Smith has called the 'materiality of consciousness'. A phrase I take to mean that consciousness is realised through artefacts, technologies and symbolic forms which provide the means for overlapping physical and virtual environments: 'The simple social acts of tuning in, ringing up and logging on can therefore have complex meanings for subjects.... In fact, what these practices point to is the way in which situated and mediated worlds constantly overlap in conditions of late modernity' (Moores 2000, p. 9). As Smith herself has said: 'Textually-mediated discourse is a distinctive feature of contemporary society, existing as socially organised communicative and interpretive practices intersecting with and structuring people's everyday worlds and contributing thereby to the organisation of the social relations of the economy and of the political process' (1988, pp. 40–1).

What this approach means is that through adopting, using, rejecting – that is selecting amongst – the performances, services and artefacts of mass culture industries practical understandings are institutionalised: 'I want to view "femininity" as a social organisation of relations among women and between women and men which is mediated by texts, that is, by the materially fixed forms of printed writing and images' (Smith 1988, p. 39). The media have thus in my view not determined our core expectations but have been essential resources in the embodiment or materialisation of those expectations.

It may also be helpful to suggest that we think of the 'products' of mass cultural industries less as texts or performances or services and more as environments. That is, they help to shape or constitute the frameworks of the everyday world. It is in the context of these frameworks that social identities – in all the different senses of individual, gendered, occupational, lifestyled and 'cultured', etc. – are established and re-established. The different ways in which who 'we' are are played out or performed is a characteristic feature of the solidity or taken-for-grantedness of everyday life and is accomplished through interaction with (or exploitation of) the facilities of mass culture industries. A further development of this approach is to say that if everyday life is intrinsically local then the borders of locality have been diffused or extended by engagements with mass culture industries which are incipiently global (Kellner 1995).

The boundaries of the 'normal' are thus being constantly expanded or changed by interactions with the exotic spectacles made available by mass culture industries. Everyday life is intrinsically local, because being grounded in the taken-for-granted setting of the here and now it is focused on the practical aspects of the matters in hand. Whereas, in contrast, mass culture industries deal in performances, services and artefacts that are either infinitely reproducible or their uniqueness can be marketed globally and thus they transcend local specificity. Textually mediated discourse is then always in a dynamic relationship between local perspectives and unanchored or free-floating signifiers. It is in the working out of these relationships that new discourses of signs and spaces are made manifest. Another illustration of changing environments is provided by the enormous expansion in telecommunications made possible by cheap mobile 'phones and expanded networks. Not only is the home no longer the conventional site for private or personal communication, but with the use of phone technology as an access point for electronic services available through the Internet individuals literally carry their global connections with them at all times. The boundaries of locality are now more arbitrarily defined.

As an example of the most fundamental shift in the institutional frameworks of everyday life, Giddens has written of the disembedding of time and space as characterising a phenomenology of modernity (1990). Phenomenology as philosophical method is off-putting for many readers as it implies deeply abstract arguments. It is relevant here though, as it captures a concern with how people engage in different sorts of experience, for, as Bull has said: 'Phenomenology is a method that permits an adequate understanding of users' habitual activities as it is attentive to the way in which social meanings are bedded down in individual forms of experience' (Bull 2000, p. 10). My own concern with the reframing of everyday life through representations in relation to the cultural changes of late modernity,[17] is an attempt at a phenomenological analysis oriented to the main objective of aiming: 'to articulate the qualitative nature of everyday life without limiting itself to localized description' (op. cit., p. 27). I hope in this chapter to have introduced readers to some of the issues in how we might go about articulating the qualitative nature of everyday life as it is represented in some aspects of cultural change. In the next two chapters I will be more specifically concerned with the topic of everyday life and how it has been represented in the modern era.

2

Everyday Life in the Modern Era

Modernity and Modernisation

I have so far introduced some issues in the interdependence of our conceptualisations of cultural change and everyday life. I have argued that culture is a conception of modernity (see for example Williams's discussion (1976)), although cultures can be found in, and indeed the concept was essentially invented for, pre- or non-modern social contexts. Thus, cultural institutions such as national museums, galleries, academies and other learned societies were largely founded in the era of the early-modern. It was also at this time that a distinctive elaboration of notions of the artist as a form of critical conscience of his (and it was almost entirely his) era was elaborated principally through romanticism. The artistic conscience may have posed as a critique of the dominant materialism of the time but was not necessarily a retreat from reality, as even the wilder flights of anguished authenticity proved compatible with a new more engaged observation of the realities of the social environment (Rosen and Zerner 1984). All these new forms of consciousness were the backdrop for my earlier assertion that the everyday as a sphere of social life only becomes problematic, or acquires a significance, in the context of better-known discourses of culture and modernity – a thesis I will develop in later sections of the chapter.

These developments in the self-conscious representation of human life in the modern era seem to me to necessitate a brief sketch of what I see to be the central features of the modern and later developments. I shall then in the concluding sections of the chapter turn more directly to the representation of the everyday. As with culture, the concept of the modern (and its variety of adaptations as in modernism, etc.) can be argued to be one of the fundamental resources of social thought. The importance of the idea of the modern does suggest that how it is to be understood is necessarily contentious (a classic account of the implications of the modern era is Giddens 1990; a more recent wide-ranging study is Jervis 1998; and see also Swingewood 1998). I will not therefore try to establish an authoritative interpretation but instead point to some basic features that seem generally accepted.

The modern is clearly a mode of social organisation that contrasts with some prior or preceding era that can be loosely characterised as traditional. This is not meant to suggest that there are only two basic types of social formation, but rather that the modern is a historical interpretation. It would be absurd to expect it to have begun at a specifiable date. There will have been a long process of transition, often referred to as the early-modern period, and the development of modern institutional characteristics should be described as processes of modernisation. I will mention three characteristics of institutional change that have commonly been mentioned as central to modernisation:

- The first is often called following Max Weber the process of disenchantment, although it clearly relates to but is probably not equivalent to secularisation. In the process of disenchantment features of the given world lose both their inevitability and any sense of magical properties. (I will in Chapter 8 look at some of the ways in which it has been suggested that aspects of cultural change have sought to re-enchant ordinary experience through forms of commercial magic.) Instead of imbuing their context with a life that makes it unpredictable and constantly needing to be propitiated, humans come to treat features of their environment as objects that can be mastered and manipulated through increasingly sophisticated technologies.
- A second characteristic is a process of institutional differentiation. What this means is that aspects of life such as work and leisure, education, religion, politics and policing of conduct become distinct spheres with their own normative expectations, discourses of expertise and systems of regulation. The process of differentiation generates a vast expansion of professional skills and training as well as a necessary specialisation that means an all-pervasive reliance upon an infrastructure of bureaucratic corporations both governmental and commercial.
- Finally, a third characteristic is a process of rationalisation which in a way combines aspects of both of the preceding characteristics. In essence the idea here is that the social world comes to be treated as something that can be rationally organised. Commercial and public bureaucracies increasingly administer the distinctive spheres of life by the use of sophisticated systems of storing information in order to effectively manage the more fragmented components of the larger-scale, less integrated, post-traditional society (Heelas et al. 1996).

These characteristics all suggest that in the transition from traditional to modern experience the boundaries to, or the horizon of, conventional social worlds are greatly expanded. The structures of order and control in small-scale integrated communal life based on a literal and visible neighbourliness are not lost, but increasingly subsumed in more impersonal

structures and networks of association. The best example is the development of a national police force with a standardised uniform, except for
minor local variations, authorised to both catch criminals and to be
responsible for the maintenance of civil peace. In the larger worlds of
nation states: social life was therefore more impersonal; governed by relevant expertise and policies, whether concerning social welfare or economic strategy, etc.; and could be assumed to be informed by rational
considerations. In this context it might be assumed that the sphere of
everyday life would also be increasingly rationalised.

Two more general processes that underlie these changes, help to make
them possible and stimulate their further development, are urbanisation
and industrialisation. By the first term we mean a process in which the
majority of the population come to live in large urban enclaves and the
growth of huge metropolitan centres in which new modes of community
necessarily develop with distinctive ways of life (Simmel in Frisby and
Featherstone 1997). The anonymity of the urban inhabitant allied to the
necessity for new forms of social etiquette in the metropolis provided a
significant inspiration for one of the major strands in the study of everyday
life described in the next chapter.

The second process of industrialisation not only means the use of new
technologies in the organisation of mass production to unprecedented
degrees, but also implies a standardisation of goods and services so that
local variations in custom, diet and entertainment gradually become
modifications of national norms rather than distinctively autonomous. In
the restructuring of social identities it is particularly significant that
urban–industrial societies generate new languages and themes of social
conflict organised around class consciousness. This in turn provides the
basis for the ideological organisation of political mobilisation through
trade unions and political parties. In all these ways the emergent worlds
of modern societies have been dependent upon technologies of communication, both physical and social, to facilitate means of interdependence
and integration on an unprecedented scale (Thompson 1995).

Of course processes of modernisation can be described from a variety of
perspectives. In what I have said so far I have sought to lay the basis for
an account of modernity – the practice of modern social life – in which the
distinctiveness of modern sociality is made the primary concern. What I
mean by this is that a distinctive consciousness of personal experience,
articulated in new modes of individuality, is constituted in modern social
formations. People come to think of themselves as having rights as well
as obligations, rights to a personal happiness, meaningful relationships,
opportunities for personal indulgence, and that the state will to some
extent underwrite and protect these privileges. But modernity is not just a
process of individualisation, it is also performed in changing forms of
community, association and other modes of formal and informal network.

Modernity is therefore played out in new languages of sociality, some of which I have previously explored as fictions of collective life (1993).

I have already emphasised that although one can generalise about the distinctiveness of modernity, that should not be read as neglecting the variety of organisational and institutional structures through which modernity has been constructed. Indeed, one of the most compelling accounts of the force of modern experience has stressed the inevitability of change, at every level of social organisation, as the founding dynamic of modern perspectives (Berman 1983; see also Nava and O'Shea 1996). The celebration of change and difference is itself in stark contrast to the perceived stability of more traditional social formations, although the lack of predictability has often been assumed to generate an all-pervasive anxiety about the management and meaning of experience that has become the dominant characteristic of both modern social thought and culture.

I have said that in modernity it is not just that new forms of identity for individuals and groups develop, but that the ways different spheres of social life are framed are also transformed. The best example of what I mean here can be seen in the distinction between public and private spheres. Of course a distinction between the public and the private already existed. But over the past two centuries it has been elaborated as new more elaborate types of cultural space each with its own dramaturgy of performance (Sennett 1976). The idea of a public sphere in which new concepts of citizenship imply an ability to engage in impersonal, rational discourse over policies in public life has been recognised to lie at the heart of ideologies of liberal democracy (Habermas 1989), and to facilitate the imagined communities of new national identities (Anderson 1983). These national communities are of course classic examples of the new collective identities of modernity and bring with them new ways of being members of society. Further developments in the public life of later modernity are the central focus of Chapters 6 and 7.

This is not the place to explore in any detail the ways in which the media of mass communication, first newspapers and then supplemented by radio and television networks, have constituted the public sphere in a nation such as Britain (Curran and Seaton 1998; Dahlgren 1995; Lull 2000). Except to say that the articulation of democratic participation in public life through the modern era has been able to preserve structures of privilege, particularly the ownership of capital, intellectual as well as financial and industrial, as well as the privileges of masculinity more generally. It is in this sense then that I would want to argue that the institutions of modernity have in the greater part of its history operated to effect a democratic compromise (it has also been called a culture of deference), in which the majority of citizens have been excluded from effective power and control over their lives.

The significance of the institutions of the public sphere, particularly in relation to the cultural changes of modernity, has been frequently commented upon. The complementary significance of institutions of the private sphere has, however, been relatively neglected, except perhaps in relation to structures of gendered relationships. The private sphere has typically been defined by a series of contrasts in which it is the world of female concerns as opposed to male, it is the world of the home as opposed to work, and it is the world of the everyday as opposed to more dramatic settings. In all these respects the private sphere has come to be associated with the development of the suburb as the dominant residential site of modern urban life (Davidoff and Hall 1987; Silverstone 1997).

Again I do not have the space to explore the implications of this perspective at this point, but note only two ways in which the constitution of the private sphere has major implications for the study of cultural change and everyday life. The first is that the home has become the primary focus of family life, leisure activities and consumer culture so that, as I shall explore in greater detail in the following chapters, cultural consumption in later modernity has been increasingly governed by values and styles deriving from the private sphere. The second is that the derogation of suburban life which has been a leitmotif of intellectual discourse virtually throughout modernity (Carey 1992), has served to reinforce the elitism of established culture and to legitimate the democratic compromise I have just spoken of, in which the privileges of social elites have not been seriously threatened by mass culture.

The Modernisation of Modernisation

In describing some of the significant features of modernisation and modernity I have begun to make connections between these changes and some sense of cultural change. This is inevitable, given (a) the way that in modernisation the cultural as a self-conscious concern with representation has become steadily more significant, and (b) the enduring sense of impermanence which we have seen pervades modern consciousness. There are, however, two specific aspects of cultural change which feed very directly into points made above. The first is that modernisation will create the opportunities for an urban popular culture. In time further technological and more importantly social developments based on the entrenchment of modern institutions will lead to the transition from urban to mass popular culture. In, however, the early phase of modernisation the existence of an urban popular culture will provide an important vocabulary for the emergent social identities of a social order being reshaped (a more developed overview of changes in popular culture is presented in the last chapter).

The second aspect of cultural change is that within the developing sphere of high cultural institutions, and partly as a reaction to the spreading commercial dominance of popular cultural forms, there was a wave of innovations in expressive resources across all high cultural forms that have come to be known as modernism (Bradbury and McFarlane 1976). I have already pointed to the confusing way in which the variety of aspects of the modern have been used in overlapping ways. While I cannot resolve this confusion, I think it is helpful for my account if I restrict my use of modernism to one type of cultural change. That is, to characterise a cultural movement that occupied a specific moment in European cultural history (if pushed to offer dates I suppose I would suggest 1880s to 1960s, although recognising that modernism is grounded in the general dynamics of modernity).

Clark has forcefully suggested that the impulse to modernism stemmed from his rhetorical question: 'is it not the case that the truly new, and disorienting, character of modernity is its seemingly being driven by merely material, statistical, tendential, "economic" considerations?' (1999, p. 8). The disorientation produced is in his view terrifying because it generates 'a system without any focusing purpose to it, or any compelling image or ritualization of that purpose' (ibid.). Thus, although a need for a vocabulary adequately to represent the reality of new social circumstances is a feature of the consciousness of modernity amongst intellectuals and those working in cultural crafts, there was simultaneously a growing realisation that those circumstances precluded the stability of order in representational vocabularies. Modernism is, for Clark then, a continual struggle with an irresolvable problem of how to represent the inherent contingency of modernity. To Clark's account I will only add the observation that art in modernity has had to generate a rationale for its existence in unprecedented ways. Thus as the various modes of artistic enterprise have shifted from economic relations of patronage to a more full-blown status as commodities sold in market relationships, artists as producers have been forced to try to reconcile contradictory expectations with consequences that I will discuss more fully in the next section.

If modernism is an anguished response to the incoherence of modernity, two further questions are necessarily posed: (a) to what extent do difficulties in finding appropriate means of representation in the high arts relate to difficulties in the representation of everyday life with which I began the previous chapter?; and (b) does the rise of postmodernism in the arts in the last decades of the twentieth century mean that the problem of representation has been solved? I will try to answer the first of these questions in the next section of this chapter. In relation to the second question, I think the answer concerns the development towards a fragmentation of culture that is one of my general themes and will be explicitly discussed in the final chapter. Generally it seems that the quest of modernism was based on an implied sense that the struggle of representation had to believe that it could be successful. That culture if you like could triumph over contingency. If the modernist impulse has now been superseded, it is more likely that the aspiration is no longer tenable rather than it has been achieved. Theorists from Jencks (1984) to Clark (1999) who have engaged with the exhaustion of modernism have emphasised that that 'exhaustion' has stemmed as much from contemporary social change as from purely expressive concerns; and it is in this sense that what has developed as postmodernism is intrinsic to the fragmentation of culture.

I have so far only touched on 'post' in relation to the modern in the cultural sphere, and thus only written of postmodernism, in an attempt to sidestep the issue of the possible end of modernity (in part because the postmodern has now generated at least as large and confusing a literature as the modern itself). Even so it will have become clear that modernity is a cumulative process. I think therefore it will be helpful in order to introduce some of the distinctive features of late modernity, to explore more fully Beck's idea that there has been a modernisation of modernisation (1992; see also 1995). The benefits of modernisation – such as greater individual freedom, generally rising standards of living, greater control of disease and pain through new medical technologies, and more democratic political structures – for a long time seemed so self-evident and unstoppable that for many social theorists there was an implicit evolutionary inevitability to modernity despite debates over the most appropriate political strategies.

Beck is writing in a situation when this faith in the future has been radically undermined, when as he says a new phase of modernisation 'today is dissolving industrial society and another modernity is coming into being' (1992, p. 10), so that: 'We are experiencing a transformation of the foundations of change' (op. cit., p. 14). The most obvious sign of this crisis of social and intellectual order is a creeping loss of faith in the ability of science and technology to always be able to master the environment for human progress. Our greater awareness of the risks of rationalisation is, however, only a symptom. It has been generated by two broader closely interdependent social processes in the new modernity of individualisation and reflexivity (I suppose strictly reflexivisation, but it is an ugly neologism). To say these are later developments might be puzzling because I have already indicated individualisation is a key feature of modernity; and I briefly indicated in the first chapter that in my view cultural forms work through reflexivity. Clearly both terms are being used in more specific ways[1] although if, as has been the drift of this section, one says that culture becomes more significant in modernity then reflexivity should also become cumulatively more significant.

Individualisation as it is being used here refers to the relative decline in significance of structural categories based in industrial modernisation such as 'class culture and consciousness, gender and family roles'

(Beck 1992, p. 87). Facilitated by rising standards of living, individualisation means a more general tendency for individuals to make themselves the
focus of their life experience and to innovate in cultural styles with different social settings. Changing structural forms do not, however, mean a lessening in social inequalities, for the 'reflexive conduct of life, the planning of
one's biography and social relations, gives rise to a new inequality, the
inequality of dealing with insecurity and reflexivity' (op. cit., p. 98, emphasis
in original – I think he means inequalities in the capacity or ability to cope
with new insecurities). For Beck the new insecurities of later modernisation
are more fundamental than the destabilisation of traditional society
induced by primary modernity.

Individualisation is therefore intensified by reflexive (in the sense of self-
conscious) insecurities. These insecurities are more destabilising than traditional fears concerning dangers of assault, want or disease, etc., because
they undermine the givenness of identity. Thus they involve the painful
and fearful reconsideration of all relationships, including family and particularly gendered relationships. Individualisation in conjunction with
reflexive insecurities therefore skirts the possibility of a dissolution of
sociality itself. But, and here is a very important paradoxical transformation, individualisation in later modernity does not in Beck's view generate
anarchy, for '*the very same media which bring about an individualisation also
bring about a standardisation*' (op. cit., p. 130, emphasis in original). This is
because a greater concern with the private sphere such as individual identity is not isolated from other social forms, but actually more firmly integrated into cultural idioms through being expressed by commodities
employed in self-conscious styles (a view I develop throughout but particularly in Chapter 4). An illustrative example for now is the greater concern
with sexual fulfilment and individual pleasure in later modernity which
has generated new forms of display and greater concern with bodily
shape, etc., as well as an industry of advice and counselling dealing with
heightened insecurities (Weitman 1998).

Thus the process of integrating individualisation appears as an effectively greater cultural conformity which in turn, and here is a further twist
in the spiral of paradoxes, generates a heightened reflexivity in social consciousness. This is because in order to participate in the semiotic intensity
of ironicised lifestyles, individuals have to constantly recognise that what is
represented in activities is not fixed or stable. They are therefore made more
insecure, an intensified anxiety that is potentially assuaged by expert reassurance. But as expertise is necessarily bracketed as limited, prejudiced and
likely to have been corrupted by corporate governance seeking to exploit
our fears, we are further driven into an infinite regress of different modes
of expertise. The idea of reflexivity is then a heightened awareness of how
what seems rational and logical is actually governed by the social conditions of its production. I gave a definition in the first chapter, and will come

back to the theme in the next, but given the clearly special importance attached to reflexivity by Beck I think it useful to give a further definition: '"Reflexivity" here refers to the use of information about the conditions of activity as a means of regularly monitoring and redefining what that activity is' (Giddens 1994, p. 86; see also Beck et al. 1994; Czyzewski 1994; Sandywell 1996; the literature on reflexivity is very clearly reviewed in Lynch 2000).

As an initial illustration of how insecurity is intensified, I will develop the point I noted above that Beck believes there has been a disenchantment with science leading to a loss of authority. This has been generated because we cannot escape knowing of the unintended consequences of ever greater rationalisation of the environment. For everybody living in Britain a succession of endemic plagues in livestock all too clearly indicates that rationalisation in food production has generated intolerable irrationalities. Almost in horror: 'everyday thought and imagination [is] *removed from its moorings in the world of the visible....* What becomes the subject of controversy as to its degree of reality is instead what everyday consciousness does *not* see, and *cannot perceive*' (1992, p. 73, emphasis in original). In Beck's account this is a very powerful dimension of the heightened insecurities of later modernity, and is most clearly expressed in the discrediting of scientific expertise in particular and institutionalised authority in general. One can see this illustrated in the loss of faith in the automatic benefits of science and in the widespread popular revulsion at both further experiments with nuclear power and genetic engineering.

There is therefore a loss of authority with rational solutions, a process that can be seen as well in the complementary turning away from established churches towards a global pot-pourri of spiritual guidance. But if we have been forced into more personal choices about what to believe, there is likely to be greater demand for new sorts of expertise and guidance. And thus a paradoxical intensification of the social process of reflexivity is a proliferation of expertise and authority in fragmented culture. The reason why a more intense reflexivity is associated with greater uniformity becomes clearer if it is appreciated that the processes of heightened reflexive consciousness are articulated through textually mediated discourses more generally.

A simple illustration of a spiral of greater anxiety leading to more forms of expert reassurance which in turn leads to further anxiety is what can be called 'the stress industry'. The invention of stress as a non-specific form of disability induced by modern living and working conditions can be dated to the middle of the twentieth century. Stress is therefore a pathology of modernity with which we can all empathise without needing to be too specific about causation, symptoms or cure. This is not say that it is not a real condition, but that it is constructed in how we talk about the experience of modernity and is therefore to some extent a self-fulfilling prophecy. The ambiguous status of stress as a response to unpleasant events or circumstances does not preclude and indeed seems to positively encourage the development of a new mode of expertise offering to diagnose and alleviate the pathology. Thus fears of litigation from workers who feel they have been exposed to inappropriate stress, amongst other factors, have encouraged the development of a stress-management industry 'to carry out "stress audits", counselling and the teaching of relaxation techniques' (Chaudhuri 2001, p. 10). This new form of expertise of course intensifies fears about the condition it has developed to counter.

A further illustration of the interrelationships between representation in the culture industry and general understanding in the processes of later modernisation I have been describing can easily be found in the narratives of popular television. Thus the process of individualisation is exemplified by how stories of major social change are told through the experiences of individuals. It may be suggested that fiction has always used this device of personalisation to create empathy, but the distinctiveness of television narratives is that individuals are depicted in their home or private settings as much as in their public roles. This can be understood as a dramatisation of reflexivity, in which it is constantly emphasised in television how organisations such as the police force or a political movement work through the actions and interactions of individuals. It thus becomes accepted in social knowledge that organisation is a performance or an accomplishment – something constructed in situations that parallel viewers' everyday lives.

I hope that following this discussion it will now be clearer that there are at least two significant themes for my general approach that I can adapt from Beck. First, although modernity is a continuous process it has at least two phases, and it is in the latter that characteristics of the first, particularly rationalisation, are intensified. Secondly, and this is particularly important, the insecurity and reflexivity of destructured social order just described have led to a number of moves towards more ostensibly radically democratic forms of public participation. This is because, and is itself a key illustration of the first theme, the moves towards democracy in the first phase of modernisation, that even so remained compromised and constrained by traditions of deference, are being reshaped towards a greater populism.

The ideological frame within which the 'destructuring' of the industrial social order has been situated is a combination of increasing rationalisation within a consumerist environment. The effect is a greater concentration upon effective marketing, most directly through the management of appearances not just of consumer goods but state agencies, political parties, social movements and, of course, entertainers. The legitimisation of these processes has been a widespread populism in education and entertainment as much as in politics or social policies more generally. The central dramatisation of these processes, as I shall illustrate in coming chapters, has been through an increasing engagement with motifs of everyday life in the cultural forms of later modernity. It is not yet clear, however, where the combined processes of greater insecurity, more reflex-ivity and consumerist populism are leading. Will they be addressed by a more effective rationalisation of consciousness as well as marketing process in which, one suspects, the egalitarianism of later modernity is merely a matter of appearance? Or will they facilitate a persistent non-rationality to the everyday which is in effect a form of resistance to the rationalisation of consciousness?

Discovering Everyday Life

I have suggested at several points that everyday life has come to con-sciousness as a topic for social thought in the era of modernity. In the first two parts of this chapter I have discussed aspects of the development of modernity that help to explain why this era has become increasingly char-acterised by an intense concern with representation – or consciousness of culture. In order to make a connection between a sensitivity to the signif-icance of everyday life and cultural consciousness more generally, I will initially take some points from Roberts's book on the history of docu-mentary photography (1998). Writing of the everyday as the characteris-tic topic of documentary photography which needed to be 'discovered' as subject matter for this relatively new medium of representation, Roberts says that: 'The construction of the category of the "everyday" is identifi-able with the major changes in social experience that take place in the twentieth century' (1998, p. 14).

On the next page he amplifies this by writing of changes in the first two decades of that century such as: 'rapid industrialisation, the deepening crisis of classical culture, the success of the Russian revolution, the opening up of the hidden world of sexuality through psychoanalysis' (op. cit., p. 15), all combining to bring 'the everyday' into the spheres of politics, science, art and social theory. This list combines elements of very different types and is therefore a little curious, but is slightly clarified when Roberts goes on to suggest that, when in 1901 Freud published *Psycho-pathology of Everyday Life*, he began a transformation in attitudes to what can be taken for granted that was itself 'inherited from the great cultural revolution of the second half of the nineteenth century [*through*] an emphasis upon the hidden significance of the prosaic and the marginal' (op. cit., p. 15).

In other words, the Freudian revolution is profound because it begins from the possibility of meaningful significance in aspects of experience that had not previously been thought worthy of serious consideration; except that Freud, as is now well known, was intent on displaying the persisting significance of what had been repressed rather than a hidden rationality. The everyday therefore surfaces as a topic because of a dawning realisation that what Berger calls the neighbourliness of mundane elements may be apparent, but any surface harmony of appearance is at least potentially ideological. That is, that the banality of the everyday – its everydayness – which is generally taken for granted is an inadequate or distorting representation. The further, more significant, implication is that the everyday poses particular difficulties of adequate representation in modernity because of its inherent irrationality. It seems that Freud might then be held to have both inaugurated and crystallised an era of radical insecurity in social consciousness – to have made explicit what I called in the first chapter troubling doubts about how to represent the everyday.

For example, Freud's influence on the later Surrealist movement is well known, as is their explorations of significance in the random juxtapositions of the marginal detritus of everyday life. It seems likely that this sense of a possible meaning in chaos and chance is what gives the documentary photography of, for example, both Brassai in France and Humphrey Spender in Britain in the 1930s an eerie, almost haunting, quality (Bate 2000).[2] Before rushing too quickly into later developments in cultural engagements with the everyday in the twentieth century, however, we should bear in mind that Roberts has also pointed to the significance of Manet and subsequent painters in the second half of the nineteenth century (see also Clark 1985).[3] The significance here is that painters, novelists and dramatists were inaugurating a great revolt in the arts or a 'cultural revolution' not by denying their own bourgeois status, but by reflexively considering how that social world was being put together and what it cost.[4] They were criticising how in making the world modern the vanguard class of modernity – the entrepreneurs and professionals of bourgeois society – had robbed the world of order.

I think that further light on this idea of a cultural revolution is thrown by Bonnett's suggestion that artists in modernity have been caught in an ideological contradiction (1992; in developing this idea I am picking up again a point made in the previous section that artists in modernity have faced contradictory role expectations). On the one hand they have enjoyed the privileges of a specialist group of producers often highly praised for their expertise or even 'genius'. On the other hand they have tended to see themselves as critics of the contingency and commercialism of bourgeois social order. For Bonnett this contradiction has typically been resolved by clinging to an idea of a specialised artistic space separate from and indifferent to everyday space. For those members of avant-garde art movements which have been particularly committed to a role of critical unmasking, and have therefore tried to reject what they saw as the inappropriate privileges of artistic status, often the solution has been to turn away from the aesthetic autonomy of artistic space and to try to confront

the reality of everyday space. Thus movements from Dadaism through
Surrealism to Situationism and aspects of postmodernism have for Bonnett
tried to represent the everyday through a merging of art and life.

I do not have the space to adequately review the variety of ways avant-
garde movements have tried to cope with the messy particularity and
irrationality of the everyday, although I will return to attempts to capture
the reality of the everyday in documentaries in the next section and discuss
the relevance of Situationist ideas in the next chapter. For now I shall only
note that Bonnett sees three themes running through avant-garde movements. These he calls spontaneism, anti-art and indifference. The first, particularly associated with the Surrealists, is a celebration of chance – literally
a rejection of order through random or inappropriate juxtapositions. The
second as a rejection of the aestheticism of art is fairly straightforward,
while the third is a refusal of any intrinsic difference between the values
of high art as opposed to popular art particularly associated with
Dadaism: 'Dada remained, as Tzara (1989, p. 247) expressed it, primarily
a "religion of indifference". "Why do you want us to be preoccupied with
a pictorial, moral, poetic, literary, political or social renewal?", Tzara continued (pp. 248–50); "We are all well aware that these renewals of means
are merely ... uninteresting questions of fashion and facade"' (Bonnett
1992, p. 74). Subsequently, the culmination of these attitudes was captured in the slogan scrawled on walls in Paris in May 1968: 'Art is dead.
Let us create our daily lives' (Willener 1970, p. 216).

A revolutionary critique on this scale is concerned with more than
responses to problems of representation. It is bracketing or putting into
question the building blocks of institutionalised knowledge – how we
take for granted differences between social classes, genders, ethnicities
and places, etc. Thus Garber (2000) has suggested that to consider something 'as such' is to be concerned with its essential facticity, and that: 'The
coinage "as-suchness", earlier found in the philosophy of William James,
has been used as a synonym for what cultural theorists often call "everyday life"' (p. 17). The cultural revolution embarked upon in the prequel to
modernism and the theme that Berman (1983) has taken as paradigmatic
from Marx and Engels both recognised that as-suchness becomes specula-
tive in modernisation. That is, the bourgeois transformation in which 'All
that is solid melts into air, all that is holy is profaned' (Feuer 1969, p. 52),
is the process in which the grounded as-suchness of experience is felt to
be being robbed of its solidity. The significance of emerging ideological
consciousness in the development of modernity is that in this perspective
nothing can be taken at face value – any value, idea or practice can potentially be reinterpreted as symptomatic and thereby significant.

I am suggesting that in the modern era scientific knowledge has
seemed to offer such wonderful opportunities for controlling the world
around us. But that simultaneously, in another form of contradiction or

paradox, for the accumulating reflexive social consciousness of modernity – that is, the ways the modern was being described in the arts and social theory – knowledge was becoming contingent and provisional. This can also be phrased by saying that the pursuit of rationality, which is the defining characteristic of modernity, has been undermined by an irrepressible suspicion that the foundations on which it rests, the everyday world, is unstable and unknowable because it is deeply non-rational or even irrational. For the dominant rationality of authoritative expertise this paradox has been unwelcome and indeed profoundly absurd. But some of the followers of symptomatic figures such as Freud and Marx have suggested that anxieties stemming from the problems of representation should not be repressed, but need to be positively celebrated as in the explorations of chance in Surrealist practice. Such a response has, however, been unusual even if we accept Clark's suggestion discussed above that the modernist movement was a long sustained cry of anguish at the meaninglessness of modernity. More generally it has been a slow and inconsistent, groping realisation in all the forms of public discourse of the problematic 'neighbourliness' of everyday life in modernity (see also Donald 1999; Frisby 1985).

Unsettled by or denying the paradox of expertise and insecurity, conventional social scientists have suppressed anxieties about the foundations of their 'science' of the world about them in their desire to be the social engineers of modernity. Traditions of suppression that have ranged from those who have sought ever better methodologies to reveal hidden order, to those who could not accept the 'irrationality' of contesting conventional realism as they believe that it undermines possibilities of purposive change. Perhaps it is a symptom of the threat perceived difficulties in representation posed for conventional social science that occasional challenges have seemed incoherent attempts at representation. Such as the, until very recently, almost entirely neglected perspective in cultural and historical analysis which is the uncompleted and possibly incompletable folders and excursions of Benjamin's *Arcades* project (1999). Here Benjamin, in seeking the roots of the spectacle of consumer capitalism, explores the ephemera of the mid-nineteenth-century Parisian everyday in pursuit of a 'profane illumination' through a documentary history that combines Marxist as well as Surrealist perspectives (Buck-Morss 1991; Gilloch 1996). Benjamin's great study occupied him through the 1930s until it was truncated by the invasion of fascism throughout continental Europe leading to his abortive flight and then suicide. Available only in fragmentary excerpts in the Anglophone world until the end of the century, it stands as a symbol of insurmountable frustration.

My argument is then that although everyday life as a topic for social thought is born in the cultural innovations of modernity, it is also largely absent from the dominant discourses of the era. Locked in the dominant

rationality of intellectual discourse, social theory has largely been unable
to acknowledge let alone use as counter-hegemonic practice the irrationality of social experience. A form of denial which is apparent in the
prejudice that the banality of everyday life, and particularly such a 'feminine' sphere as consumption, has made it unworthy of grand social
theory. It should be acknowledged, however, that the denial has not
been absolute. The everyday has been a subterranean strain kept alive as
I discuss more fully in the next chapter by those who sought a 'dirty realism' (and recognising that the phrase was coined for literary rather than
sociological writing). And as the everyday has become more prominent in
the dramas, entertainments and discourses of later modernity, slowly it is
emerging as a major theme in social theory.

It is also true that grand theory has always been complemented by the
studies of social reformers who believed disease and crime could be alle-
viated by more efficient planning and management of the environment,
particularly of the poor. This impulse to analyse the imperfections of contemporary social conditions was supplemented by the exhortations of
moralists such as temperance reformers to generate a variety of fact-find-
ing initiatives. These ranged from surveys of the living conditions and
working practices of the poor (Booth 1889), to more documentary studies
such as Hine's use of photography to record the everyday life of recent
immigrants to the United States (Stange 1989). My argument is, therefore,
that although the study of everyday life was not completely absent from
the social discourse of modernity it was predominantly directed, at least
until that rupture in the confidence of modernisation the First World War,
towards the problematic 'others' of modernising society (I think this generalisation holds true even for those rare studies such as Veblen's of the
commercially based new leisure class that involved him looking
'upwards' rather than down (1924)). The anthropological impulse to chart
the living conditions of these alien elements was undoubtedly regulatory,
in that it sought to manage their improvement more effectively, but it was
also humane in that it sought to discover people, at least partly, in their
own terms (Tagg 1988).

Documenting Everyday Life

I mentioned that Roberts's book is on the history of documentary
photography – a genre that is particularly concerned with everyday life
and indeed based in a technical medium that paradigmatically captures
in representation the mundane and the accidental (Sontag 1978). Documentary, as I have just noted, has often been used as a campaigning medium
against social injustice through the depiction of poor social conditions.
But it has also been used in attempts to represent a poetry in everyday life

despite being clothed in an aura of factuality. In this, documentary can be differentiated from representations of everyday life such as soap operas on television that, however much they may mimic the accents and styles of everyday life, are fictional in their melodramatic structure. It seems likely then the tradition of work in film, literature, photography, sound and other media that we generally call documentary can provide a guide for how we should attempt to represent the culture of everyday life.

In this section I want to show that in seeking to discover at least some aspects of what is involved in taking everyday life seriously, we will find it helpful to begin with traditions of documentary practice in the twentieth century. The central reason is that, as I have said, art that has rejected the idea of an aesthetic autonomy to the artistic enterprise and the corollary of a distinctive artistic space has been driven to try make art in the terms of the everyday. In such a project the distinctiveness of the documentary enterprise is particularly thought-provoking. My intention here is not to attempt a history of documentary or even various modes of representing everyday life (I am for example omitting any consideration of important work in oral or documentary history; see for example Terkel 1970 and Kaledin 2000).[5] It is rather to argue that in their commitment to representing everyday life documentarists have raised questions about the form of representation that have become more relevant as the motifs of everyday life have become more prominent in later modernity.

What I mean by issues about the form of representation can be grouped under two main headings: as themes of cultural practice, and as sites of cultural practice. I have already asserted that documentarists have in general taken the everyday as a theme of their cultural practice. While this is not inevitable as one could have a documentary about something quite exceptional such as innovative surgery, however, in showing the activity as something done as a co-ordinated social practice documentary renders it everyday through the display of neighbourliness. A more significant innovation and one that is more difficult to achieve comes in taking the everyday as a site of cultural practice. By this I mean holding everyday life up as a model for cultural intervention that can be used to change society. In this respect it is not a surprise that the first major illustration of this use of documentary came in the cultural ferment of the early years of the Russian Revolution. In seeking to theorise and exemplify the making of a new social order, a whole series of struggles over how to appropriately represent social reality threw up new forms of documentary practice. Not all documentarists are necessarily committed to this ideal, but it offers a different understanding of involvement to which I will return at the end of this chapter.

The various strands of social consciousness in representation came together with the coining of the term 'documentary' in the inter-war years. The documentary movement or impulse drew upon a number of traditions in literature such as social realist novels, various forms of usually sensationalist confessions in popular literature and self-consciously proletarian writings, but combined them with the work of photographic pioneers such as Hine to provide a dramatisation of the facts of ordinary experience: 'Documentary is a radically democratic genre. It dignifies the usual and levels the extraordinary' (Stott 1973, p. 49). The documentary movement therefore bridged the previously separate literatures of social science, exposé (muckraking) journalism and popular sensationalism. It was a reaction within modernism that was undoubtedly inspired by the social commitments of an ideologically polarised era but also purported to offer an objective vision. As such it was felt to be a corrective to the excessive individualism of modernist abstraction, but neither was it a disembodied taxonomy of social description.[6]

Instead documentarists aimed to use the significant detail of personal experience to dramatise social truths: 'Those who practice documentary tend to be skeptical of the intellect and the abstractions through which it works. Like artists, they believe that a fact to be true and important must be felt' (Stott 1973, p. 12). While the focus of this way of seeing was generally on the 'hidden' groups of mass society that were felt to be missed by the agendas of popular journalism – thus for example the well-known studies of the dispossessed rural poor by agencies of the New Deal administration – and in this making connections to the studies of urban 'low-life' stimulated by the ethnographic sociology of the Chicago School, the documentary impulse could encompass the everyday life of ordinary people more generally (Corner 1986).[7]

This is brought out well in certain aspects of the documentary movement in Britain in the inter-war years. The film unit initially organised under the auspices of the Empire Marketing Board and then the national Post Office may well have had confused relations with nascent ideas of public relations and the advertising industry, but under Grierson's leadership it did produce a number of accounts of the mundane accomplishments in work and leisure of the contemporary working class (Sussex 1975; Swann 1989). There are a number of obvious criticisms to be made of these films (in addition to weaknesses that inevitably stemmed from cumbersome technical facilities). For example, Flaherty's film of *Industrial Britain* was a romantic account of craft production rather than what is promised by the title, and the famous film of the overnight postal train to Scotland, *Night Mail*, was largely mocked up in a studio, and in any case was overlaid with modernist pretensions so that it is very dubious as a piece of reality reportage. Even so, and particularly in contrast to the pictures of the working class available in the commercial cinema, the films were an innovation in showing the people to themselves (more generally on the radicalism of documentary, see Winston 1995). It was an innovation strengthened by pioneering efforts in finding new sites for exhibition outside commercial settings. Another documentary innovation that more directly stemmed from the concerns of social theory was the Mass Observation movement founded by Madge and Harrisson (two young men – a poet and a botanist) in 1936 explicitly to provide an anthropology of ourselves (Chaney 1987b).

Once again it would be too great a digression to explore the history of Mass Observation in any detail, but there are certain aspects of their work in the early years that raise very clearly central difficulties in the study of everyday life. There were two themes to the early work of Mass Observation – a group of observers living in Bolton – in a form of participant observation and a national diary project in which volunteers were requested to record happenings in the world around them on particular days and occasions (e.g. Jennings 1937). Partly drawing on these sources and their observations and analyses, the leaders produced the first sort of national ethnography or popular culture of everyday life (Madge and Harrisson 1939). The conventional critique of these innovative modes of social research is that they generated material that lacked order or structure, that it was a primitive romanticism that had to be superseded by more professionally trained social scientists. I have, however, previously suggested with my friend and colleague (Chaney and Pickering 1986; see also Pickering and Chaney 1986) that in their use of fragments of naive observation a more profound challenge to the privileges of authorship was being enacted. Mass Observation was, without fully grasping its own potential, in effect attempting to remain faithful to the practical order, or irrationality, of everyday life rather than bend that lived experience to the rationalism of a quasi-science.

I have been trying to show that however laudable the documentary impulse to imbue the facts of everyday life or ordinary people (the terms were used interchangeably) with social and political significance was, it could not rest content with naive empiricism. The facts had to be given a narrative structure, or authorial frame, in order to tell the story for which they were significant (Atkinson and Coffey 1997). To attempt to leave the fragmentary incoherencies of the profusion of detail in everyday life *as the story* means approaching the meaning of modernity in another way. Going back to what I said earlier about the everyday offering a different perspective on modernity, the implication of Mass Observation practice was that it was trying grasp a more radically democratic potential for cultural discourse.

An interesting contemporary to Mass Observation's attempt to theorise some of these ideas more directly was a group of intellectuals meeting in Paris as the Collège de Sociologie (Hollier 1988). Drawing on Durkheimian traditions in French social thought and contemporary surrealist commitments to the significance in the everyday of 'fragments, curious collections, unexpected juxtapositions' (Clifford 1988, p. 118; a

perspective that is, Clifford suggests and citing Susan Sontag, the fundamental modernist sensibility and is of course 'irrational' in its lack of
order), members of the Collége sought to find what they called an eth-
nology of the quotidian. This would, they believed, provide a unique vantage-point for disturbing the closures of dominant consciousness in mass
society (a search for radical disruption within the forms of everyday
life that was explicitly shared within the Mass Observation movement).
This tension between seeing the forms of the everyday as structures of
reality and as the means of transcending those structures will be discussed more directly in the next chapter and be a persistent theme in subsequent chapters.

In this section, I have been trying to show that the documentary movement, working in the gap between sociology and fictional representations,
attempted to complement academic sociology's theories of modernity
with representations of everyday life. In so doing, certain aspects of documentary practice have raised fundamental questions about discourses of
the everyday. What I mean by the latter phrase is how to talk about, represent or theorise everyday life. I have already said that I assume that
everyday life is that part of our daily activities that is so widely shared
that it becomes unremarkable.[8] If knowing a language is knowing how to
go on, then we can routinely speak the everyday. However, the history of
documentary practice helps us to see that as soon as we attempt to step
back and find meaning in everyday utterances, then we are forced to consider the nature of the language we are using. In the following chapter, I
will discuss later twentieth-century attempts to confront order in everyday
life more explicitly.

Conclusion

Before going on to that though, I should acknowledge that my concentration on the documentary movement in the inter-war years is misleading
if it implies that the documentary has been exhausted. Not only would
this miss the vitality of more recent documentary (see for example Bruzzi
2000; Hassard 1998; Nichols 1991; Rosenthal 1988), it would also miss the
extent to which television, as the dominant cultural form of the post-war
years, has been both consumed in the everyday setting of the domestic
home and has pioneered dramatic entertainment based on representations of everyday life. I will discuss this latter point more fully in later
chapters, but just note very briefly now that television's use of documentary
has been very varied and has ranged from narrated authoritative accounts
such as wildlife programmes to personal fragments by anonymous authors
as in video diaries.

The premise of this chapter has been the ambiguous status of everyday life in accounts of modernity. Of course there are very frequent references to what happens in normality as happening in everyday life, but its very predictability has usually been taken as meaning that it does not need explication. Guy Debord, a leading figure in the Situationist International, has drawn a distinction between 'specialised activities' and the everyday to argue that the majority of sociologists have concentrated on the former, to the extent that everyday life for him is 'the sphere of the [sociological] specialists' resignation and failure' (1981, p. 71 quoted in Bonnett 1992, p. 69). (Recently there have been a number of other 'discoveries' of neglected themes within sociological discourse such as those aspects of the everyday – the body and the things we use (Shilling 1993; Turner 1984; Dant 1999).) If everyday life is equivalent to normality then it might seem that one runs the risk of either labouring the obvious or of imbuing the mundane with inappropriate complexity and/or significance. I think it is relevant here that the routine nature of everyday life means that it is likely to be focused on the home or the private sphere, whereas social theorists, largely being men, have tended to concentrate on the more masculine world of the public sphere where important things happen. One of the effects of feminist interventions in social thought has been an at least partial rescue of domesticity and the everyday as serious topics (Willis 1991).

The further implication of making this point is to assert that there is a politics of knowledge, and a politics of all sorts of knowledge. Who decides (and how they decide) what is significant in social life is the most basic level of political control. The more substantial point should now be becoming clearer – and that is that *one cannot determine the significance of the everyday just by collecting details of what people do*. The distinctiveness of the everyday lies in the attitudes of inhabitants, what actors routinely employ in living or doing it – that is, the representations they employ. The main question therefore shifts from 'what is everyday life' to 'how is it possible' or 'what does it take to be possible'? A relevant analogy can be found in reconsiderations of the sociology of knowledge. Some years ago Berger and Luckmann pointed out that this field had been overly concerned with what determines or explains improper or biased knowledge. They argued it was more fundamental to ask how something was accepted as knowledge: 'an adequate understanding of the "reality *sui generis*" of society requires an inquiry into the manner in which this reality is constructed' (1967, p. 30); that is, that the forms of reality – however banal – are always a representation. The difficulty with charting changes in the forms of residence or neighbourliness of everyday life is that we cannot rest content with observation but must engage in how they are being constructed.

In effect, a recognition of the distinctiveness of everyday life requires, as Maffesoli has said, 'less a new form of analysis than a specific perspective on things' (1989, p. 1). A perspective that begins with a concern with the conditions of possibility and includes what Maffesoli calls sociality – a celebration of all the elements which go into the practice of coexistence and which 'obliges us to take into account everything which was generally considered as essentially frivolous, anecdotal or meaningless' (1989, p. 1). Once again making the point very explicit: this means beginning with the experience of irrationality rather than rational discourses. But in order to restructure the frivolous and meaningless we have to find a way of working from within. Unlike traditional aesthetics we cannot stand back in disinterested contemplation, but can only sense shifting associations of significance through personal involvement. We cannot presume in advance that the overwhelming detail of lived experience can be wrestled into intellectual consistency or coherence, and must therefore accept that any narrative is necessarily arbitrary and fragmentary.

Maffesoli goes on to elaborate a theme of sociality in a way that will be important when I return to the topic in the next chapter. He argues that what he calls 'the recrudescence of the everyday does not involve a restriction of analysis to the individual subject but its exact opposite' (1989, p. 11). Mundane social interaction, I will show, requires a broad perspective in which the most routine 'bit' of social life is seen to necessitate an equivalent complexity in inter-subjective management as anything more exceptional. In subsequent chapters I will argue that the focus on the everyday in the social and cultural discourses of later modernity should not be taken as evidence that issues in the staging or construction of mundane reality have been resolved. This approach is intensely political in its concern with the ownership and operation of power in the making of social life, and it is intensely social in a concern with inter-subjective organisation. In the following chapter I will discuss broad perspectives in how social theorists have grappled with issues in the representation of the distinctiveness of everyday life.

3

Social Theory and Everyday Life

Constructing Everyday Life

In the previous chapter I began with a characterisation of modernisation and later modernisation as an introduction to why everyday life can be seen to have posed distinctive problems of interpretation in the modern era. This was intended both to help to explain some of the character of cultural change and the status of the topic of everyday life in the cultural consciousness of the modern era. In particular I discussed aspects of the tradition of documentary representation in order to illustrate one particularly powerful approach to the everyday. While documentary has often been used as a means of social critique and indeed social mobilisation, the stress on raw experience has not facilitated a more wide-ranging interpretation of how we know and understand the forms and order of social life. I have begun to make clear that for me the essence of the problem is that there is an incompatibility between the messy particularity of everyday life – the ongoing interpretive dialogue of making meaningful – that I have loosely characterised as irrational or disordered, and the drive to order and control, the rationalism, of dominant public discourse.

A contrast between the intensified rationalisation of consumerism and the irrationality of ordinary lived experience is not being presented as absolute. In the following chapters I will have a lot to say at various points about the irrationalities of rationalisation. And in this and subsequent chapters I will discuss various types of research study which have brought out the orderliness of meaning-making in ordinary social experience. My use of irrational is not then meant to suggest that ordinary everyday life is crazy, but rather that this sphere of life is owned by its members in ways that may not be conformist.

It seems that in the machineries of government by both agencies of the state and corporate enterprise, the technologies of production and marketing, and the dominant intellectual paradigms used in accounts of both natural and social processes, there have been interdependent assumptions about the essential need for rational discourse. As an alternative, I have begun to show how there have been subterranean traditions in both artistic practice and social theory, emphasising that the study of everyday life involves a concern with the construction of reality that has to encompass a more complex sense of the texture of lived experience that may appear disordered or 'irrational' (see also Crook 1998 in this respect). Such an alternative does not necessarily promote irrationality or meaninglessness, but it does ask whether a questioning of how we decide what is meaningful, sometimes against the grain of hectoring discourse, can be emancipating.

In this chapter I will survey the main works to be found on library shelves of social thought that have discussed the character of everyday life. I want to bring out first, and less controversially, that they have all in a variety of ways been concerned with the construction of reality or more prosaically asking 'how is it possible?' Secondly, and more contentiously, I want to consider how a reconciliation between the orderliness of everyday life and the rationalisation of the wider order of institutionalised social life has been considered. In particular, whether increasing rationalisation means a suppression of the creativity of everyday life. I am in this laying the basis for illustrations in later chapters of how the changing ways of representing everyday life in the culture of later modernity are profoundly concerned with struggles over its meaning.

In the terms I am using I have been influenced by Berger and Luckmann's rethinking of the sociology of knowledge oriented towards the social construction of reality (1967). The book, at least in part, is intended to introduce readers to the work of Alfred Schutz and served to introduce Schutz's phenomenological sociology to a wider audience. The phenomenological project, in its concern with the raw materials of consciousness, is particularly relevant for any attempt to excavate that which consciousness takes for granted. Berger and Luckmann begin with the realisation that all of us are familiar with a multiplicity of realities through shifts in the nature of our consciousness. They illustrate this idea with the example of dreaming, but might also have cited the potential for absorption in imaginative fiction. These alternative realities may be very powerful and all-absorbing, but in normal circumstances they are recognised to be inferior analogues to a paramount reality of everyday life which 'imposes itself upon consciousness in the most massive, urgent and intense manner. It is impossible to ignore, difficult even to weaken in its imperative presence' (op. cit., p. 35).

It may seem a digression from my review of writing about everyday life, but it might be worth noting at this point that the idea of paramount and alternative realities is extremely relevant to any study of cultural change. I think it uncontroversial to say that cultural performances in all societies will often provide representations or explorations of alternative realities. These may be designed to reaffirm the rightness of conventional accounts of normality or to act as a means of escape from an oppressive normality, but in either case cultural performances may function as a means of vicariously envisaging what is both alluring and frightening. One form of cultural change will then be the story of changing ways of articulating alternatives to normality (see Chapter 8). One could be interested in how, for example, the cinema has developed a genre of gothic narratives concerned with both life after death and the human creation of life. A second type of study of cultural change will be concerned with those situations in which cultural forms have been able to be influential in changing the conceptions of paramount reality.

In this respect I think it could be argued that the development of the novel in the eighteenth century provided opportunities for the exploration of inner consciousness, that both facilitated and articulated changes in the normality of notions of individuality and responsibility, etc. In this view the novel was a catalyst for the general spread of a new way of understanding individual identity. In relation to more recent innovations in cultural forms, Miller and McHoul suggest that an 'equivalent moment of epistemological rupture ... [has] ... produced a new textual form' (1998, p. 121), that is the television talk show. In their view this provides for audiences a complex morality play about self-revelation. These shows illustrate Beck's point discussed in the previous chapter that the pursuit of individualisation can lead to more rigorous doubts about the legitimacy of forms of order. The point of these illustrative examples is to repeat the point emphasised in the first chapter, that representations of normality are not just located in everyday situations but are continually being articulated in what were called textually mediated discourses.

The paramount reality of everyday life is for Schutz therefore both awesome and hedged around with discordant intimations. It is, however, self-evidently an inter-subjective world populated by others who can be presumed to share my natural attitude of confidence in the self-evident routines of everyday life. Although everyone, at least within the normality of my life-world, can be presumed to share this natural attitude, I do not know everyone equally. Indeed the social environment can be conceptualised as a series of ripples radiating out from each individual, and as one moves further away from the core the individual's grasp of the other is increasingly governed by typifications: 'Social structure is the sum total of these typifications and of the recurrent patterns of interaction established by means of them' (Berger and Luckmann 1967, p. 48). This world is further structured by frameworks of space and time that provide a distinctive architecture of order for patterns of interaction. Above all language is an essential element (but by no means the only element – think for example of the significance of visual culture) in what Schutz calls the social stock of knowledge of a society (see for example Schieffelin 1993). These create frameworks of relevance and significance that further structure the social construction of reality.

Doing Everyday Life

Although Schutz's work was generally only published in English quite late in the century, and as we shall see a lot of work also concerned with the study of everyday life pre-dates this, it can stand as a heading for a tradition because it was quickly established as a central point of reference. For example, it would be mistaken to see all those projects that have been loosely grouped under a heading of ethnomethodology as solely inspired by social phenomenology, but it certainly functioned as an important influence (Garfinkel 1967; Sudnow 1972; Turner 1974). The collection edited by Jack Douglas explicitly oriented to a theme of everyday life (1971b) is a good indication of the diversity of background and perspective of those committed to understanding everyday actions and situations. Douglas's thematic paper introducing the collection struggles diligently to hold together what he calls phenomenological and existentialist sociologies with ethnomethodology and even symbolic interactionism, and he does bring out a common concern with the significance of practical actions in mundane settings.

Douglas argues that what is common to the various strands of what I can call interpretive sociology is a move whereby the researcher suspends a naturalistic or scientific stance in which features of the everyday world can be taken for granted as factually present. Instead of blindly accepting scientific precepts, interpretivists make a commitment to a theoretic stance: 'To take the theoretic stance is to treat the everyday world as a phenomenon' (1971a, p. 15). The theoretic stance is then another way of putting what I suggested is the basic sociological question in the study of everyday life – how is it possible? Further, the theoretic stance involves approaching the everyday world on its own terms, not that is in taking over the vocabulary of everyday life but accepting that life as a meaningful enterprise. The ethnomethodological concern with practical actions in mundane settings is clearly then an exception to my generalised view that everyday life has been neglected in the human studies. There have been a number of publications that have acted as introductions to or overviews of the ethnomethodology school (Button 1991; Livingston 1987; Psathas 1979) and it would be crass to attempt a thumbnail sketch here.

I can, however, point to two key concepts that run through all ethnomethodological work – indexicality and reflexivity – and show why they have a broader relevance for accounts of cultural change than just to those committed to what sometimes seems the sect-like concerns of ethnomethodology. I wrote previously that the study of everyday life must assume that actors respond to one another in terms of their interpretations or what they think actions, signs and settings, etc. mean (to do otherwise would involve suspending any concern with everyday life in favour of those factors such as genetic inheritance which could be held to determine it). The issue captured by the notion of indexicality is that meanings are not specifiable in ways that are independent of the situations in which they are formulated. Communications (that is, expressions of meanings in whatever form) are enigmas to be unravelled on each and every occasion, so that 'to make sense of these and other communications members pay artful attention to the available contextual features to achieve an interpretation' (Benson and Hughes 1983, pp. 101–2). At first glance this might seem to sufficiently explain what I have described as the disorderly or irrational character of everyday life, in that generally people are striving for pragmatic and therefore situational interpretations.

There is, however, a danger of endless regress here. Indexicality is opposed to rationalising theories of human expression which hold that signs, such as words, are comprehensible either because they always stand for particular meanings or because they are governed by structures which work like laws of communication. I do not have space to explore the problems here (see Winch 1958 for a concise account), but if one accepts meaningful communication always and necessarily involves creative adaptation then a different sort of problem arises. In order for any communication to be possible, expressions, to be meaningful, must display within themselves the means through which they are to be understood. And in this way we come back to a concept used earlier, that meaningful expressions are reflexive. Another way of putting this is to say that accounts (and all meaningful expressions are accounts of social phenomena) use formal resources to elucidate how they are to be understood. The consequence of this is that indexicality and reflexivity are inherent features of all interaction, although 'in the ordinary run of affairs people do not attend to the fact that, for example in the course of a conversation, they are 'constructing' the sense, the flow, the orderliness, the rationality, and so on, of what they are engaged in' (Benson and Hughes 1983, p. 116).

The relevance of this analysis to the more general concerns of this chapter is that cultural phenomena – whether they are initiation rites, the etiquette of dining or a situation comedy on television – are constituted through the ways in which they named, recognised and categorised: 'Of course the notion of culture is, thereby, transformed and relocated in the very doings of members, in their talk, their descriptions, their formulations ... fragmentary and contingent as they may be' (Benson and Hughes 1983, pp. 148–9). I hope it will be recognised that this is another way of phrasing the point I made in the first chapter that culture is always being constituted through various modes of discourse rather than being found as an already made entity: 'we are concerned to show that culture is constituted *procedurally* – by its techniques – as much as *substantively* – in terms of its contents' (Miller and McHoul 1998, p. 159; see also Moerman 1988).[1]

Everyday Life Seen More Pragmatically

I have been very briefly sketching some of the key themes in a representation of social reality that begins with and indeed refuses to go beyond the practical matters of mundane experience as resources for social life (see also Potter 1996). Not only does this intellectual project seem to repair what I have pointed to as an absence in sociological accounts of modernity, but it also seems to address the discrepancy between rationalising theory and the particularity of everyday experience that I have identified. The ethnomethodological perspective, particularly conversation analysis, does this by identifying formal structures to the management of interpersonal interaction that show the orderliness of personal circumstance; and indeed show a 'rationality' in the everyday.[2]

Given these accomplishments, it becomes appropriate to ask why my own work is not more directly located within the ethnomethodological canon. The answer is found in the contrasts between the use of reflexivity in the discussion of developing character of modernity and that which has just been briefly sketched. For writers such as Giddens, Beck and Lash, reflexivity is not confined to the practices of interpersonal interaction.[3] The reason is that they seek to elucidate meanings and identities at institutional levels that are not as focused on processes of interpersonal interaction as studies in ethnomethodology and conversation analysis (although see Boden and Zimmerman 1991; Drew and Heritage 1992). For critical theorists of the broader sweep of modernisation the process of rationalisation is central, and it is this dimension that is missing from the ethnomethodological project.

It is clear that for all the major strengths of ethnomethodological concerns with the constitution of everyday life there is virtually no sense of historical change and how that may be accommodated. Thus the institutionalisation of rationalisation in the management of appearances by various forms of public body cannot be considered. Although the development of conversation analysis has made significant strides in the identification of formal resources in the management of interaction, the failure to address issues in institutional change, other than in the sphere of language, has meant turning away from the character of everyday life in modernity. The discrepancy I have identified between the rationalisation of modernising change and the messy irrationality of ordinary life has been swept under a carpet of detailed analysis. It is important to recognise how structures of order are employed in the construction of social reality, but not at the cost of effectively neglecting what I have called the doubled character of representations. As I have made clear, for Giddens and the others, while reflexivity may in some sense be a cultural universal, there is also a crucial emphasis on the idea that in processes of social and cultural change reflexivity is becoming more significant at every level of social organisation.

The general approach in this book is that an account of cultural change needs a level of analysis of social and cultural forms as institutionalised practices. It may be helpful to explore the use and interpretation of photographs here. In a great deal of everyday life photos are of family or household members either posed in relatively formal settings such as celebrations or the school photograph, or in more informal snapshots often taken on holiday or in other leisure situations. These photographs are indexical and reflexive resources used and interpreted much as other expressive resources in the negotiation of immediate situations and members' identities. Photographs are, however, extremely portable 'texts'. Not only are they easily reproduced but they can be 'pasted into' a variety of settings to illustrate other discourses. Thus in an obvious example an image of a young woman in a beach setting can function as a family memento, an objectification of gender and a record of changing fashions, etc., thereby expressing meanings that move outside the immediate concerns of viewers.

I have suggested in the title of this section that I will be concerned with more pragmatic accounts of everyday life, and I therefore now turn to symbolic interactionism which was included by Douglas in his review of phenomenologically inspired sociologies. While I do not think this is strictly true, clearly symbolic interactionism is part of a broader interpretive tradition and interactionists (again a label that covers a variety of types of work) have contributed a great deal to our knowledge of everyday life situations (e.g. Truzzi 1968; Glassner and Hertz 1999).[4] I include them at this point in the narrative, although the broad sweep of the interactionist tradition pre-dates many of the publications already cited, because they direct our attention back to both the everyday as representation and the creativity of everyday life. Both are themes that provide a crucial bridge to ideas developed in later sections of the chapter. Generally I think it fair to say that interactionists are less interested in everyday life as a phenomenon in its own right than in the sorts of ways actors interact to make life's situations routinely manageable. Their stance is if anything naturalistic rather than theoretic – they begin with members' assumptions of normality and ask how they go about sustaining the orderliness of it. So interactionists do share an interest in the overriding question with which we began – how is everyday life possible? – but really focus on how actors make situations have the quality of the everyday.

Really instead of saying they begin with members' assumptions of normality I should have said they begin with members' quest for the orderliness of normality. I think this explains why it is that interactionists have often been drawn to research what ordinary people might see as abnormal or deviant situations. Indifferent to the morality or physiology of drug use or prostitution or selling funerals or achieving orgasm, etc., interactionists show us that these are bits of social business that have to be managed usually by being routinised so that for those concerned they become everyday life. An example can be used to illustrate this characterisation (Birenbaum and Sagarin 1973). In a collection of studies oriented to the sociology of the familiar, we find work on sleep, errands and intimacies as well as drinking and gambling. The overall emphasis though is on managing life's diversity: 'The study of man in his most familiar settings can be called situational sociology. It makes social life into a drama but one in which there is no clear line between actors and audience' (Birenbaum and Sagarin 1973, pp. 9–10).

Two further aspects are brought out in this quote: the first is the emphasis on situations which are treated as a resource framing actors' difficulties rather than indexically as in ethnomethodology; and secondly an assumption that the management (of situations) is a form of performance signalled by the slip into dramaturgical metaphors. In this the editors, as they explicitly acknowledge, are developing a perspective on everyday life derived from Goffman's study of the presentation of the self in what has become one of the best-known books in sociology (1959). Particularly in his early works, Goffman is concerned to provide a sort of taxonomy of types of space and social occasion through a play between telling example and structured analysis so that he can direct our attention to the means of the production of social order (e.g. 1971, 1974). As Manning puts it, for Goffman the predictability of everyday life 'is neither natural nor assured; instead it is an astonishing collective achievement' (1992, p. 10). In so doing he generates a sense of wonder at the creativity of everyday life that might well be taken as a starting point for all sociological curiosity.

Although Goffman does not sit straightforwardly within the interactionist tradition his studies of the strategies and rituals of interpersonal relationships have been enormously influential, as has his practice of taking instances eclectically from 'everyday life' (that is what he takes to be familiar) rather than using data generated by research practices. Goffman's significance as a social theorist is that he greatly enhanced our understanding of what Giddens has called the reproduction of institutions (1984, and in this extending Simmel's conviction that society is constituted in forms of sociation), although his joy in the minutiae of 'performance' also generates 'a kind of map to the uncharted world of everyday life' (Manning 1992, p. 4; or 'a new way of thinking about the obvious and the common-sensical' (Weigert 1981, p. vii)).

Rationalisation and Everyday Life

I have been briefly outlining sociological work which has not only treated everyday life as important but has also showed how the variety and unpredictability of ordinary creativity are not chaotic. This work therefore leads us to considerably modify the rather glib use of irrational in relation to everyday life. I do not, however, want to drop the usage altogether for reasons that will become apparent in this and the following section.

My main criticism of sociologies inspired by phenomenological ideas has been that they have neglected or been unable to accommodate the significance of institutionalised practices or discourses in framing meaning. In particular, the ways in which developments in modernisation have intensified pressures to rationalisation in marketing and consumption as well as production. A more general way of formulating the consequence of these pressures is a recognition that the meaning of the world at hand can be seen to be systematically distorted. While what I will call the Marxist perspective is rather arbitrarily named, as is the body of work characterised as phenomenological,[5] I use the label for one definitively important reason. This is that the writers I include in this group emphasise that the consciousness of the ordinary individual will generally be oppressed by the character of everyday life (for a much fuller account see Gardiner 2000). That is to say that social circumstances will routinely operate to ensure that individuals cannot perceive or evaluate their life circumstances appropriately.

This idea, that the structures or forms of everyday life can work to perpetuate a false consciousness, I take to be inspired by Marxist critiques of capitalist society and is significantly absent from the phenomenological tradition. Which is not to say that that tradition cannot encompass a concept of ideology, but the idea that consciousness is systematically distorted so that everyday life is oppressive rather than the ground of our being would generally be untenable in the interpretive perspective.[6] (Any typology generates anomalies and in this case the contrast I am drawing between phenomenologists and Marxists is inadequate to encompass a writer on the everyday such as Dorothy Smith (see 1987).) To speak of systematic distortion raises the question of whether the consequential constraints can ever be transcended. I will not attempt to survey the full range of ways of answering the question of ideological closure, instead I will be concerned with those who see everyday life as a site of dialectical tensions or conflicts between oppression and resistance. We are then looking at social thinkers who have been led to a concern with the determinations of consciousness, a theme that has become attractive in critical theory in later modernity interestingly largely because it has offered a way of interpreting cultural change.

Marx's thesis that the contradictions of the capitalist economic order would lead to a polarisation of conflict between the two main social classes was clearly wrong as a prediction of necessity. The potential for conflict has been masked by the considerable proportion of the working class at any one time who did and do not feel themselves exploited by the economic order, and by increasing standards of living of the working class throughout the twentieth century. Consequently the thesis has been supplemented by an emphasis on the use of cultural resources by the powerful to ensure that workers or employees do not fully appreciate the nature of their economic exploitation or their alienation from the full potential meaning of their productive labour. There has in this sense been a turn to culture within Marxism designed to explain developments in the capitalist social and economic order post-Marx.[7] This has clearly taken a number of forms most of which are not immediately significant for my account here; but one version of this critique of conventional knowledge has concentrated on everyday life – summarised by Silverstone as: 'The worker is seduced by, and into, the false realities (or real falsehoods) of the culture of everyday life and into believing in his or her own freedoms and authenticities' (1994, p. 161).

It is important to appreciate here that this is a development of broader themes in the sociology of knowledge. When concluding the previous chapter I said that Berger and Luckmann's dissatisfaction with an ideology-critique of cultural or intellectual knowledge had led them to explore what they called the social construction of reality. The developments of Marxist critique I am outlining are also concerned with the social construction of reality, but this time through enhancing or strengthening an ideology-critique. By this I mean that conventional understandings of the forms of reality are depicted as ideological because they work to maintain social and cultural consensus. It follows from this that: 'If we accept the quotidian passively we cannot apprehend it *qua* quotidian; we have to step back and get it into perspective' (Lefebvre 1971, p. 27). In saying this Lefebvre is distancing himself from the *Annales* school of French historians such as Braudel who have written histories of cultural change in Europe from the perspective of aspects of everyday life such as sexual habits, cleanliness, home furnishings and costume (Braudel 1981).

Lefebvre is also though, and more relevantly for my purpose, envisaging a level of representation that is probably completely alien to its subjects and is in effect a critical history of everyday life. In this perspective he argues that style has come to dominate culture resulting in, amongst other features, 'anguish arising from a general sense of meaninglessness, the proliferation of signs and signifieds failing to make up for the general lack of significance' (1971, p. 39; a considerably more authoritative account of Lefebvre's several publications has been published by Shields (1998) who also brings out the clear connections to the intellectual context of critical theory). Although the inadequacies of the culture of modernity stem for Lefebvre from the fact that culture is the ideological face of what he characterises as a bureaucratic society of controlled consumption, he does differentiate between those who are completely immersed in the trivialities of consumption and those who sense the possibility of using the material world as a means of actualisation. It is, though, necessarily a vastly unequal struggle, because the forces of governance have come to appreciate that rationalisation can be disguised by instilled needs to endlessly consume novelties fuelled by the insistent rhetoric of advertising: 'Publicity does not only provide an ideology of consumption ... [it is also] ... based on their imaginary existence; it evokes them and involves a rhetoric and a poetry superimposed on the act of consuming and inherent in its image' (1971, p. 90).

The critique of everyday life can now be understood to be a critique of the alienation and inauthenticity inherent in a culture of consumption (and in this making connections to a broader critique of mass society and mass culture). It is argued that the forms and rhythms of material practices grounded in local circumstances have been broken up and swept aside so that culture itself becomes a commodity and part of an infinite spectacle: 'every object and product acquires a dual existence, perceptible and make-believe; all that can be consumed becomes a symbol of consumption and the consumer is fed on symbols, symbols of dexterity and wealth, of happiness and of love' (1971, p. 108; and again one can see how this critique has fed into later critical accounts of consumerism such as that of Cross (1993) and Haug (1986)). In this account everyday life comes to consciousness in modernity because for the first time moderns have to choose how (or at least how to try) to act authentically. While it is true that the spectacle of consumerism offers to transcend the constraints of work, this is not emancipating because the free space of everyday life cannot be represented. Actors are pitched into a world of leisure that is either frustrating because it cannot be controlled or it is hallucinatory in its self-absorption.

I have said that this critique of everyday life in the modern world has been attractive (and have tried to indicate the broader sweep of the critique which has also clearly become part of the debate about the meaning of the postmodern condition), because it signals an important development in Marxist analysis by shifting the location of the crucial site of alienation from labour relations to relations of consumption. Although everyday life has been presented as lying at the heart of the ideological regimes that hold modern society together, I think it is actually seen as occupying a more complex mediating role. This is because it is really the institutions of mass culture and consumerism that are held to constitute the society of the spectacle – while it is true that they are made tangible in the practices of everyday life, it is also in the ways people consume that ideological regimes can be seen to be being resisted or transcended. As Roberts says: 'Lefebvre begins from the premise that the alienating forms of everyday life contain within them real, if unconscious and fragmented, desires' (1998, p. 8). Some of this ambiguity can be found in the politicisation of Lefebvre's ideas (allied with other sources) in the manifestos of the Situationist movement that have now become irremovably linked to the 'interruption' of ideological closure in May 1968, Paris (Plant 1992).

In the previous chapter I noted how the Situationists can also be seen as an avant-garde art movement, although one dedicated to the destruction of art in favour of a creation (or re-creation?) of everyday life (Gray 1974;

Vaneigem 1979). Although in their role as a call to arms to overthrow the society of the spectacle these manifestos offered a revolutionary promise, they were also very pessimistic about the power of oppressive ideology. They did, however, act as a catalyst for a combination of social theory, revolutionary social movements, anti-art artistic practice and a politics of the everyday that has been crucially important for a reconsideration of the nature of popular experience in cultural change that has resulted, amongst other initiatives, in the present book. In considering their influence it is also important to note the significance of intermediaries, particularly in relation to accounts of complex accommodations to the aestheticisation of everyday life such as in Britain in Hebdige's exploration of youth subcultures as spectacular sites for absorption in, and yet resistance to, the signifying potential of consumption (1979).

I hope it is by now clear that writers who adopt a critical stance to the everyday do so from two motives. In part because they wish to show that it is in the reproduction of alienation in the most basic tissues of ordinary experience that the more general inauthenticity of modernity becomes possible. And in part because they believe that in the sphere of the everyday the alienation of authenticity can at least potentially be transcended, as Gardiner puts it for the critical tradition: '*it is the everyday world itself* that is open to redemption, to positive and empowering transformation ... {*because*} ... The everyday exhibits a certain strength and resilience that enables it to resist domination by identity-thinking' (2000, p. 15, emphasis in original). Such a recovery of meaning is possible through what I have called the persistent 'irrationality' of embodied life which, because it is independent of discredited scientific expertise, can provide an alternative basis for processes of cultural contestation based in personal experience.

I have said that in the critical perspective it is the distinctive alienating features of modernity that have created a problem of everyday life, a problem that was absent in the more integrated social worlds of traditional society. A further elaboration of this perspective comes in Heller's book on the sociology of everyday life (1984), where although she shares the general stance that everyday life is the site of alienation for modern consciousness (a theme she develops from the writings of Marx and Lukacs), she argues it would be mistaken to reduce this alienation to being merely the consequence of consumerism and privatisation. Everyday life is not seen to be equivalent to the private sphere, but rather consists of a passive acceptance of the particularity of experience and situations. Thus although everyday life is where actors labour at the reproduction of social life, the effect is the reproduction of alienation unless and until they can find ways of transcending particular consciousness to attain a form of generic consciousness. This seems to be a form of reflexive (in the sense of self-conscious) consciousness in which actions are oriented to social (or communal) needs and values which can be authentic rather than alien-ated. Interestingly, though, this approach has two consequences which I pick up in the following sections. The first is that social theory needs to attend to the particularity of life-practices rather than presume their meaning on purely theoretical grounds; and secondly that the everyday is seen to have a potential, indeed almost a utopian promise, for the recon-struction of meaning that transcends alienation.

Celebrating the Irrationality of the Everyday

So far I have described two broad traditions of approach to the study of everyday life within social theory. I have tried to bring out one major dif-ference between these traditions in the attention they pay to processes of rationalisation in the modern social order. There is of course a further corollary of this distinction, which is the different ways in which the 'irra-tionality' of the everyday is conceptualised. While the differences in style and practice between these traditions are very evident they do, however, bring out distinctive difficulties in the study or representation of every-day life, and help to clarify Maffesoli's insistence on everyday life need-ing a unique and innovative analytic stance. One way of conceptualising what is needed here would be to see the discrepancy between rationalisa-tion and irrationality as the perennial sociological issue of how to recon-cile competing perspectives between structure and agency. Thus as Silverstone has put it, the problematic of everyday life 'is the expressions of activity and creativity *within*, and constitutive of, the mobile forces of structure' (1994, p. 164). I think what he means by this is how to give appropriate recognition to the practical creativity of ordinary people while also recognising the constraints of their social and ideological con-text. In fact I think it is of only limited use to see rationalisation as exter-nal constraint; rather I will in the concluding sections of the chapter, and in the following chapters, argue for a more complexly dynamic account of the representations of social normality.

I have emphasised that writers within the Marxist tradition, while beginning from a perspective on the everyday that sees it as the sphere of alienation, allow that it has the potential for transformation and transcen-dence; as Roberts puts it: 'the sense that the routine, commodified and alienated everyday experiences of late capitalism contain the suppressed and unformed potential of emancipatory transformation' (1998, p. 6). I stress this point because it is consistent with my view of cultural change as a remaking by actors of their life-worlds. It seems to me that Marxists (and the wider sphere of Marxist influence), because of their commitment to the study of social change, have been more able to recognise the prob-lematic character of the everyday in modernity, although the dominant strand of economism has also led to a neglect of both the feminine sphere of the everyday and the implications of popular creativity. A completely pessimistic analysis, to which some have succumbed, is, however, obviously self-defeating and so the institutions of mass culture must be limited in their effectiveness, thus allowing a potential for resistance or subversion, with the further implication that the everyday has to be understood as a site for contesting meanings.

It is therefore appropriate to devote some space to writers who have thought more closely about the creativity of everyday life. Creativity is particularly important, because by definition it is open-ended and unpredictable and thus likely to be troublesome for rationalising tendencies seeking coherent order; indeed, disorderliness in the everyday is likely to seem irrational to social authorities and to be prized by social actors as a way of preserving some sense of distinctiveness or authenticity as a form of resistance to those authorities. One author whose writings on the everyday have been influential in this respect (although not in the Marxist tradition and who shares an interest in Wittgensteinian philosophy with ethnomethodologists) has been de Certeau (1984). Unlike the dominant strain in the Marxist tradition which is not interested in the specifics of everyday practices, de Certeau is particularly concerned with how they are typically performed – that is with the ways of doing rather than what is done. He therefore directs our attention to how people routinely negotiate the meanings of mass cultural institutions (Buchanan 2000; Gardiner 2000; and I have previously discussed this approach in greater detail as part of an analysis of theories of lifestyle practices in 1996, Ch. 6). There are three points that I will take from de Certeau's interpretation of everyday life as they are particularly relevant to the interrelationships with cultural change.

The first is a distinction he makes between two characteristics of social actions: strategies and tactics. The former are clearly intended and more easily understood as rational, whereas tactical actions are short term, haphazard and situational (indexical). He argues, however, that tactical actions are more characteristic of everyday life, and it is in these unremarked incidentals that one is more likely to find the evasiveness that escapes the logic of instrumental rationality. This leads on to the second point that the everyday is in effect invisible to the analytic gaze. Because the everyday is the marginal taken-for-granted backdrop to more 'significant' happenings (what Debord calls specialised activities), to become a focus of inquiry requires a shift in perspective (as we have seen Maffesoli also maintains) so that 'to make tangible the exact status of everydayness ... it must be compared to the status of dreams in Freud's thought' (de Quieroz 1989, p. 33). This in turn leads on to a third point that a study of the everyday requires a transformation of the intellectual stance of the observer: 'The very nature of the object revealed by a sociology of everyday life alters from the inside the relation that the scientist holds to what he knows and to the idea of knowledge of the social world' (de Quieroz 1989, p. 35). Issues around the manner of representation become as relevant to the practice of social theory as to the practice of more conventional cultural forms – and here at last we can see the full relevance of issues raised by different modes of documentary practice discussed in Chapter 2.

The cumulative effect of these points is a rejection of the belief held by Lefebvre and inherent in the self-consciousness of a vanguard intelligentsia beloved of Marxism that theory alone can adequately represent everyday life. In bringing this out, de Certeau abandons any commitment to the 'rationality' of social theory, as well as undermining any pessimistic account of the power of surveillance authorities to completely encompass social discourse. It follows that in de Certeau's account of everyday life the accomplishment of processes of cultural change becomes central. For de Certeau the nature of cultural changes provides the materials through which everyday life is at least in part constituted, rather than acting as determinants from outside the sphere of the everyday. This idea has also been expressed in two other projects by British social theorists in ways that help to clarify it. The first comes in two books by John Fiske (1989a, b; see also 1996; and the study reported in Willis 1990; see also Hearn and Roseneil 1999), explicitly oriented to the interpretation of cultural change, particularly popular culture. Fiske argues that the popular should not be evaluated by reference to aesthetic criteria derived from other cultural spheres, and neither should it be evaluated by its class consciousness or revolutionary potential or not. Instead, popular cultural performances can be differentiated by the extent to which they facilitate rereading or renegotiation by audience groups. That is the extent to which the popular can be adapted as a resource in the making and remaking of everyday life.

This idea of the popular as resource is also central to two editions of a book by Cohen and Taylor on the 'theory and practice of resistance to everyday life' (1978, 1993). As this subtitle of the book makes clear, the initial assumption is that the everyday is oppressive, but here it stems more from the iron cage of bureaucratic rationality rather than the sometimes more apocalyptic sense of alienation in Lefebvre. Although Cohen and Taylor do not cite de Certeau as a source, their account of the tactics of resistance interestingly overlaps – for ordinary people 'fights against reality are rarely frontal assaults, running battles or planned campaigns. They are more often interruptions in the flow of life, interludes, temporary breaks, skirmishes, glimpses of other realities' (1978, p. 24). In their play with contrasts between dominant and alternative realities, Cohen and Taylor are taking us back to our phenomenological starting point, but here the interplay of realities is explicitly politicised. Such breaks in normality are often commonly pursued, as their chapters illustrate, through opportunities available in the spectacle and entertainments of cultural industries, and in particular through a search for freedom in leisure. So although mass culture is not condemned as only offering overwhelming suppression by inauthentic illusion, the authors retain a clear sense of the limitations of escape and the conflicts and contests it entails.

It is arguable how 'everyday' the pursuit of escapes is (certainly the phenomenological status of the possibility of an escape is an essential element in those alternatives that help to constitute the normality of everyday life – see below and Chapter 8). A theme of evasion is, however, significant in three ways: first, it suggests that the normality of everyday life is never complete, it is always provisional and hedged around with uncertainty; secondly, it follows that in the performance of everyday life actors have choices while making it up as they go along; and thirdly, that the meaning of choices made helps to constitute who 'they' (whether as individuals or instances of more collective categories) are, so that the choices become in effect battlegrounds over what are seen to be legitimate or appropriate decisions. An example will, I hope, help to make these rather abstract points more concrete.

In one of her contributions to a collection on consumption and everyday life, Finnegan (1997, 1998) reports some research on the sorts of stories people in Milton Keynes tell about aspects of their lives. The incidents reported are not necessarily of dramatic occasions, but they are accounts which help to make sense of the person doing the telling: 'A fragment of a *story* about a life can tell us so much more than one hundred pages of *information* about a life' (O'Neill 1998, p. 128 emphasis in original; see also Berger 1997 and Hepworth 2000). The stories Finnegan researched she came to appreciate as personal engagements with identity as a totality: 'personal narratives can be regarded not as *reflections* of life but rather as a way of *constructing* it' (1997, p. 75 emphasis in original). The authorial impulse is not, however, autonomous – the form of the tale is not just a whim of the speaker's imagination but is based in available conventions and repertoires. This is the main point I want to take from her study for this context: 'these stories were both personal and yet not *purely* personal. In that they were cultural constructs, not "natural" phenomena, their tellers were able to draw from ... a culturally recognized art-form to organize personal experience and the development of a life' (op. cit., p. 93, emphasis in original).

Everyday life is a creative project because although it has the predictability of mundane expectations, it is simultaneously being worked at both in the doing and in retrospective reconsideration. In order to see how the details of personal experience get to make sense both to actors and others, we have to frame those details in the forms of conventional accounts. My general approach, then, is to stress that the shift of perspective required in studying everyday life is not a search for new sorts of 'data'. It is rather a recognition that interpretation requires a sensitivity to both what is going on and the ways in which that which is going on is simultaneously being framed, articulated and staged (see Smith 1987). Thus coming back to the problem of creativity of personal experience with which I began this section, I feel able to say now that particular studies will require close attention to the frameworks or ecologies of space and time within which the narrative conventions and material embodiments of identity are being formulated.[8] Here I have been concerned with changes in the formulation of experience that we label as everyday life that have been consequent upon modernisation; and in the next chapters with how some of these 'formulations' have been elaborated and re-elaborated in what I am calling the textually mediated discourses of a culture of mass entertainment.[9]

Conclusion

In drawing this discussion of everyday life to a close I hope to have shown that in the variety of writing on the topic, despite the frequently opaque terminology of social theorists, there is a consistent commitment to the distinctiveness of the social, and to an engagement with the idea that the experience of sociality is not an unchanging 'essence'. This is, however, a lofty ambition, and it is doubtless reasonable to ask if there any more immediate achievements in relation to the study of cultural change. I believe that there are and I will therefore set them out as a series of points:

- The first is the clear consensus running throughout the authors I have reviewed that the topic of everyday life must be approached as something that is constantly being renewed rather than treated as an accomplishment.[10]
- This leads to the realisation that one is more properly concerned with how processes of construction, constitution, are undertaken, for the very banality of the accomplishment of everyday life masks its significance.
- Those who seek to interpret these processes have to forgo a stance of disembodied observer using their own framework for distinctions between what is or is not significant, and instead seek significance in the uncertainties, hesitations and mistakes of practical actions.
- The fourth point is that although I have emphasised the making of meanings in everyday life, this process uses forms or structures which can exist at a number of levels.
- Form is perhaps best understood as a resource – a mode of order that makes sense appreciable – and this idea of resource can be explicated as a discourse or means of expression.
- Forms do not, however, float in a potential social space unanchored until they are called upon, but are generated in the pursuit of practical

interests, and in this sense a crucial part of what they represent and articulate are competing interests.
- Forms in everyday life give it its character of predictable, orderly routine and indeed make communication of new meanings possible, but they do not necessarily lend themselves easily to being rationalised, so that everyday life may retain the impression of being disorderly or irrational when seen from outside.
- Overall, it follows that change in relation to those forms we call cultural is not something that happens independently of everyday life (or is a representation of everyday life) but is part of the discourses that constitute the everyday.

In conclusion, I can now hope that the project for a sociology of cultural change from the perspective of everyday life is clearer (although we might still agree with Crook (1998) that the topic of the everyday as such is best left alone). I might have been read as saying at the beginning of the book that I sought to explore the interrelationships of cultural change and everyday life. Although this way of putting it is commonsensical, I have tried to show that neither cultural change nor everyday life can really be thought of as entities existing independently that can have effects on one another. I have tried to bring out instead that instances of both cultural change and everyday life utilise both sides of that pairing in order to be comprehensible. In order to see how the various styles of 'normality' are made to seem so, we have to be sensitive to the interplay of the discourses that are formative. I will in the following chapters introduce some illustrations of what might be involved here by discussing several institutionalised spheres of the everyday in contemporary Britain.

4

Everyday Life and Personal Setting

The Household as a Moral Economy

In the opening chapters I have introduced aspects of the social and cultural changes of modernity and their implications for our understanding of an idea of everyday life. In lots of ways we feel, with Berger, that there is an implicit order in everyday life that we can describe through the metaphor of neighbourliness. I have, however, suggested that in the social and cultural developments of modernity how to articulate or represent this sense of order became problematic. The difficulties did not just stem from the inadequacies of our means of representation but were inherent in the forms and structures of modernity. The difficulties were not therefore peculiar to the projects of intellectuals, that is those who have acquired some mastery in the use of public discourse, but were present throughout the experience of ordinary people. In the remaining chapters I will explore how in later modernity the everyday has become both more prominent in the entertainments and commentaries that make up the popular culture of ordinary people, as well as increasingly providing the idioms of public discourse. While this is in itself a mode of cultural change, it should not be taken to signal either that the meaning of the everyday has been settled, or that Britain has become a popular democracy.

I hope in these chapters to bring out how disputes over how the everyday is to be interpreted and represented lie at the heart of the management of cultural change. Initially I will develop this overall perspective through some notes on how changing frameworks of private and public spheres are indicated by how ordinary people use technologies, artefacts and discourses to negotiate their environments in the process of dramatising identities and subjectivities. It seems to me that an interplay between the physical terrain we inhabit and the textually mediated discourses we consume is the most tangible sense of everyday lived experience. I believe the various examples I will discuss are linked by a notion of the household as the setting in which two modes of inhabiting places and using culture can be seen together. I have pointed to Berger's metaphor of neighbourliness as implying a network of commitments and responsibilities, a moral order, in relation to those with whom one shares somewhere. I therefore think it is important to consider how the process of cultural change might have modified the moral order, not just in terms of behaving towards others but also in using the facilities of the domestic environment. It could be argued that both a heightening of consumer acquisitiveness and a loss of local commitments and identities through a massification of culture have meant that moral frameworks have been undermined in ways that make individuals more susceptible to exploitation by corporate interests.

I am thus in this chapter going to be concerned with whether moral frameworks can be found to persist in everyday life, and how this relates to the tension between rationalisation and everyday rationality. I have briefly suggested previously that the character of modernity has been grounded in a fundamental differentiation between public and private spheres. The interdependence of these spheres has not, of course, remained constant throughout the modern era. In subsequent chapters I explore some aspects of the changing character of public discourse. If the representations of authority and legitimacy are changing as part of a more radical democratisation of public life, it will follow that there will have been complementary changes in the institutionalised conventions of the private sphere. My argument throughout this book is that in an era of cultural fragmentation the interface of public and private spheres has been reconstituted. In this chapter, I shall use the idea of the household as the primary locus of the private sphere as an initial framework for an exploration of the changing conventions and discourses of this sphere of everyday life.

The basis for the development of a distinction between public and private spheres was provided by an innovation within particular social groups of physically separating work and the family. More technically, we can say that the structural basis for a differentiation between public and private spheres lay in moves away from the household as the main centre of productive activities, and a related restriction of a household to a single family. The implication of these processes is that the household in modernity has been projected primarily as a centre for consumption – not only of household goods and services but also increasingly of leisure activities. I say projected because of course the household is not a work-free zone. It takes a considerable amount of labour to organise and sustain a household, both its functional and leisure activities, and that labour is predominately provided by female members. So that for women, particularly the mother, a household is a site of very active and demanding production, but it is unpaid labour and oriented towards the constitution of a consumption environment. That this generates different ways of using a social environment is brought out very clearly in relation to television watching by Bennett et al.: 'For men, the home is a place of leisure, and watching television is something that is done attentively and as a self-contained activity. For women, even those in the work-force, watching television is more likely to be an activity which ... has to be fitted into all manner of domestic responsibilities, or which has to be done in more disengaged or sociable ways' (1999, p. 75). The dominant ideology of a household as leisured zone also underlies a second assumption that it has provided a site for more 'authentic' social life in contrast to the artificiality of more public interaction.

I hope I can now make it a little clearer why I have called this section 'a moral economy'. Moving households into the private sphere has not robbed them of all economic significance. Indeed they have retained a central role as the probable motor for important economic decisions concerning, for example, motor cars, furnishings, leisure practices and lifestyle diets (Lunt and Livingstone 1992). The discussion and decision-making processes around these acquisitions and investments are not, however, governed by a concern for the maximisation of profit, but rather by concerns for what is seen to be appropriate and desirable for this group of people. Economic decision-making in modern households is therefore governed by norms of desirability and good conduct (both ethical and aesthetic), much as Thompson originally argued that markets in early-modern Europe were often governed by moral as much as economic considerations (1971). (Although saying this is not meant to neglect the obvious considerations of necessary economy that doubtless influence many household decisions.) Indeed such has been the moral significance of the household in the private sphere – not just in relation to the staging of domestic life but, as I have just said, as the locus for what have been perceived to be more 'natural' relationships – that I think it provides a good analytic framework for any discussion of the implications of cultural change for the institutional structures (or moral order) of everyday life.

While I will in the next section look at some aspects of how homes and families have been constituted through textually mediated discourses, the reason for using the household more generally in this chapter is that it is the spatial setting which mediates between public and private spheres. The household is an ecological universal, necessarily common despite a gamut of living arrangements. One's home may well be a part of the larger entity that the household inhabits, and not share kinship ties with some or all of other household members, while one's family will be dispersed through several homes and households. What this means is that the household has increasingly become the crucial social form that mediates between public and private spheres. This is particularly significant, as so many of the innovations in the marketing of leisure facilities and consumer goods have worked to privatise or individualise consumption in household settings – in effect culture has been privatised. New technologies such as radio and television, various forms of music-player, more recently the personal computer and above all the revolution in transport inaugurated by the private car, have all brought public culture into the sphere of everyday life.

This then is one sense in which the everyday has become more prominent, in that it has become the primary site of cultural participation rather
than more public specialised settings such as concert halls, cinemas, audi-
toria and sports stadia. In addition to the personalisation of cultural consumption, we will have to locate this change within broader processes of
enormously expanded consumer facilities that have been characterised as
a consumer culture (on the significance of consumer culture for traditions
of social theory, see Slater 1997 and Chaney 1998). As I have said, the
increased significance of consumption as a medium for social values cannot be separated from a gradual substitution of leisure activities and
styles for what had previously been the centrality of work. All these interrelated developments focus around the development of the suburban
estate as the dominant ecological environment for household forms. In
considering the cultural changes of late modernity we will have to be concerned, therefore, with both the social organisation of cultural activities
and the articulation of distinctions between public and private matters. It
will be my argument that the personal experience for ordinary people of
what I will call cultural fragmentation will be based in complex reconcil-
iations of constraints and opportunities.

Staging Homes and Families

It may well be surprising that I have picked out the household as the
crucial institutional framework for everyday life in the private sphere.
Although the home or family are often used synonymously, these terms
strictly refer to different types of entity. A home is essentially a normative
concept, while a family is a structural concept and a household is both
ecological and economic (although in a system of moral economy). The
family is, of course, a notoriously imprecise term and has never been
simply coterminous with a household. More recently, changes in the structures of family relationships which are familiar from widespread journal-
istic commentary, and are intrinsic to the process of individualisation
discussed above (Beck-Gernsheim 1998), have meant that it is not uncom-
mon for families including nuclear families to be spread across several
households. This has meant that individuals may have several homes
simultaneously, the use of the term being governed by the context at hand,
and one's immediate family may have several sites with whom one is
involved in household arrangements to differing degrees.

The constitutive social arrangements of the private sphere are therefore
in a process of transition, so that we need to note some of the ways in
which terms such as home and family are being restaged in a privatisation of public culture[1] (both Silverstone 1994 and Morley 2000 are important and influential books in this area). I have said that home is a

normative concept, and by this meant that what counts as home for any-one is defined by an emotional affiliation ('home is where the heart is'), and is therefore an arbitrary attribution. It may be a village, town, region or landscape, but for most people is generally understood to be a private habitation (on some of the ambiguities of the social construction of homes as lived environments, see Chapman and Hockey 1999). Because it is nor-mative and therefore special one's home is a privileged place, but as we have noted in practice, many of us have more then one home simultane-ously. This is not just because homes overlap, but different parts of one's family will have separate homes with different claims upon affiliation. (Perhaps sentimentally there is a tendency to speak of where one lived with one's mother as at least one home.) What is to count as a home will be constituted through certain symbols and rituals – thus times of family reunions at 'the old home' will usually be celebrated in a ritualised meal as at Thanksgiving and Christmas. My point here is to suggest that the private means of public culture – pre-eminently first radio and then tele-vision – have become both symbols and a focus for ritual in the domestic home. It is in this that we can recognise how certain consumer goods have become at least partly constitutive of a normative ideal.

Two further points about this process should be made. First, there is as always a politics to cultural change. The promotion of a radio and then a television set as a focus for domestic life was actively encouraged by the service provider(s), who in Britain was a public authority, as part of train-ing listeners in how to be the 'right' sort of audience (Frith 1983; Moores 2000, Ch. 3). Right in the sense that they were expected to listen and watch with appropriate seriousness, even when it was a comedy performance, and in the sense that it was believed by moral reformers that a home focused on broadcasting could nurture family values for an institution seen to be under threat. Secondly, the significance of a television as a focus for home life is not constant. Initially, the cost of the television set and the fashion to design the cabinet of televisions to emphasise substantial bulk allied to the novelty of television use all helped to make the televi-sion a prized possession (Forty 1986; Morley 1995). As they have become cheaper they have proliferated throughout the household and consump-tion has become more individualised. Televisions have more recently, then, become a necessary element in home life although not necessarily still the central focus; whether this will change again with large-screen digital mini-film centres will have to be seen.

The interrelationships of ways of using entertainment facilities with the social organisation of home life lead on to a consideration of how the privatisation of culture has helped to formulate family relationships. I have described the family as a structural concept because it consists of a hierarchy of roles with differentiated responsibilities and expectations that change in the course of the life cycle. The family is also of course an institutional sphere, commanding a strong normative commitment to certain ideals of relationships that are more intense, emotionally unfettered and wholehearted than the more calculating or strategic relationships of the public sphere. As I have said, it is apparent that the stability of family structures has been undermined first by a greater mobility both physical and social, so that families are more likely to be dispersed and not share a common social space. Secondly, there is both a greater willingness, and more institutional facilities, for individuals to change sexual partners or live singly for longer periods of adulthood. This is probably not because of disillusion with ideals of family relationships but because, as Giddens has argued, of an endless search for their fuller realisation (1992). The simplicity or naturalness of family life has also been thrown more into question by a greater awareness of how these relationships embody structures of power, so that they can and have been used exploitatively, sexually and physically, both between adults and by adults towards children.

Clearly, a strong example of an argument that the everyday has become prominent as a cultural theme in later modernity is that family relationships have become such a dominating topic of televisual discourse. This is likely to have been a response to the problematic character of interpersonal relationships, particularly family relationships, in late modernity. I use the phrase 'televisual discourse' because I want to indicate that the range of representations of issues concerning family life on television is not confined to authored dramatisations but also includes documentaries, advice programmes, interviews and news reports, etc. Authored dramatisations also cover a range of genres and problematic relationships from adultery and abuse to comedic presentations such as Victor Meldrew and Terry and June. In all these different genres the anxieties of audience members can be seen to be being flattered, reassured as well as accentuated. This is particularly relevant in explaining the most distinctive genre innovation that television has developed – the continuous serial or soap opera in which family life is frequently found to be nasty and brutish but always endless.

While this perspective is obviously relevant, I want to go a bit further by emphasising the distinctiveness of television as a mode of dramatic representation. Television up until now has largely been watched on a small screen with poor picture quality. The characteristic mode of address both of the camera's distance from its subject and the performer's way of speaking has been conversational. That is, the television in the corner of the main leisure room of the household has been an element in the network of relationships that swirl through that space. I think it is unsurprising that it has largely mimicked the dominant interactional mode of its environment: 'Broadcasting, unlike cinema, is "intimate" and familiar – part of the furniture of ordinary daily life in private homes rather than a site of spectacular public entertainment' (Moores 1997, p. 216). Family relationships are therefore both the main topic of the flow of television, and a dramatic space within the living space in which social relationships are represented. In this continuous interplay of lived and dramatised relationships, it is unsurprising to discover that the use of the television has become a medium in the dynamic organisation of family life: 'television in the family ... is beginning to be seen both as a focus of family activities and as a resource' (Silverstone 1994, p. 37; see also Ang 1996; Gauntlett and Hill 1999; Hartley 1999; Morley 1992).

The argument here is that within a household and most typically within a family setting the use of a television and other technologies will become the medium of political interaction. The politics here are the micro-politics of interpersonal relations rather than party programmes, but are no less agenda-setting in terms of the management of a shared environment. As would be expected, precisely because the nuclear family is generally organised around gender distinctions, so the politics of leisure and television use in particular focus on differences in gendered power and expectations. It is not just that researchers such as Morley (1986) and Lull (1990) have found that control over the use of a shared resource is unevenly distributed, with male members of the household generally exerting more influence than female counterparts. It has also been established that television can act as a symbolic focus to integrate the household unit, or to pacify potentially demanding or troublesome household members such as children or the elderly (Lull 2000). It is also clear that there are distinctive styles in ways of using the television as, say, between it acting as a focus for conversation or absorbing attention. In a whole variety of ways, then, it seems that the passivity of the television set, waiting to be switched on or off, masks its more active role – or its institutionalisation (Moores 2000, Ch. 2) – in what I have called the moral economy of household life.

The Meanings of Material Culture

I have, then, begun to suggest that the textually mediated discourses of everyday habitation are informed by moral concerns. Would such a perspective be inconsistent with the view of everyday life being colonised by rationalisation? In this view, moral concerns with authenticity are inevitably either sacrificed altogether or at best made counterfeit by the seductions of material culture. In considering this perspective, I will consider more fully why what I have called the constraints and opportunities of cultural change have come to be focused around goods and services. I do not want to too glibly discount rationalising tendencies but neither do I want to assume they are completely dominant. In this part of the chapter, I will initially discuss why I and others have come to use the term 'material culture' to describe the resources and facilities made available to many people by consumer culture. The section largely consists of an account of the social organisation of using or appropriating television as an illustration of the mediation of moral concerns between viewers or consumers and the facilities of mass entertainment. This will lead in subsequent sections to a more general discussion of the appropriation of goods in consumer culture.

The idea that commodities are material objects that are given meaning by being embedded in social practices is not of course new. It is well established in disciplines such as archaeology and anthropology (see for example Hodder 1991 and Hoskins 1998). In the former case social theory may be confronted with artefacts, or fragments of artefacts, but no living respondents to explain their uses, decorations or ritual significance. Although social theory in anthropology is considerably more likely to engage with living practices, their respondents are also likely to lack historical records, indigenous secondary interpretations and systematic archives. In both cases, then, the study of material culture is a necessary mode of hermeneutic analysis of objects that have been in crucial respects made dumb by being distanced from the way of life of the interpretive analyst.[2] It is, however, true, as Dant has recently argued (1999), that the study of material culture has been relatively neglected in sociology or the social theory of contemporary societies – perhaps because their availability as taken-for-granted features of personal experience has made them seem self-evidently meaningful.

The main way in which the social or cultural significance of the material props of the everyday environment has been addressed in social theory is as part of a critique in which objects function as the mechanism of new forms of exploitation which is generally referred to as commodification (more generally on the exploitation of desire as a means of precluding full human self-expression, see Marcuse 1969; Cross 1993; Haug 1986; more generally on the intellectual history of the critique, see Miller 1991). I think there are two distinct strands to this critique: first, that ordinary people have been duped into treating commodities as the goal rather than the means of social interaction; and, second, that commodities have been made attractive as a form of spectacle that is open to all and thereby lacks any possibility of distinctive engagement for individuals. Both strands of the critique are illustrated by the example of the rise of dating agencies selling what should be a creative engagement as an interpersonal service. In this case the moral dimensions of reciprocity and communal value become superfluous. The idea that there have been innovations in the nature of the exploitation of the relatively powerless by the more powerful in the course of modernity effected through the changing meanings of objects obviously then must form a theme in any consideration of cultural change.

If objects marketed as commodities are changing their meanings to figure in new relationships of representation, the crucial factor must be more than there are lots of them. The innovations in representation lay in illusions of desirability promulgated by advertising and the encouragement of fashions in every aspect of life, and new emphases on fun, indulgence and the ease of gratification. In all these ways features of everyday concerns came to dominate the general cultural climate, although it can also be argued that in combination they have created new and more insidious forms of alienation. The trouble with this critique, as with the related critique of mass culture that will be discussed in the following part of the chapter, is that it is a view formed from the top down. That is, it is an intellectual account generated by those who feel themselves estranged or distanced from the everyday lives they are criticising. This is not to say it is necessarily wrong; it may well be that estrangement is necessary to get any sort of grip on the ideological closures of conventional understanding. But it is likely that in an era of cultural fragmentation when the authority of intellectual elites has been radically discredited, it will be seen to be necessary to counter this critique with a view based in the experiences of everyday life – that is from the bottom up.[3]

In order to begin to develop an alternative I will briefly discuss some of the themes in Scannell's (1996) account of the incorporation of radio and television in modern life (the representations of broadcasting are not, I suppose, strictly objects but they are only available through material facilities and they are certainly marketed as commodities). In a move that should by now be coming familiar, Scannell begins by emphasising that the institution of broadcasting (conventional expectations on form, content and use, etc.) was not present unproblematically from the beginning. Rather (in a way that exactly parallels the study of everyday life) it had to be developed through time as a discursive resource – so that while it is obvious that 'radio and television are intelligible in just such a way that anyone and everyone can understand them' we still need to 'explore the conditions of intelligibility of any radio or television programme' (p. 3). These conditions are addressed through case studies of the organisation of intelligibility of different types of programming. The great virtue of Scannell's book is that he sidesteps the conventional emphasis upon ideological persuasion of most media studies to consider the more fundamental issue of what he calls the sociability of broadcasting – how it has become part of the back- as well the foreground of everyday knowledge.

Essential to this process of constituting the sociability of broadcast experience are the ways in which listeners/viewers are addressed, or we could say included, in the dialogic frame of representation (a way of conceiving what I have elsewhere called 'audience-ing' (1993, Ch. 5) that is quite different from the positioning of audience members as passive victims of Althusserian interpellation – for an introduction to the latter approach see Strinati 1995, Ch. 4). Scannell picks out two aspects of this address that have been fundamental to mass communication – speaking[4] to anyone-as-someone (that is to a generalised other) – but at the same time making as though it is has a personal relevance to any particular me. Because, by the nature of mass communication, the particularised others cannot be present in the interactional frame (it is what Thompson has called a mediated quasi-interaction (1995, Ch. 2)), their attention is drawn, or we could say implicated, in the representation by devices of making it seem intriguing – frequently magical. This sociability of address is grounded in frameworks of predictability such as the routinisation of schedules and the serialisation of production (using the serial form as the dominant narrative structure) across a number of genres (on the organisation of televisual experience see also Abercrombie 1996; and a very different type of study of the use of television in everyday life – Gauntlett and Hill 1999).

I have talked of the sociability of broadcasting working to implicate viewers/listeners, and by this I mean that a form of involvement is being generated through a sense of what Scannell calls a mood of care. More particularly, this sense of care – which is by no means inevitable so that it has to be continuously worked at in broadcasting practice – is articulated in a number of perceived qualities: sociability, sincerity, eventfulness, authenticity and identity. (The bulk of Scannell's book is taken up by illustrations of how these qualities have been constituted in different practices – thus he writes of Vera Lynn's perceived sincerity as a singer in wartime Britain and how a documentary recording police treatment of a rape victim sustained the authenticity of its account.) The main point I want to take from Scannell's analysis is that the qualities he identifies in broadcasting practice are essentially a set of moral attributes. They provide a way in which the moral order of everyday life is echoed and reflexively displayed in broadcasting practice (see also Allan 1999, esp. Ch. 5).

Material Culture and Personal Experience

In saying that there is a reciprocity between how people use broadcasts and their general moral concerns is not to say that we as audience members, or as broadcasters, approach the provision of entertainment as a moral exercise. It is rather that the moral order of everyday life is unproblematically accepted as a way of making sense of the materiality of broadcast entertainment. That is, the commodities of broadcasting are made meaningful, at least in part, through the social practices and expectations of the households in which they are consumed. A stress upon the moral reciprocity of broadcast entertainment is not an attempt to deny its ideological closures or all the ways in which the complexity of everyday life is short-changed in broadcast representations. It is, rather, to seek to show that commodification is not necessarily incompatible with an investment of moral significance in the practices of use in everyday life: 'Its use is not simply a "using up" of the "good" but a releasing of what has been embedded; it is not a consumption so much as a reproduction' (Dant 1999, p. 14). Something as diffuse as mass broadcasting can be seen to offer different ways in which it can be made to seem appropriate for, and relevant to, the specific concerns of different household settings.

I hope this way of approaching the changes in material culture of late modernity is more useful and productive than more apocalyptic denunciations of the seduction of innocent masses into the pursuit of false needs. I think it can be accepted that an investment of forms of meaning and significance in the objects and environment at hand (that is, a material culture) is a universal feature of all social experience. So that what is distinctive about the changes of the contemporary era is that there has developed what Lury has called a process of stylisation of use, which 'refers to the production, design, making and use of goods, that is, their design, making and use as if they are works of art, images or signs and as part of the self-conscious creation of lifestyle' (1996, p. 77; on lifestyles as new ecologies of social order see Chaney 1996, and for an early reading of the cultural politics of these changes see Melly 1972). A process of stylisation is, then, a trend towards using material goods as means of representation, that is making the everyday into symbolic displays of taste and social affiliation and thereby accepting the everyday as the terrain for cultural discrimination. In the process of stylisation, although symbolic aspects are being exaggerated for the purpose of display, they are also being brought back into the everyday and treating that as primary cultural concern.

An illustration of what I mean here can be provided by summarising Lury's discussion of the ambiguities for women of the development of consumer culture (1996, Ch. 5). As a complementary contrast to my now familiar theme that technologies or objects in general are not given meaning in isolation, she begins by pointing out that consumers are not isolated individuals but members of networks of relationships. Crucially, as I have already emphasised in this chapter, women as members of households have typically had distinctive responsibilities. For example, both in relation to the provision of consumer goods for other members and through being expected to provide further work on those goods – for example by generating meals or clean household furnishings. But it is in this second sense that the process of stylisation becomes clearer. It is not just that household facilities, whether it is food, furnishings, clothes or entertainment, are expected to be functionally effective, they must also be seen to be appropriate for the perceived character and identity of the household in terms of the expectations of significant others. In other words that these facilities, and indeed the way that they are used to control the behaviour of household members particularly children, have all become imbued with moral and aesthetic significance as a mode of representation.

Lury goes on to point out that consequentially women become connoisseurs of appearance, of the representations, of others and themselves. Thus not only do women have particular responsibilities for the moral and aesthetic consistency and appropriateness for the appearance of the household and its constituent parts, but their very identity also becomes part of the economy of appearance. A more contentious way of putting this is to say that women become trailblazers in iconography of representation in an intensified material culture through being consumers of themselves. Although it is true that women have always been particularly concerned with everyday life through a joint association with the private sphere, as the everyday has become a more prominent theme and source of motifs in later modernity the frailties of order and ambiguities of representation in its various modes of dramatisation will become particularly significant. As Lury says: 'This argument has important implications for the issue of how consumer culture may have helped shape contemporary ideals of personal identity as a possession, reflexively created in practices of self-fashioning' (op. cit., p. 132).

Such an emphasis upon appearance and representation can of course be experienced as oppressive, and I will return to some of the implications of excessive concern with others' expectations in relation to management of the body in the next chapter. But it is important to recognise that there is a crucial ambiguity in seeing others' expectations as just constraints; for they may also offer an opportunity in that appearance can be exploited as a masquerade. This mode of dramatisation can be played with creatively, not solely in the manner of heroic self-aggrandisement which may be a more masculine project, but as a series of simulations of identities so that, as Lury concludes, what it is to be a social being will also be 'in part defined by the individual's relation to self-identity, a relation closely linked to notions of authenticity' (op. cit., pp. 255–6). It seems to me then that Celia Lury is making two points in this regard. The first is that appearance and representation have been made more problematic by the cultural changes of late modernity which have been described as a radical destabilisation of both the boundaries and the structures of personal experience. While the second is that this does not necessarily lead to an anomic fragmentation of the moral order, but rather new ways of making relationships through more reflexive consideration of the significance of authenticity.

It seems to me that the more we look at research evidence on how the material culture of everyday life in later modernity is being used, it becomes apparent that it is too simplistic to believe that it functions effectively as illusions that lack any personal meaning. I hope that in concluding this section I can both strengthen this argument and develop my concern with practices of representation through a brief discussion of Miller's theory of shopping (1998). Miller's account is derived from an ethnographic study of household shopping in a street in north London.

Rather than seek to infer moral effects from the facts of new structures of marketing, Miller uses the everydayness of shopping 'to be a means to uncover, through the close observation of people's practices, something about their relationships' (op. cit., p. 4). But he goes further in trying to show that the use of commodities as a mediation of relationships is not a sign of alienation, or more strictly reification, as the Marxist tradition of the oppressive character of everyday life holds. Rather, the use of commodities should be seen more positively as an 'argument that objects are the means for creating the relationships of love between subjects' (op. cit., p. 128).

In developing his theory, Miller combines his ethnographic evidence with a sophisticated reconsideration of the nature of sacrifice in a society of spectacle. This latter cannot be adequately summarised and is not essentially relevant to my present purposes. The more relevant part of his theory seeks, in a way that is analogous to Scannell's rereading of everyday television, to show that shopping is conventionally misrepresented. This is probably because it is typically associated with women as a gendered skill, and enthusiasm for shopping is usually thought of as an indulgence, prone to irrationality and almost a frivolous use of leisure time as opposed to more instrumental activities (see also some of the papers in Falk and Campbell 1997, particularly Campbell's). In order to develop an alternative, opposed view, Miller uses the ubiquity of the presence of a treat (perhaps a small purchase or a coffee and a cake) as a small piece of self-indulgence in the course of shopping. Miller argues that a contrast between the 'selfishness' of the treat and other shopping activities shows the latter to be principally concerned with others – not just anticipating their needs and desires but in shaping these perceptions to a more general sense of how the specific other, the loved one, should be.

Shopping is, therefore, in his view a devoted activity in which the shopper is sacrificing personal interests for 'the labour of constituting both the immediacy and the dynamics of specific relations of love' (op. cit., p. 155) – a paradoxical conclusion that is most effectively conveyed by an interpretation of the values of shopping as being an exercise of the skills of thrift. Far from being an occasion for indulgence, except for specifically framed occasions such as leisure shopping on holiday (and even then one is often seeking to bring back souvenirs as contributions to the household as a biography of relationships), shopping is typically governed by a desire to save and exercise caution in defence of the collective interests of a moral economy, leading to a 'conclusion that thrift has come to supplant the house itself as the process by which economic activity is used to create a moral framework for the construction of value' (op. cit., p. 137). As this last quoted remark suggests, it may well be that rather than marking the alienation of moral concerns in intimate relationships, the stylisation of material culture in consumerism has provided new opportunities for ways of dramatising the significance of the moral concerns of those relationships.

The Boundaries of Personal Experience

In the first part of this chapter I suggested that the idea of the household provides a useful frame within which the dynamics of changing aspects of everyday life can be more clearly established. The household works in this way because although particular households vary in size, composition, internal organisation and social status, etc., they all act as a stage for the dramatisation of more contested institutions such as home and family. In previous parts of the chapter I have broadened the account of how we might understand how themes in the consumption of goods and services might concern the forms of relationships as well as moral and aesthetic and practical concerns. In this part of the chapter I will extend this analysis by making some connections between the ways in which practical activities are ordered (that is, given structure and organisation) and the dramatisation of environment in personal experience.

A household is physically located in space and time and is based on a site and the possessions of individual members (either brought to the unit or that can be claimed by an individual at a time of restructuring or dissolution). It is given identity by a name and a distinct style concerning, for example, forms of order, noise and vitality. Possessions are like flesh on the bones of household relationships – they give them identity and character and in their relations with each other they imply the sorts of order Berger notes in still lifes. Television documentaries that have asked people to comment on the order represented by their household interiors have found them highly concerned with, and reflexively aware of, meanings conveyed in this mode of representation (Parr and Barker 1992; Painter 1986; Csikszentmihalyi and Rochberg-Halton 1981). Although commitments from the public sphere will clearly structure household rhythms and help to determine resources, the central concerns of ongoing household life will be occupied by the overlapping activities of consumption and leisure.[5] It is in relation to the purchasing of goods and services from daily foods, through more occasional acquisitions of records of music to various forms of player and other more specialised goods, that the household as well its constituent members will develop as a distinctive entity.

A household mediates between public and private spheres by acting almost literally as a conduit in which publicly available resources and systems of signs are translated into personal experience. It also reverses this flow in that it acts as the base, and through media facilities as the lens for viewing the wider environment. It is in both these senses, then, that we can say that the household frames the staging of everyday life. (There is rather a neat parallel here in that domestic photography, the pre-eminent medium of the representation of household members and activities, also 'frames' its subjects in distinctive ways and in so doing constitutes an archive of everyday life (see Chaney 1993, Ch. 3).) The framing here is of course not necessarily literal, in that it is not presumed that an individual's interaction with the world outside always takes place within the spaces colonised by their household. Leisure activities, tourist trips and shopping expeditions, etc. all range out far and wide from the household base. It has often been remarked that the cultural range of modernity has both shrunk and vastly expanded the personal experience of space; I will illuminate this idea through a discussion of two aspects of the dramatisation of space through new elements in material culture.

The first is provided by Bull's ethnography of the use of personal stereos (2000). Although they can be used in households often in ways that parallel some of the uses of television to control relationships, personal stereo systems were invented for, and have been primarily seen as, resources for public spaces. Most obviously, they provide a personalised form of entertainment that enables the user to carry their private tastes with them, and act as a form of shield insulating the user from both the incidental hubbub of public space and unwelcome address from strangers. Such a neutral summary of function would, however, leave the technology acting solely as a passive buffer and miss how 'Personal stereos are used effectively to extend the range of management that users have over a wide range of personal experience' and how their use 'enables the user to transform both their relationship to themselves and the world beyond them' (Bull 2000, p. 43). In this more active sense the stereo system and the products of a culture industry it makes available are used as forms of resistance to the drudgery and indeed the fragmentation of experience in the routines of everyday life. They enable the user to overlay personal meaning upon impersonal necessities and thus dramatise public space with moral concerns.

One of the most important of these strategies of personal ordering comes through the way personal stereos facilitate a non-reciprocal gaze in public spaces. One of the most frequently commented upon aspects of modernity is the way in which metropolitan life not only makes us available for constant inspection by the gaze of others, but also throws us into a close intimacy of looking and being looked at by a constant stream of strangers with whom one has only fleeting acquaintance. Personal stereos enable those wearing them to withdraw from the stress and anxieties of fragmentary intercourse. By giving an aura of both invisibility from the looks of others and a form of superiority, personal stereos enable them to carry on looking without conventional obligations of mutual regard: 'Personal stereo use appears to reflect a transformation in the rules surrounding forms of everyday social recognition' (Bull 2000, p. 98).[6] As I shall emphasise throughout, the cultural changes of late modernity are changing the structures and forms of everyday life through expanding their frames and horizons. Rather than, however, seeing this as just a process of dissolution, we must be constantly alert to the renegotiation of frames of experience by actors seeking 'through their efforts to negate the perceived contingency of the everyday that lies in wait for them, [and] create habitual forms of cognitive management based on personal stereo use that blurs any distinction that might be made between inner and outer, the public and private areas of everyday life' (op. cit., p. 153).

The second example of the dramatisation of space, and its significance in the context of the more general exploration of changing forms of everyday life, can be illustrated by a brief discussion of the provision and consumption of food. Probably the most universal as well as the most manifest way in which households indicate their community is by sharing a meal together. Heightened in traditional societies as Falk has emphasised by often eating simultaneously from a common pot, this practice has largely disappeared with the development of individual meals although until recently still sharing a common table (Falk 1994). The 100 years or so of the modern era have been ordered by increasing access to foods not grown locally, to foods unconstrained by seasonal growing cycles and by the provision more recently of convenience meals. This has taken the form of fully or partly pre-cooked meals available from specialist retailers or supermarkets. Originally developed in the USA as a labour-saving device and to facilitate leisure activities, particularly watching television, in Britain the facility has been very successful in broadening access to more exotic styles of cuisine – particularly associated with Indian, Chinese or Italian dishes.

It is clear, then, that the marketing of ingredients and private consumption of meals (ignoring for now the vast expansion in ethnic restaurants for public eating) has in a way that is consistent with other trends in modernisation led to a shrinking of the universe of global culinary diversity. Simultaneously the diet and personal experience of exotic foods of ordinary people have equivalently expanded. In a powerful study of changes in the social organisation of eating, Mennell (1985) has proposed that there has been a complementary interrelationship between a process of greater homogenisation across the social spectrum allied to a process of greater variety in range of foods. Although this thesis is initially attractive, Warde's major study of food and taste (1997) argues persuasively for the continuing persistence of class differentiation in diets. This is not to deny that change has taken place and is continuing particularly in terms of the discourses governing how food is to be appreciated, presented and consumed. In terms of managing change and the proliferation of expertise concerning values in food, Warde finds 'four "antinomies of taste" provide a systematic basis for these contradictory messages. These oppositions – novelty and tradition, health and indulgence, economy and extravagance, care and convenience – are values which can legitimize choice between foodstuffs' (op. cit., p. 55).

The opening up of a global cuisine for everyday personal experience is obviously a major form of cultural change that has dramatically expanded the boundaries of everyday life. It is consistent with other changes to find a process of stylisation in relation to food choices. I have suggested that, generally, a process of stylisation involves turning everyday items into symbolic displays of taste and social affiliation. Warde's study emphasises that even so traditional associations with the meanings of food remain remarkably powerful, and in this perhaps the provision and choice of foods on different occasions are part of a negotiation of a moral order in relationships. It is, though, undoubtedly true that these choices have become more thoroughly implicated in a commodification of food in that meals are increasingly being supplied as standardised mass products through supermarkets or fast-food outlets. This seems to be the main point in relation to the impact of commodification on what I have called the moral economy of the household. The rituals of eating – its preparation, rules over ingredients and combinations of foods, and the organisation of shared consumption – all provide a powerful exemplification of the moral order of the household.

It could be argued that the globalisation of everyday eating has weakened the moral significance of the household in three ways: some members of a household are less likely to need to collaborate together in the making of meals; individuals can more easily eat by themselves and at times to suit personal convenience, thus fracturing the meal as a collective occasion; and the relationship between any particular meal and the locality of its consumption has been vitiated. As Warde has said: 'Commodification involves precisely the increasing dominance of the social relations associated with production in the formal economy over those fostered by communal or domestic production' (1997, p. 192).

This idea of commodification has, as I said above, a second strand in that some argue that plenitude of choice in consumer culture disguises the poverty of the experience being offered. One trenchant and deservedly widely read instance of such a critique is available in Ritzer's engagement with what he calls the rationalisation of new means of consumption (1993, 1998). Ritzer's account is pitched more at the level of societal change rather than focusing on the meaning for households, but it is relevant here as one of the central themes of his analysis is that there has been a commodification of interpersonal interaction in ways that necessarily lead to a weakening of the moral order of everyday life. I think it is also relevant to my general account, although not part of Ritzer's concerns, that everyday matters such as eating food – and in particular eating everyday food that requires no obvious skill or artistry in presentation – have become dominating motifs in public culture.

Drawing from themes in classical sociological accounts of modernisation, Ritzer has argued that there are four dimensions of the rationalisation of production and marketing of 'fast food'. He labels these dimensions – efficiency, calculability, predictability and control – and in brief they refer to how processes of producing and marketing food have been so tightly calculated and controlled that no individuality in making and in effect consuming seems possible. Ritzer argues that this attitude to eating out has been pioneered by McDonald's and has underlain its phenomenal global success (1993). Further, this drive to rationalise the consumption of personal services will continue to gather pace and will spread (has already spread) to a variety of other consumption environments: 'Spearheaded by, and modeled after the fast food restaurant, we ... are seeing ... an acceleration of the rationalisation process' (1998, p. vii; see also Schlosser 2001).

Why should this matter? Because the drive to rationalisation produces a range of irrationalities including an alienation of the workforce through the deskilling of the preparation of food, an emphasis on ersatz flavours and a homogenisation of cultural diversity. More generally, his analysis can be summarised by saying that the new means of consumption have sought to treat personal experience as a commodity, with the effect that distinctiveness becomes illusory and individuality is packaged in ways that we cannot appreciate and are beyond our control. (I will discuss in Chapter 8 his development of this thesis that the illusions of commodification are an attempt at a re-enchantment of disenchanted modernity (Ritzer 1999).) The moral critique of this way of marketing food is, then, that it simulates the satisfaction both of desire and individuality. Neither is adequately addressed, because what is offered lacks the complexity of a structured meal[7] and is inevitably effectively standardised. In combination, therefore, the significance of food as a focus of communal life is trivialised – commodities have been substituted for the pleasures of interpersonal interaction. Plus of course eating at McDonald's will reinforce the three ways outlined earlier in which the moral significance of the household is being undermined by convenience foods more generally.

Appropriating Material Culture

Ritzer's critique of the implications of cultural change is clearly powerful and takes us back to analyses of the negative implications of the intensification of consumption (more generally on social theories of consumption in modernity see Slater 1997). It is not, however, exhaustive because his focus on the rationalisation of means of consumption leads him to neglect the practice of consumption. Although he is proud of his roots in classical accounts of modernisation, he seems unaware of the extent to which he is also grounded in a more recent tradition often known as mass culture critique (the contending positions between optimistic and pessimistic interpretations of mass culture were collected in Rosenberg and White 1957 and 1971; on the broader intellectual context of American responses to the massification of culture see Ross 1989). Thus although he recognises that

his account can be criticised on the grounds that it is too modernistic and lacks sufficient awareness of what he calls a postmodern fragmentation of cultural markets (1998), he misses the extent to which he is part of a longer-term critique of the dangers of letting the masses have untrammelled access to cultural goods. Cultural pessimists such as Ritzer neglect the ways in which audiences/consumers use cultural facilities – whether it is televisions, fast foods, universities or credit cards – to constitute new sorts of environments (see Fiske 1989a, b; Tulloch 1999). The pessimistic neglect of use stems from a prior reading of change that assumes a conviction that in effect more means worse.

I hope it will be apparent that there is an intimate connection between the criticism of the commodification of food and other critical reactions to consumer culture. It should therefore be unsurprising that my response will be similar to that I have already explored in the several discussions of the social organisation of television use and other new technologies. More generally seeing these technologies as part of textually mediated discourses, and in this respect Moores's argument that we need to rethink the processes of mediated interaction in a new cultural geography of symbolic environments is helpful (2000). The point can also be developed by reiterating a remark from the opening of the book when I noted that it is now commonly accepted that technologies do not determine their use.

Indeed there has been a considerable amount of interest recently in how technologies, particularly the new information and communication technologies which are supposed to be transforming the spaces of the private sphere, are being adopted and institutionalised (Silverstone and Hirsch 1992; Mackay 1997; see also du Gay et al. 1997). In constituting what a technology is going to be expected to do, there are at least two levels of interpretive organisation. The first concerns factors such as perceived relevance, functionality and legitimacy as they are formulated in specific social settings such as households. The second concerns the promotion, design and policies for technologies by manufacturers, state regulators and providers of associated ancillary facilities. Both levels can be seen in interaction in relation to emerging expectations of how telephones should be used earlier this century (Flichy 1995), as much as in relation to new communication technologies more recently.

It has been implicit throughout the discussion in this chapter that the clarity of traditional distinctions between public and private is being lost. I have suggested that if this lack of clear boundaries is challenging, the household as a frame provides a way of concretising the abstractions of changing meanings of spatial context for everyday life. What this means is that the social activities of the household involve interpersonal relations that are both political and moral. Political in the sense that power is being deployed to maintain structures of control and freedom, and moral in the sense that some way of justifying a division of labour is, often implicitly, appealed to and confirmed. Justifications are usually based in expectations associated with who people are or more precisely what types of person they are. Thus in formulating how things are to be done (whether it is using the telephone or providing a meal), the moral dimensions of identities – both individual and collective – are also being contested (see for example Moyal (1989) and Rakow (1992) on conflicting gendered expectations concerning sustaining relationships in relation to the use of the telephone).

So that if we return briefly to the example of the use of food in a household, we should note that I have written so far of members collaborating together on preparation, etc. But of course this labour is unlikely to be equally shared and in practice we know that it has traditionally been part of gendered role differentiation that women both take responsibility for food preparation and cater for male tastes. An option of 'convenience foods' will therefore offer more opportunities for increased leisure for women, although it may in practice be that the opportunities (or the necessities) are for more commitments in paid employment rather than untrammelled leisure. The argument is then that the identities, roles, responsibilities and expectations of household members are being reformulated and actively contested in relation to the commodities that cultural change makes available. It is in this way that a moral economy of constraints and opportunities is constantly being reshaped in the institutionalisation of materials at hand.

The central theme of my argument here is not to presume either an optimistic empowerment through cultural change or the impoverishment of commodification without recognising that these moral orders are always networks of relationships with commodities that we can characterise as a material culture (cf. Dant's argument that 'material culture involves taking on cultural practices in relation to material objects which define the uses and the values of those objects in everyday life. Their importance ... emerges through grasping the way that objects are fitted into ways of living' (1999, p. 39)). While I obviously cannot begin to write out an ethnography of material culture in late modernity, I have been able, I hope, to begin to show how everyday life has itself become a theme of cultural concern in adapting to and incorporating the material complexity of this era (a considerably more sophisticated interrogation of the material culture of everyday life has been published by Attfield 2000).

The jumping-off point for my account has been a view of the household as a stage for the moral order of everyday life. This has enabled me to argue that the cultural changes of consumerism, that is a more intensively stylised material culture, have to be seen as being appropriated within an adapting moral economy. But any household as social ecology does not exist in an abstract space – in order to function as a stage (and the idea is not entirely metaphorical) the institution has to be grounded or embodied in the physical environment of a dwelling. It follows if this approach has any substance that dwellings will also be imbued with moral qualities or organised in terms of a moral order. To go back to the starting point of the book, the way a dwelling space is structured will itself provide a mode of representation of the order of everyday life – it is literally a form of resi-dence. One of the classic studies that has helped to formulate this idea is that by Bourdieu of the structural division by Kabyle tribespeople in Algeria of their dwellings into gendered spaces (Bourdieu 1973).

Although not as symbolically structured as the Algerian situation, the conventional distinction in British households between front and back stage spaces with access to the latter being restricted to close intimates has certain parallels (see also here Mary Douglas's (1966) account of the power of these distinctions). Thus there has been a powerful division of labour in terms of household tasks so that certain spaces, such as kitchens, bedrooms and bathrooms, have typically been seen as more female areas. This coding of space is likely to be expressed in terms of colour or deco-rative order, with male spaces being conventionally furnished in more rectangular shapes and using deeper more neutral colour shades. Strong gendered differences in expectations for what the home should represent have been found in Bennett et al.'s study of Australian everyday cultures:

> It is clear that men and women hold very different views about their ideal homes. ... Women's preferences ... reflect an orientation that cen-tres inward on the home and its relationship to family members. ... The attributes which men prefer more strongly than women, by contrast, mostly relate to the display functions of the home – its role in presenting an image of the self and of the family to the outside world (1999, p. 44).

Generalisations about spatial order obviously have to be qualified by cross-cutting variables such as age and the presence of young children. Thus, it seems common that households that contain young children are increasingly focused on their activities and accomplishments – that is, they are less likely to be segregated into specialised areas. One effect will be that children's paintings and their photos will dominate the decorative order often to the extent that the dwelling feels like a temple dedicated to their creativity. Such arrangements also have the effect of making the environment less formal, more haphazard in its decorative order, and this is consistent with Dant's observation that the lack of professional skills in home maintenance and decoration often results in what he calls, follow-ing Lévi-Strauss and de Certeau, an effect of *bricolage* so that 'the material culture of dwelling involves both an aesthetic of appearance and an ori-entation to functionality – but neither are learnt as abstract, institution-alised knowledge' (1999, p. 71).

I think it is clear that the personal investment in the lived environment is becoming more significant. In part this is an inevitable feature of the increasing significance of lifestyles as forms of social categorisation. In a previous discussion of how lifestyles are distinctive forms of the organisation of social space (1996, Ch. 9), I suggested that sensibility – a perceived affiliation in taste and style – is a crucial dimension in making judgements about appropriateness and relevance. The decoration, furnishing and organisation of the lived environment are one of the most explicit exemplifications of sensibility, and it is therefore unsurprising that a considerable theme in public discourse, including magazines, television programmes and press reports, etc. is taken up with advice on the range of style choices and how they might be accomplished. What I have called a greater investment, and a more acute awareness of choice of style and decorative resource, does not seem to lead though to a more widespread commitment to coherence in styling. Of course, some people do take over templates from manufacturers and style experts, but the more common effect is of what I called in the previous paragraph bricolage. While there might be an organising theme in the dramatisation of the lived environment, there will also be a confusion of objects and images drawing upon sentimental and nostalgic associations as much as a decorative order (Attfield 2000, Pt. 2).

The significance of this point is that an increased sensitivity to the meanings of elements of material culture, what we could call an intensified aesthetic awareness in everyday life or as we have seen what Lury calls the stylisation of use, does not necessarily lead to a greater orthodoxy or conformity to dominant norms. As I shall argue in the following discussion of fashion more generally, there is instead an almost paradoxical combination of sensitivity and indifference. In a way that exemplifies what I have called the destabilisation of boundaries and structures to personal experience, it is as though a greater consciousness of the arbitrariness of choice both makes every choice more important and less significant. I think it is important to mention here that the increasing suburbanisation of lived environments (see generally on suburbs in mass society Silverstone 1997) has meant a close connection between the moral aspirations of suburban life and more elaborate explorations of ways of differentiating a semiotics of identity and authenticity. Thus I have argued in a previous paper (1997) that the dominance of the suburban environment has generated a search for authenticity – being used here to mean a truth to personal integrity – as new forms of tradition. I will develop and clarify the significance of a search for authenticity in the altering cultural environment of everyday life in the next chapter.

5

Dramatising the Self
in Everyday Life

The Democratisation of Fashion

In the previous chapter I have been exploring some of the changes in the basic themes of the lived environment that can loosely be described as cultural. One general point that recurred throughout the chapter is how these changes have led to a blurring of boundaries between public and private spheres, this process associated in turn with the everyday becoming a more prominent theme in cultural idioms. I was also concerned to try to establish the extent to which it would be appropriate to describe everyday experience as rationalised, or as becoming more rationalised by the commodification of interpersonal relationships that has been an inevitable feature of the cultural changes of later modernity. While obviously one cannot make a summary judgement given the diversity of everyday experience, I have pointed to various ways in which studies have deduced that the textually mediated discourses of local experience continue to display distinctive moral and aesthetic concerns. In effect, that the greater massness of contemporary culture has not meant an overwhelming uniformity in everyday life. In this chapter I shall develop this approach by looking more specifically at aspects of how personal experience, in particular how individuals might think of their self in relation to social expectations, has been caught up in cultural representations of everyday life.

I shall begin with stylisation again, that is treating material goods as symbolic markers, but this time more specifically concerned with the presentation of the self that for many is conveyed by the greater significance of fashion in later modernity. To attach any importance to fashion has for many critics been possibly the clearest indication of the power of what I have called the commodification or, more generally, the capitalist logic of commercial modernity. Fashion has been condemned as alienating for a number of reasons. First, because it leads people to invest objects and styles with significance which is unrelated to their functional efficiency; second, it is necessarily ephemeral and is not concerned with things that have any lasting value; and, third, because it blinds its 'victims' to the way their energies and resources are consumed in the pursuit of what, effectively, serves only to bolster the profits and the dominance of an exploitative and inequitable social order.

While not necessarily disputing the truth of these charges, other commentators have pointed to the way the institution of fashion has functioned as a means of practical creativity in popular culture – most typically in sorts of symbolic creativity of engagements with style by young people charted by Hebdige (1979) and Willis (1990). Secondly, fashion has been seen as a means of reflexive engagement with the forms of identity in modernity – an idea explored through the emblematic figure of the *flâneur* or dandy (Tester 1994; see also Negrin 1999). And, thirdly, as languages of community and collective affiliation in a radically secular social order leading to a radical conceptualisation of the oft-touted phrase of the aestheticisation of everyday life (Chaney 1996; Featherstone 1991; Gronow 1997). I will expand upon and clarify at least some of these contrasting ideas, but my purpose here is not to resolve debates about the meaning of fashion. Instead I will work from the significance of the institution of fashion in the constitution of modernity to consider how the moral and aesthetic concerns of fashion have been institutionalised in everyday life.

One reason for suggesting that fashion lies at the heart of the process of modernisation is the way that fashion stimulated trade and thus economic development. The idea that goods are valued whether they are clothes or decorative or functional household items or whatever because of the judgements of a membership or reference group, that is social judgements, rather than because of the intrinsic utility of the good, has been recognised to have been a crucial stimulant to economic development (on the role of material culture in intellectual innovation in the Renaissance see Jardine 1996; see also Campbell 1987 for an influential account of cultural transformations of material goods in European modernisation). The impetus to acquire prestige goods both stimulated exploration and manufacture to make such goods available in new markets – for example the spice trade in the eighteenth century and the contemporary search for a way of making porcelain (Gleeson 1998). The same impetus also stimulated the enhancement of design to differentiate goods within a market – for example the exploitation of fashions in his decorated china by Wedgwood (Forty 1986). Fashionable prestige not only stimulated trade in these ways, it also, crucially, provided a means by which differentiation or stratification amongst consumers could be perpetually renewed.

The reason that social concern with fashion releases unsatisfied and indeed unsatisfiable desires is that giving certain elements of the material culture a symbolic prestige that is wholly secular (in that fashionable items do not in general derive their prestige from religious associations or ritual function), is effective in providing a means of affiliation that differentiates those who recognise the prestigious object from those who do not. This awareness or knowledge cannot, however, be controlled and inevitably it will diffuse to a wider awareness diluting the distinctiveness of the original group. Social elites will therefore have to invent or develop new sources or objects of prestige in order to reassert the differentiation. Simmel amongst others pointed to the cyclical character of fashion as a means of differentiation both within a community and as a semiotics of stratification between classes or status levels (1971; see also Blumer 1969), and used a cycle of expansion and contraction in relation to prestigious objects as an illustration of his conceptualisation of social forms (Nedelmann 1990). The cycle of fashion is particularly relevant to changes in later modernity because in an era of extensive mass communication, knowledge of different forms of prestige will necessarily be one of the major staples of public discourse.

The cycle of change in every field from entertainment to clothes to cooking, etc. will therefore continually accelerate. Further, in a constant search for innovation, traditional hierarchies of status will be circumvented by new forms of cultural capital, so that otherwise socially marginalised or excluded groups may be able to usurp the role of symbolic innovators and sources of prestige. All this has meant that the institution of fashion has become more pervasive in the course of modernity (Craik 1994; Edwards 1997; Wilson 1985). If primarily but not exclusively focused on clothing the body, it will become increasingly dynamic in relation to other aspects of lifestyle elaboration such as household furnishings and decoration, food, holidays, language and of course the whole range of cultural choices in entertainment and leisure. The dynamism of fashion will mean in one sense that it will become increasingly ephemeral, and given the relatively narrow range of sources that recycling of previous fashions will become a dominant characteristic as has happened for example, in the popular music industry. The ways in which fashions are necessarily ephemeral and create desires that cannot be satisfied have been sources of alarm for those who have seen modernity as dangerously unstable, and where what they see as a consequential volatility of everyday life is likely to be exploited as a means for intensive marketing.

I think, though, that rather than stress an instability in everyday life it is more significant to see how fashion has stimulated a pervasive relativism. I suggest that a more general relativism in values and standards becomes dominant in three ways. First, it has become apparent that norms are historically contingent – every judgement is specific to time and place and can be assumed to be increasingly indexical. It further follows that judgements are also relative to the social group in which they are grounded. This second form is, therefore, an ideological relativism which has extended from the secularisation of belief in the development of the public sphere to become pervasive in all aspects of everyday life. In both of these processes a third form of relativism has also become apparent, and this is a self-consciousness or reflexivity of relativism. In this version the very awareness of the arbitrariness of judgements ceases to be an unfortunate defect to be repaired if possible, and glossed over if not, and instead becomes celebrated.

A good example of this process comes in the discussion of post-tourism (Urry 1995; Munt 1994). Tourism as a consumer industry trading on fashion has been criticised for taking people to places that had been more or less artificially designed or manipulated to appeal to their preconceptions. Tourism therefore promoted an inherent inauthenticity for its critics and was consequently deplored by more discriminating travellers. The idea of post-tourism is that the value of authenticity, as a concern with real, has been superseded by a recognition that tourists may not only be aware of the dramatisation of which they are consumers (Rojek and Urry 1997), but actively welcome it as a form of entertainment that is judged by criteria other than truth (Chaney 2001b). If this has been true in relation to this industry might it not be more generally true of other types of fashionable consumption? Thus one could argue that with the dominance of institutionalised fashion the languages of social life will be increasingly ironicised. What this means is that the dominant coinage of appearance – technically called the semiotics of social identity displayed through sexuality, gender, desirability and eroticism as well as all the connotations of class, culture, locality – will be increasingly accepted as relative. Such an ironic consciousness creates opportunities to subvert traditional associations and thus once again work at the destabilisation of structures and boundaries of personal experience (Finkelstein 1991).

A thesis that the semiotics of style have been used increasingly playfully (amongst other terms that have been used are ironically and cynically) in both professional practice, as in architectural innovation (Jencks 1984), and personal experience has become a defining characteristic of postmodernism. My point here has not been to write of cultural eras but suggest that this trend is inherent in the logic of the role of fashion in consumer culture. I also want to go further and suggest that the several modes of relativism I have briefly described help to explain two paradoxical combinations. First, although material goods have become more important, they have in an important sense dematerialised in the multiplicity of uses and meanings to which they can be put. Secondly, there is a process of extreme sensitivity to, and yet comparative indifference to, stylistic norms in everyday life. Although fashionable codes are capable of infinite gradations and internal differentiations within any particular group, it has been assumed that the demands of fashionable conformity work to create a sort of uniform. The very attractiveness of the metaphor of uniform and its implied expectations of conformity should not, however, blind us to the way that the relativism of fashion both individualises as well as communalises.

To grasp this more clearly, I think we have to go back to what I have referred to rather monolithically as 'a fashion'. Innovation in symbolic prestige is never a once-for-all event but a process of innovation, acceptance and eventual decline. Davis, for example, has set out a five-stage model (particularly directed at fashions in the clothing industry) of innovation and change. He emphasises, though, that any structural frame is arbitrary and we need to concentrate on the intermediary roles of influentials both in textually mediated discourses and local communities; thus he concludes that: 'it would seem on balance that contemporary fashion leadership is profoundly polycentric with respect to its social locations and decidedly polymorphous as regards its thematic materials' (Davis, 1992, p. 149). That is, there is neither a homogeneous leadership dictating fashions or a consistent set of tastes constituting its substance, not least because of the development of various forms of what has been called anti-fashion (Benthall and Polhemus 1975). What is meant by this term are determined attempts to use local styles as ways of signalling rejection of conformist orthodoxy including: 'utilitarian outrage, health and fitness naturalism, feminist protest, conservative scepticism, minority group disidentification, and counterculture insult' (Davis 1992, p. 168). A paradoxical conclusion is then that while recognising the dominance of fashionable concerns, it seems that in later modernity we need a populist model of fashion in which rather than general trends it is the local meanings of a diversity of styles that is more significant.

Self and Others

I hope it will by now be becoming more apparent that the key element in my account of the significance of a dominating concern with fashion for everyday life lies in the opportunities it provides for more complex vocabularies of social identity. Rather than see fashion as only something dictated by style leaders in metropolitan centres and usually publicised through various media channels, I would suggest that fashion is better understood as a semiotics of inclusion and affiliation that has provided the basis for new modes of social grouping called lifestyles (Chaney 1996). I have previously suggested that lifestyles have thematic concerns, some of which I have summarised as surfaces, selves and sensibilities. If lifestyles are concerned with the representation of identity then a theme of dramatisation of the self should not be puzzling. The idea of sensibility as a mode of affiliation may not, however, be so apparent, but I have been fortunate with a recent apposite example. Writing as somebody on the Left, Charlotte Raven (2001, p. 5) describes a new political landscape in which:

the old left–right allegiances are rendered even more meaningless than ever. When I think of who my opponents are, I don't conjure up a party or a class so much as a sensibility. ... It's hard to pick them out on sight so you have to learn to spot them by their responses to the things around them. One technique I use is to ask them what they think about Madonna. If they think she's sexy, they're unlikely to be real human beings.

I think this reads as a classic illustration of new groupings typically using cultural icons as criteria of us and them. It is also relevant that it has been suggested that issues such as gun control, defence of family values and religious commitment were more effective discriminators in the recent American Presidential election than traditional factors such as class or race. Markers such as these are expressed or articulated through the use of goods and services that carry resonances and connotations for their local environments. Not many of these choices need be fashionable in the sense of something intensely of the moment, but they will be manipulations of symbolic prestige in the judgements of significant others and as such be continually drawing boundaries between what is and how it could be otherwise. Precisely because these vocabularies are so mobile, imperfect and flexible, they will rarely if ever be used completely consistently but will function as an idiosyncratic form of performance.[1]

In trying to argue that fashion as an institutional form has become more significant or more pervasive in everyday life (with a corresponding proliferation of communities of taste, see Gronow 1997), and yet less rigorous more self-consciously relative, I am not trying to deny that there are fashions or looks or styles that characterise an era. There is, for example, the well-known 'hippie-look' forever associated with late Beatles and 'flower-power' of what has become loosely called the 1960s. Although grounded in an era it was initially associated with particular localities – metropolitan bohemian enclaves – and then diffused through student communities to mass publics exemplified in a few features such long hair for men, loose colourful clothing and a lot of jewellery for both sexes. The style therefore characterised both a time, places and in progression different types of social spaces. In an important sense 'the look' for social actors is analogous to brand identity that marketing agencies try so hard to develop.

Although necessarily having an initial specific temporal grounding, the look does not disappear but survives not only amongst certain elements in that generation as they age, but as a resource for quite diverse younger groups to be picked up and adapted periodically in occasional recyclings of stylistic motifs. These looks, both specific and general, with their associated expectations of language, attitudes and other cultural preferences, will be experienced as normative expectations such that individuals will try to conform in order not to feel incompetent, but they will be at best baggy language-games. My point is then that fashions or styles are in effect textually mediated discourses. Formed and diffused, however much intertwined with local networks of influence, through cues and ideas made available by media sources, fashions become environments or social spaces in which affiliations can be recognised and sustained. As such they are extending the boundaries and structures of local or personal experience through a stylisation of use that is radically rewriting distinctions between public and private spheres. I think this becomes particularly relevant in relation to our interpretation of the power of perceived cultural expectations in relation to attitudes, tastes, behaviour, etc. It is an issue that is central to any account of the moral order of mass society and particularly when it is suggested that expectations can become so oppressive that they generate forms of self-abuse.

Generally in this book I write of textually mediated discourses as vocabularies. While a vocabulary can be criticised for a lack of breadth the metaphor generally implies an expressive resource. It is, however, possible to see textually mediated discourses as oppressive in the sense that they only allow for certain forms of expression, or they promote normative expectations which cannot be met by groups within the participants or users of the discourse. It has, for example, been a common criticism of the racial stereotypes employed within media discourses that the representations of ethnic minorities have worked to perpetuate images that legitimate structural inequalities (Ferguson 1998). Another version of oppressive representation, and one that is particularly relevant to forms of symbolic prestige in consumerism, has been identified in certain ideals of femininity that have privileged a thinness that is necessarily unattainable by most women (Bordo 1993; Hesse-Biber 1996; Wolf 1991).

A consequence of this normative imagery has been held to be an all-pervasive anxiety amongst women, particularly young women, about their size and weight. This leads in turn to an obsession with dieting and other forms of bodily control that leads to widespread feelings of low personal esteem, and in extreme cases to a pathological obsession with body image that can lead to severe forms of physical abuse and even death from self-inflicted starvation. It would be inappropriate for me to pretend to an expertise in relation to this problem that I do not possess. There are, however, certain comments that flow from the account of cultural change that I have presented so far. Initially we must recognise that there does seem to be a widespread anxiety particularly but not exclusively amongst young women about the need to control bodily appearance.[2] In addition to the numerous articles and programmes aimed at women that deal with dieting, weight loss and body shape, the huge number of companies offering exercise programmes, diets, massages, etc. as aids to weight loss all speak to the degree of interest in weight as a 'problem' in everyday life. Not only does the problem clearly exist it also seems to be a textually mediated discourse, in that however much peer judgement is used to reinforce norms about the desirability of thinness, the issue of appearance and associated normative expectations has become constitutive of femininity in public discourse.

The norms of thinness in public discourse will be reinforced by being articulated and literally embodied by those who are presented as beautiful and desirable whether as models, actors or other types of public figure. There is therefore no doubt that what it is to become a woman will in a mass-mediated culture have to be negotiated through a normative climate that necessarily creates anxieties about conformity. This does not mean that all women will feel these anxieties to the same degree, but it does mean that dealing with others' expectations in this respect, whether from a generalised other or local peers, will be at least a component in the moral orders of self and collective identity. It does not, however, follow that those who take their anxieties about eating or body weight to the degree that they force themselves to reject food in a variety of ways are doing so *because* they feel that this is a cultural expectation or *because* they feel that this is a necessary form of compliance to perceived expectations. It may well be that food is too easily seen as a medium for dramatising a low self-esteem, either because of or interrelated to interpersonal tensions and/or anxieties about sexuality and gendered identity more generally. My point is that fashion as a generalised name for cultural expectations over secularised forms of symbolic prestige will become more significant in a populist climate of radical democratisation, but this does not mean it will generate greater conformity; rather that its use as a means of performing self and identity will become more complex – more reflexive.

Individualisation of Commitment

My account of how the borders of the private sphere have been opened out by new textually mediated discourses has been led to the institutionalisation of the body as part of the presentation of the self. More generally, it seems that the normative organisation of the body will inevitably be a central theme in everyday life. It has been widely noted (Turner 1984; Shilling 1993) that the character and forms of the organisation of embodiment, as with so many aspects of everyday life, has been relatively neglected in traditions of social theory. It seems likely that the recent 'discovery of the body' in social theory is itself at least in part a response to a more widespread concern with the character of civility in a culture where the public sphere is becoming dominated by private concerns (Finkelstein 1989; Sennett 1976). While this opens too many questions for now, it is relevant to ask whether, and if so in what ways, the nature of everyday embodiment – that is whether we feel our bodies to be things we can control, whether they give us pleasure and whether they are a source of shame and/or guilt – has come to seem more problematic in late modernity (Scott and Morgan 1993). Another way of phrasing this is to ask about the ways in which our bodies are used in everyday experience as representations of our selves. I think these questions deal with presentation and authenticity in representation and, for reasons I shall endeavour to bring out, if so it is also helpful to consider the presentation of bodies in sporting activities.

Modern sport has become extremely significant in mass culture for three reasons. First, it provides an ideal source of content for media of mass entertainment. Performances are highly structured, easy to follow and inherently exciting given their indeterminacy of outcome. Sport does not require great creative talent in production and is relatively cheap to write about or film even if access becomes more expensive through competition. As media proliferate, sport, as has been seen in relation to marketing satellite television, provides an ideal attraction that is both formulaic and unpredictable. Secondly, sport provides a relatively non-contentious but still gripping form of identification for mass publics – whether people are identifying with individuals or local or national teams. In the imagined communities of mass communication sport can serve as a focus for religious, ethnic and national sentiments as well as more placid forms of vicarious participation. A third factor stems from the ideological transition that sport has undergone. As a model of honourable conduct it has been commodified by fully realising its potential as commercial spectacle; but simultaneously sporting values have been individualised to provide a normative vision of commitment and community, that, I will go on to show, is a distinctive embodiment of authenticity.

I want, therefore, to develop an argument that sport has been seen to articulate values through forms of disciplined endeavour focusing on the body that both individualises and transcends other lines of structured differentiation. Although as always it is important to remember the social patterning of participation in different sports (illustrated for example in Bennett et al. 1999, Ch. 5), I will illustrate the individualisation of sporting values and my more general theme of embodiment in everyday life by turning to a study of the advertising of Nike sporting goods (Goldman and Papson 1998). Nike is interesting in a number of respects as it has become globally successful very recently by managing to imbue what might have been thought to be extremely functional objects such as footwear, clothing and other sporting accessories with high symbolic prestige. As a consequence very high prices can be charged and extremely discriminating communities of taste have grown up around particular products. In an innovative appreciation of what it is that is being sold, the Nike corporation decided not to be a production organisation – subcontracting production to others – but rather a design and marketing enterprise committed to developing values to be associated with the brand and in particular its semiotic exemplification the Swoosh.[3]

Nike therefore exemplifies certain postmodern themes by being centrally concerned with appearance and fashion; the functionality of its products would be hard to assess, but is in any case largely irrelevant to those urban style-warriors who primarily or perhaps exclusively wear the goods in city streets and clubs. Furthermore, the marketing of appearance is not only necessarily articulated through advertising but also has to display a reflexive awareness of the ambivalencies (what I called in the previous section the relativism) this entails by using a style that is 'situated at the intersection between public and private discourses where themes of authenticity and personal morality converge with the cynical and nihilistic sensibility that colors contemporary public exchanges' (Goldman and Papson 1998, p. 3).

One reason why the audience is necessarily cynical about Nike advertising stems from a contradiction that concerns the privileged space of the game – a form of social space in which all participants are equal under the rules. And yet of course the advertising, in being concerned with stars and their exceptional achievements and more or less explicit endorsements, pictures those who are far removed from mundane reality. Rather than bridge this gap in the manner of traditional advertising by saying that purchasing the good will magically transform us, the audience, Nike advertisements use the normative ethos of the game – what I have called its ideological discourse – as a model of more general social values. Goldman and Papson bring out a number of ways in which this works of which I will describe two. The first is that the equality of conditions of sporting competition provides an opportunity for the individual, through strength of will and effort, to transcend social disadvantages: 'For Nike performance is always about the will, about self-affirmation, about exceeding limits by refusing boundaries. As noted earlier, Nike has positioned itself against the boundaries associated with the social construction of race, class, gender and age' (op. cit., p. 157). Of course we know that this is impossible and are thus cynical, but the promise of exceptional luck, will, talent is so built into the promise of radical democracy (see the next chapter) that it remains an inspirational image – morally and aesthetically.

The second way in which Nike uses sport as an idealised vision that can transcend our cynicism about the persuasive message to posit more enduring values is to present the sporting life as a form of community in which there is a camaraderie of commitment. An example of how this happens is to present the experience of sport – both front and back stages – as a form of cultural alternative to mainstream society with its over-adherence to norms of convention. It is consistent with Nike's strategy of selling itself as a sign that advertisements do not concentrate on product or product features, rather the products are implied to offer a way into new perspectives so that 'Nike ads concentrate on hailing viewers about the aesthetic and discursive practices of each sport subculture' (op. cit., p. 37). And it is also consistent that television advertising is neither narratively consistent nor didactic, but instead accumulates images through collagistic associations and often seemingly unrelated voice-overs and subtitles. This associative style allows a wide range of references to the sensibility informing this choice of product. As advanced examples of what Messaris (1997) has called syntactic indeterminacy, they facilitate the seeming resolution of incompatible values and deflect attention from ideological contradictions. This process is perhaps seen most clearly in the way in which one of the most sophisticated examples of consumer culture presents itself as an icon of sport and thus allows access to otherwise unobtainable forms of authenticity: 'Nike beckons viewers to seek out unregulated spaces and deep, unstructured experiences that only pure and wondrous Nature can provide' (op. cit., p. 164).

I have described the Nike vision of sport as idealised both because of the way it resolves contradictions in its own version of the sporting life, and because the values articulated are striking chords with at least some of the audience who either do not live the sporting life or use the products in non-sporting settings. The idealisation is ideological because it involves marrying themes of communal integration with individualised competition. In the incompatibility of this association the discourse of the advertising is following in a long tradition of normative inconsistency in the values of sport. The theme, or one could say the surface, on which these discursive tensions are played as if they are being resolved is the competitive body. Whether the performers are shown as young or old, male or female, black or white, physically endowed or disabled, it is in the exertion and grace of the body in action that sport is being shown as a practice that transcends conventional society. It is part of Nike's bid for idealism that it refuses to be constrained by general advertising norms as to what is a conventionally desirable body to symbolise desirable products. In an important sense, though, the desirable body is being replaced by the authentic body. It is essential for a broader perspective than that used in this rhetoric that sport offers an otherwise inaccessible space for authenticity. The body is thus being used as a sign for and medium of authentic identity.

In writing about sport in modern culture I have so far neglected its role in relation to the constitution of gendered identities. Sport in both its traditional and modern forms has typically been played by men, with organised competitions often excluding and only reluctantly allowing female competitors (Hargreaves 1994). An example is the slow and unwilling opening up of all the branches of the Olympics to female participants. And the idea of open competition between men and women at the same event has usually been treated with the same sort of horror as that occasioned by miscegenation. The physicality of sport has typically been seen as constitutive of masculinity and antithetical to femininity. A distinction that is somehow confirmed by the greater strength and aggression of the typical male. As a form of entertainment for spectators sport has also generally been consumed by men, this being particularly true of the mass sports for working-class audiences such as football, baseball and rugby league. In this context it is therefore unsurprising that sport has been a central theme in masculine culture, providing one of the few taken-for-granted topics of common interest, and an essential medium for bonding between fathers and sons, other male family relationships and masculine communities generally.

The constitutive role of sport for masculinity shows no sign of diminishing and indeed may become more important as other sources of male privilege, in particular greater occupational earnings and prowess, are disappearing. It may be expected that associated ceremonials of exaggerated masculinity at sporting occasions such as dressing in team colours and generally behaving badly will continue or grow, but the salience of sport in mass entertainment is changing its popular character. While televised sports can still attract large male audiences they not exclusively male, and the broadcasting of sport, and the organisation of sporting occasions, is increasingly designed for women as well as men. More generally, the numbers and popularity of female competitions in all sorts of sports are increasing (although there are still marked discrepancies in the amount of media attention – and related earnings – that male and female competitors attract), and the normative discouragement of exercising the female body is being swept aside. If the training of the body and pride in its appearance and accomplishments are becoming normatively significant in late modernity, it is a more general cultural value than being predominately focused on constituting masculinity.

Discipline and Hedonism

Sport has clearly become one of the major forms of entertainment in everyday life but my main concern has not been with sport as a form of drama. Rather my concern is with the distinctive values articulated in sport; for example, Bennett et al.'s respondents answering why they enjoy participating in sport, use 'the four most salient categories... "fitness", "health", "relaxation", and "competition" ... [and] ... give us with all their banality, a sense of the differences between the pleasures that different social groups take' (1999, p. 135). Overall, I have suggested that sport offers a vision of a form of authentic experience, perhaps a form of *communitas*, that addresses the constraints of everyday life (perhaps through this the possibility of the extra-ordinary in everyday experience as Miller and McHoul suggest 1998, Ch. 3; see also Berking and Neckel 1993; and my Chapter 8 below). There is here, though, a crucial paradox in representations of the body in everyday life. In pursuit of authentic experience bodies are increasingly being rationalised, but, at the same time, also providing a means of self-fulfilment that is 'irrational' for a disciplined social order. Further, the complexity of the redemptive vision focusing on the physicality of the body is attractive to, and being pursued by, both sexes.

In support of this last proposition I am not just pointing to the popularity of televised sport amongst both sexes, or the greatly increasing numbers of both amateur and professional female sports performers, but the very widespread pursuit of bodily training amongst men and women. Indices of the latter are the plethora of health clubs and training gyms, the popularity of aerobics classes, the numbers of people diligently pounding city streets often burdened with extra weights to increase their purgatory, the popularity of activity holidays for adults and families and, of course, the taken-for-granted assumptions in everyday conversation that 'working out' and keeping fit is socially desirable and a necessary element in taking care of yourself. Conversely, the unproblematic sneering at those who are overweight, inactive or just lazy speaks to the same normative hegemony.[4] In all sorts of ways, then, it seems that the form of our bodies is both becoming more important and more normatively constrained (see the research collected in Nettleton and Watson 1998).

Traditional assumptions that as bodies aged they lost the taut muscularity of youth and indeed collapsed into the parodic features of middle age with expanding waistlines and softening of body contours are no longer taken for granted. Our bodies have also become 'plastic'. In addition to regimes of exercise, training and dieting there are also of course increasingly widely available types of surgical intervention which make it possible to change bodily shape and appearance: 'The increasingly common use of transplants, prosthetic and/or mechanical body parts, and various reproductive technologies (not to mention developments such as virtual reality) bring into question what our bodies are, and thus what our relationship to them might be' (Wilson and Laennec 1997, p. 1). Such a range of concerns with manipulation and modification can easily suggest that the secular values of idealised appearance require, and indeed it is part of their redemptive force, a regime of punishment and mortification. Perhaps in contrast to the indulgences of a consumer culture and a world in which involuntary pain is seen as something to be banished or at least controlled whenever possible, the voluntary pain of the disciplined body is welcomed as a necessary cost of a semiotics of the body (on the persistence of certain themes throughout the modern era in proselytising for a more healthy or authentic diet, see Gusfield 1992).

Miller and McHoul (1998) take the idea of discipline involved in privileging the body further, by suggesting that the increasing salience of control in this sphere of everyday life is part of broader processes of the disciplining of modernity. They make a connection between the development of new knowledges such as medicine and psychology and new disciplinary regimes in prisons, hospitals and asylums, etc., with what I have called the bureaucratisation of modern sport: 'The governmentalization of everyday life in Britain during the eighteenth century pacifies sport via the imposition of organizational and behavioural rules' (op. cit., p. 69). Following in the footsteps of Foucault, they go on to argue that the elaboration of time in sporting contests is an analogue of the increasing efficiency with which modern bodies are controlled and become effectively machine-like in the ways they are deployed. In their view, therefore, the mortification of the body involved in its management and constant challenging through setting new hurdles is less a redemptive search than a more pervasive mode of subjugation. In this way, then, the body can be seen as providing an opening for the rationalisation of the everyday, and it would seem only consistent that their emphasis on the body as a machine makes other interesting connections to accounts and explorations of the technologised body in cyber-culture. Although the paradox of rationality here is that for many commentators the virtuality of the cyber-body offers avenues for emancipation rather than disciplinary control (Featherstone and Burrows 1995).

The numerous ways in which the body has become a plastic resource in contemporary lifestyle practices opens up an enormous field for study, from a stylisation to more literally treating the body as a work of art (Featherstone 2000). Sometimes the latter project involves an eye-watering mortification of the flesh, although more generally, practices such as piercing, scarification and decoration are less self-consciously avant-garde and more aimed for a greater authenticity of personal embodiment (Myers 1992). It seems, then, that a recognition of the significance of disciplinary controls and asceticism in the institutionalisation of the body in contemporary everyday life is part of a rationalisation of the everyday that makes a bridge between corporate marketing and new modes of social order. At the same time, however, the individualisation of the body clearly involves a greater reflexivity about the dramatisation of identity that is both personally experienced as emancipating and may be functionally 'irrational' for social order. In the remainder of this section I will discuss three further aspects of the individualisation of bodies. My aim is to show that in making our bodies more plastic, because it is more important that we get them 'right', we both burden ourselves with constraints and provide emancipating expressive opportunities.

I have emphasised that in certain respects making one's body a project rather than something one just has imposes constraints. One of the most important that I have not so far discussed, and is the first of the concluding points in this part, is that not just the appearance but the health of the body becomes an individual responsibility. This theme is exemplified in a number of ways, such as health promotion campaigns urging people to take more exercise, to only engage in 'safe sex' and to abandon 'abusive' practices such as smoking and excessive drinking. The idea of responsibility is taken further in the formulation of public policy when medical intervention is denied on the grounds that an individual is overweight or continuing to smoke and thus failing to display sufficient seriousness. More generally, it can be argued that health responsibility is part of a more general shift in social attitudes towards a consumerist emphasis in social policy on individuals taking charge of life circumstance including pension provision, health insurance as well as healthy practices. An interesting adjunct of increased personal responsibility is the likelihood of a greater awareness of the threat posed by others' unhealthy or 'irresponsible' practices. This I think helps to explain the increased intolerance to the point of paranoia of those who smoke or let their dogs defecate in public places (Edgley and Brissett 1990).

If the idea of responsibility as I have described it so far is understood only as a constraint however, then I think important aspects are being neglected. I think if we recall the discussion of Beck's ideas of the increased perceptions of risks in the second or reflexive phase of modernisation then it will not be surprising to reflect that a greater concern with health, and the deployment of increasingly elaborate technologies of health intervention, has been bracketed with a more pervasive discrediting of conventional medical expertise. It is as though the very search for meaning in a healthy life and privileging bodily concerns more generally cannot be contained in the scientism of orthodox medicine. Surrendering control over one's body to experts whose mistakes and bureaucracy are too well known is both threatening and denies a search for personal authenticity in body matters. It is in this context that there has been an enormous increase in interest in forms of alternative medicine – not just drawn from other modes of expertise than the scientism of the European tradition but also involving less materialistic ways of conceiving relationships between self and body. While frequently scoffed at by health professionals, these more spiritual ways of exploring and disciplining the experience of the body as in, for example, yoga or other exercise regimes have interrelated with other aspects of the changing culture of everyday life.

Contesting how health is to be understood and complementarily expanding notions of what might constitute 'ill health' in the sphere of everyday life has involved a politics of the body. This is because the authority of expertise deploys various forms of power in order to defend its hegemony, and any form of resistance by mounting a countervailing view involves querying the right to define central elements of the relevant intellectual agenda. This comes out clearly in relation to the second aspect of bodily concerns in contemporary culture. Feminist writers have frequently pointed to the ways in which conventional discourse has tended to align cultural or more intellectual, rational characteristics to men while women have been associated with natural or elemental characteristics. While seeking to contest such an agenda, feminism has been led to consider the discursive control of women's bodies in a variety of ways.

For example, how specifically female concerns such as childbirth and diseases such as certain cancers have been organised and made subject to regimes which have not necessarily been benign. Alternatively, the representations of women's bodies as objects of desire and thus as subject to various forms of controlling gaze in the breadth of popular culture have been a topic extensively explored in women's studies. Once again, though, in making a politics of the body the feminist movement has found these concerns a focus for mobilisation that has been emancipating.

The politicisation of the body is also relevant to the third aspect of complex institutionalisation that I want to mention at this point. This picks up what for many will have been the most obviously liberating aspect of changes in the regulation of the body in later modernity, that is what has been experienced as a greater tolerance of the pursuit of pleasure in the body – largely but not exclusively sexual.[5] Once again this has taken a variety of forms of which I can only mention a few, but a good starting point is the more overt celebration of sexuality for both men and women in mass media of popular entertainment such as the press, magazines, film and television (Weeks 1998; Wouters 1998). Other aspects of the same trend include a fairly general acceptance that sexuality is not and need not be confined to marital relations; a greater acceptance of same-sex sexuality amongst men and women, although the persistence of discrimination has led to the development of effective social movements pressing for recognition of gay and lesbian rights; and a general recognition of the legitimacy of diversity in the discourse of sexuality. A widespread recognition that controls on sexuality are arbitrary has even so run into persistent battles over the representation of sexuality, particularly in ways that might be labelled pornographic. The huge market for pornography is shown by the importance it has had in the development of new technologies for distributing television and the rise of the internet, although of course this hidden trade has not ceased to be politically contentious in terms of the manner of its depiction of sexuality.

An emphasis on the pleasures of sexuality allied to more general values about the emancipation of the body, and a belief that bodily indulgence can act as a means of transcending the constraints of everyday life, might be expected to particularly privilege youthful bodies. And to some extent an increased explicitness about sexuality has been part of values emphasising youth as the most desirable stage of the life cycle. And yet of course people do inevitably age, and other changes in working patterns, household structures and leisure facilities have all meant that a concern with the body, its appearance and regulation, etc. has not been confined to the young (Featherstone and Hepworth 1991). Indeed the 'grey market' and particularly the young old sector have become very attractive to advertisers and an important part of changing consumerism (Featherstone and Wernick 1995; Nettleton and Watson 1998, Pt. 4). It might be appropriate, then, to suggest that the various ways in which we have seen that the normative organisation of the body is changing in later modernity constitute a search for greater authenticity in which the everydayness of the body becomes a powerful idiom for cultural dramatisation.

Mellor and Shilling (1997) have argued that in the changing forms of dramatisation of community in modern European history it is possible to detect three eras of embodiment which are also forms of sociality: 'the emergence of what we can refer to in ideal type terms as the "medieval body", the "Protestant modern body", and what we call the "baroque modern body"' (op. cit., p. 8). In this context I shall only briefly describe the third of these types because in their formulation it captures some of the ambivalences of embodiment I have been trying to describe. Mellor and Shilling see the baroque modern form of embodiment as combining the banal rationality of bureaucratised everyday life with what they call the sensual solidarities of more indulgent celebrations of physical experience that can be sufficiently bacchanalian to undermine conventional social order: 'The baroque modern habitus has provided us with the potential to exert an unprecedented degree of control over our physicality, but has also thrown into radical doubt our knowledge of what our bodies are and how we should control them' (op. cit., p. 24). It may be true that in the cultural changes of later modernity we have a rediscovered sensual appreciation of physical experience, but we have not formulated a coherent discourse about the meanings of embodiment in everyday life nor have we come to terms with the differentiation of institutionalised bodies in private and public places.

Conclusion – Informalisation

I have suggested that the everyday has become considerably more prominent as both a theme of culture and as an idiom of public discourse in later modernity. This is in itself an indicator of cultural change, but it also raises questions about the significance of representations of everyday life in the practical negotiations of that life. These questions are heightened by the realisation that culture is no longer something out there to be enjoyed on special occasions, but is instead embedded in the identities and vocabularies of 'normality'. In order to illustrate this in this and the preceding chapter I have looked at a range of mundane activities in everyday life such as watching television, organising household relationships, going shopping, exercising personal taste and being concerned about one's body. Clearly all these activities, and other aspects of everyday life could be mentioned, have been reshaped by culture industries, and this is what I meant when I said earlier that the boundaries to 'normality' have been enlarged through textually mediated discourses. I have tried to show, though, that they have not been robbed of any local distinctiveness by these changes. Everyday life has not been gutted of any vitality and emptied of any significance for its participants. In this concluding section I will use the formal character of everyday practices to develop a discussion of a more general theme of change which I shall call informalisation. This I will argue is a crucial aspect of the increasing prominence of the everyday in cultural change.

In the opening chapter I recommended an approach to cultural change that is concerned with institutional change, that is with how the forms of social experience adapt in incorporating new materials and situations. What connects form and institution is that both are things detectable in the actions of individuals – they are an organisation or pattern to the actions of a number of people which they may not be aware of but which even so structure and give meaning to interaction. When the guests at a wedding group themselves in a particular arrangement of individuals and pose for a photograph they are conforming to formal concerns. Even more when they correct the misalignment of someone who has made a mistake about where they should be they are displaying the normative force of formal concerns. The point of formal analysis is that themes in institutional concern can be shown to be meaningful in ways that the individuals concerned could probably not articulate. It is in this sense that institutions can be said to constitute the sense and sensibility of everyday life. Of course individuals can form habits, even obsessions, that are meaningful in that they are open to a deeper reading, but these patterns are responses rather than constitutive. In addition to Simmel's classic essays already cited (1971), perhaps the most celebrated example of formal analysis in cultural change is Elias's reading of forms of guidance on personal manners as exemplifying the development of a new language of individuality (1978, 1982).

One way of linking the several aspects of formal change that I have discussed in these chapters is to point to a recurrent concern with authentic identity. More precisely, it is with ways of expressing, presenting or performing identity more authentically so that individuals can feel that they are being truer to themselves. It seems to me consistent with the populism of consumerism that I stress throughout that the expression of authenticity comes out in a variety of settings as modes of informalisation. By this I do not mean a deliberate attempt to break down or violate the normative order of institutional life, but rather to no longer accept the force of many codes or conventions of public life. In this way the more relaxed 'naturalness' of private life is becoming more the vernacular of public settings.

A good example of the process I am thinking of grows out of the salience of sport and exercise to presentation of the self. It seems that it is because being active is seen to be taking responsibility for oneself, to be stretching the body in desirable ways, that being dressed for exercise unproblematically carries connotations of being dressed naturally. It follows then that previously quite rigid demarcations between exercise clothes and more conventional street wear are being disregarded. It is now common to see possibly primarily but by no means exclusively young people in streets, bars and other public settings in the stripped down clothing of exercise. In part, of course, this is a form of display as it draws attention to the sexual connotations of muscularity, sweat and physicality. And in part it is a taking to the extreme of the fashion of wearing leisure clothes as relaxed, informal comfortable clothing, but not thereby precluding the role of fashion as differentiation, for as Visser has wittily pointed out: 'The modern "business" suit for men was an ingenious device for disguising the appalling physiques of the sedentary nineteenth-century rich.... Now that the top people ripple with expensive health, they want "casual" or streamlined clothes, to enhance their splendidly fit forms' (1997, p. 24).

If the wearing of exercise clothes in public settings, and taking exercise as in the common habit of jogging and associated exercises of stretching and flexing, etc., are seen to be part of a more general acceptance of the *desirability* of unstructured, classless communal anonymity in dressing, then exercise can be said to be a fashion of anti-fashion – a semiotic of authenticity as opposed to the artificiality of more fashionable dressing-up. Becoming less formal can then be seen as part of a more general disregard for the defining features of situations and identities. A good further example is provided by the way that many of the conventional constraints on gendered identity are increasingly ignored. Although wearing trousers had become common in leisure wear by the 1960s, it was still generally expected that women would wear a skirt as a badge of their gender in the workplace. Recently a woman who was sacked because she refused to conform to this expectation was awarded damages for unfair dismissal.

Other constraints on gendered identity such as women not being expected to do 'male' things like swear in public, drink pints of beer in pubs, talk loudly in public places, go unaccompanied to meet friends or partners in public places and initiate conversations with strangers are increasingly disregarded. To the extent that these constraints were ways of constituting female subordination, their rejection is obviously part of political struggles to establish equality of citizenship; but they are also indices of less finely differentiated social vocabularies. It seems that it is part of the transitions of a mass society that the fine texture of structural differentiation between social actors is becoming blurred in an informal egalitarianism. I want, then, to argue that informalisation is a general name for institutional change that works across a number of settings and can be summarised as a process of what I called earlier blurring the boundaries and structures of personal experience.

One objection to the term 'blurring' is that it might be taken to imply subverting or destabilising social order. While there are aspects to the changes we are exploring that can be said to be generating anomie, that is not the dominant impression I wish to convey. It is rather that many of the rigidities of social order are being made more permissive through an opening up to personal choice that results, in a paradox familiar to us from Beck's work, in a blander orthodoxy or greater conformism. The reason is of course that in a mass society where convenience is pursued at every opportunity we all end up driving the same small cars, eating the same pizzas and wearing the same jeans. The logic of consumerism is, as I have argued, a radical democratisation which does not transfer substantive power to the people but translates prestige into the conventions of everyday life. In the process of transition from a class to a mass social order in later modernity there is then a deep connection between democratisation and informalisation through the common use of motifs of the everyday.

I further suggest that this complex of connections is clarified by a recognition of the extent to which the informalisation I discuss involves a de-legitimation of the sacred or a greater dominance of the profane in everyday life (on this see Martin 1981). One example of what I mean is provided by all the ways in which profanity has become commonplace. There has, of course, always been profane speech such as swearing, ribald and blasphemous humour and a general vulgarity in behaviour and attitude. The expression of profanity has, however, been highly structured by social class and between genders. Above all sexuality – either its expression or representation – has been carefully regulated in public settings and discourse. What has changed in the informalisation of cultural fragmentation is that profanity has become commonplace in public speech, there are no longer words that are taboo from utterance in public prints, and sexual behaviour – in particular the display of sexual organs and acts – is a standard feature of public drama (I will come back to this relaxation of the boundaries of the ordinary in Chapter 8).

Another aspect of the same process is the changing character of humour. Jokes have typically depended upon breaking rules on what is sayable or appropriate. There has had to be a shock element in the joke being told so that what makes it funny is both a reversal of conventional expectations and a frisson of pleasure at contemplating the illegitimate. Humour has therefore traded upon institutional norms such as rules prohibiting premarital sexuality or the chastity of priests. When these norms no longer have any force or significance because they are no longer observed in the wider society, jokes about their violation lose any dramatic impact. It is in this context unsurprising that 'stand-up' (individual address to an audience) humour has shifted to narratives of personal experience trading upon audience empathy and thus sympathetic laughter at the vagaries of everyday life rather than a structured joke.

One way of describing these changes is as a consequence of the efflorescence of permissiveness in the 1960s. But rather than attach too much significance to a moment it is more useful to recognise that there are periodic rebellious phases, as in for example the 1840s across Europe, which promise much but are actually subordinate to longer-term processes of more orderly transition. In practice, a willingness to consider the relaxation of sexual mores, more open relations between generations and a greater freedom of personal expression as themes in lifestyle concerns can be interpreted as consistent with individualisation in the European civilising process (Elias 1978, 1982). It would be too much of a digression to explore informalisation in Elias, but it seems likely that informalisation operates (not necessarily consistently) at a number of levels of social complexity, and that there may be a spiral, as Wouters has suggested, between different aspects of formality through time, across a social formation and in relations between cultures (Wouters 1986, 1990).[6]

However, it is because the process of change I have called informalisation is situated at the level of form that it displays the characteristic Simmelian paradox of contradiction. In one perspective a consumerist refusal to accept the automatic authority of conventions of public places and identities has meant an undermining of social differentiation which has resulted in a pervasive conformism. In a large crowd of young people particularly at a leisure setting such as a pub or club, status differences based on say education, wealth, family background and occupation will not be immediately apparent in appearance. Of course in a country like Britain where social class is finely engraved in consciousness, voice or accent has traditionally functioned as a means of social location more precise than appearance, but even here these distinctions seem to be being overlaid with a more general inarticulate estuarial orthodoxy that is generational rather than regional. From another perspective, though, the distinctions of structure are being replaced with more ephemeral fashions or tastes that are displayed in areas such as types of food eaten, when it is being eaten, what is being drunk and in general the undermining of conventional distinctions between public and private eating (Warde and Martens 2000). Time, place and company no longer structure eating as a social occasion, but it rather becomes a matter of style – an opportunity to display a sensibility.

The process of informalisation therefore involves a new play of social distinctions, new forms of social spaces. If the everyday is primarily a spatial concept in that it is concerned with the ecology of normality, then as the everyday becomes more prominent in cultural discourse it will be apparent in changing frameworks of social and cultural spaces. As is well known, Bourdieu has developed a notion of habitus as a form of lifeworld that structures the meaning of everyday life at different positions in the social formation (1984). While it would be foolish to deny that there are patterns in use of culture associated with all the major lines of social differentiation (for example Bennett et al. 1999), my discomfort with a notion of habitus lies in the way that a dominance of what I have called textually mediated discourses has meant that patterns of taste have become less firmly differentiated, less stable and more subject to the self-conscious relativism of fashion. It is for these reasons that I have described the use or consumption of cultural resources in the institutional structures of everyday life as environments. That is, ways of bridging personal experience to the broader, less tangibly graspable spaces of public culture.[7] In this way environments straddle the boundaries of private and public spheres and help to reconcile and make comprehensible or at least reasonable each in relation to the other. In the next chapters I will show the increasing dominance of the everyday in public culture.

6

Authority and Expertise in Public Life

Introduction

I have been trying to show why a fruitful way of interpreting cultural change in later modernity is through the boundaries of normality. That is, change should be understood in relation to what I called the borders of locality or the frames of everyday life; and I have further argued that these are shifting and becoming more ambiguous in the experience of all-pervasive mass-mediated cultural forms. My approach to the sociology of everyday life can in this sense be described as an attempt to provide an ecology of unremarkable assumptions. Beginning with the household, I have embarked on an ecology or study of the use of space which is concerned with representations of selves and other social identities and social situations including more explicitly public environments. In this and the next chapter I will continue the approach of looking at the boundaries of normality, this time how they are being formulated in certain aspects of public discourse.

It may well be thought that the worlds of politics, corporate commerce and the government of spheres such as crime and social policy are not part of general conceptions of everyday life. And yet, of course, the ideologies and programmes enacted in these worlds do have major implications for the forms and quality of life-practices, not least in relation to an ideology of the need for rational solutions in all aspects of social life to which I have referred several times. I have, though, also argued that increasingly the dramaturgy of public life is being played out in terms of the idioms of everyday life. There is therefore at least a potential for contradictory tensions in how the vocabularies of everyday life are interrelating with the multitudinous voices of public discourse. It is in trying to explore these tensions that this and the next chapter are concerned with the populism of radical democracy. I shall argue that the medium that concretises these textually mediated discourses of radical democratisation is the changing character of public identity. In order to develop this interpretation though, I need to consider some more general aspects of a notion of public order and link these to a notion of legitimacy in public discourse.

By the term 'public discourse' I mean all the ways in which collective life or public life is talked about, represented, symbolized and enacted, principally in the media of public communication. The public discourse of modern societies has supported and sustained the legitimacy of the institutions of public order, indeed has so presumed the normality of the structures of power embodied in these institutions that it can be said to have been functioning as an ideology of consensus (Thompson 1990). This ideology is articulated through a dominant tone that is tolerant of the diversity of cultural styles in complex societies and neutral between competing perspectives on public policy. The power of the ideology is that it seeks to present an impersonal authoritative perspective which masks the way in practice it promotes a normative consensus around white middle-class heterosexuality. Not only is such a consensus increasingly criticised, there also are influential groups in all democracies who seek to curb liberal diversity in favour of what are seen to be more 'traditional' values.

The dominant liberalism of public discourse is therefore embattled so that its position is increasingly precarious. A factor here has been the persistent moral panic engendered in public discourse by dramatisations of the hazards of metropolitan life (on moral panics see Thompson 1998). Such a sense of fear about the dangers of public life is one negative aspect of mass society, although it is in contention with a more positive view that the very heterogeneity of multicultural life has engendered a greater tolerance of difference and diversity. It seems, then, that a more populist public discourse will not exhibit the same consensus as the limited democracy of modernity. It follows that we need to pose the question of whether the changing ways in which we participate in public life in the discourses of more radical democracy are equivalently destabilising public order.

Public Order

In the introductory chapter I described what I take to be some of the normative assumptions of everyday life as a way of pulling together the diversity of practical circumstance. It is clear that several of them involve expectations, such as a desire for security and a predictability in the orderliness of interaction with others, that are about the broader public context of personal experience. One of the defining features of modern society is that the main responsibility for the maintenance of public order has been devolved to or appropriated by agencies of the state, as part of that process that Weber famously saw as the monopoly of legitimate violence by the national state. This process of specialised agencies being charged with a responsibility for the maintenance of public order is itself part of a more general shift towards specialisation by new modes of professional expertise. The elaboration of social control in the modernisation of modernisation has involved a combination of the proliferation of both public and private control agencies, increasing amounts and types of information held on individuals by commercial and public agencies, and increasingly elaborate networks of surveillance of individuals in both public and private settings (Lyon 2001).

In this context I am not going to be concerned with the effectiveness or not of this apparatus in differentiating between conformist or deviant (or with how that distinction gets to be made (Fiske 1998)), or with the implications of a complex control apparatus for mythologies of citizenship (although the character of citizenship is a theme I shall come back to in the next chapter). I want, though, to briefly note two aspects of public life that have perhaps surprisingly survived and then discuss each in turn. The first is that the complexity of mechanisms of control has not precluded widespread fears of various sorts of dangers in everyday life. Neither, secondly, has the elaboration of controls precluded outbreaks of summary assault upon those who may be seen to pose threats or be dangers to the moral order of everyday life. I have already discussed Beck's theorisation of why the perceived dangers of various forms of risk have been accentuated in later modernisation. In relation to the legitimacy of public order I am thinking more of accentuated perceptions of moral dangers possibly stemming from a weakening of the authority of liberal consensus just mentioned.

It is clear that the development of the public sphere in later modernity through proliferating media of public discourse has not led to a triumph of rationality. Two examples of what I suggest are a pervasive irrationality in public discourse are, first, the dangers supposedly posed by immigration – most recently, at the time of writing, from perceived threats from refugees. When it is possible for the leaders of mainstream political parties to suggest that the refugees concerned – whether they are 'genuine' or not – are in danger of 'flooding' or 'swamping' indigenous culture,[1] then clearly the frameworks of collective identity have been felt by at least a substantial proportion of the population to have been destabilised. This is why I have written of this perceived danger as deriving from suspicions of a loss of cultural integration because it seems that the fear is moral rather than pragmatic (moral as in the sense of moral panic). There is some grumbling at immigrants taking advantage of state welfare provisions funded through general taxation, but the dominant resentment seems to concern threats to the hegemony of established culture. This is obviously a confused sentiment as there are also many perceived advantages to cultural diversity, but it is inevitably related to the persistence of nationalism when national economic and cultural boundaries are being eroded. English football hooligans may be an extreme version of this sentiment, but they are dramatising an outrage of threatened identity as both men and citizens.

A second example of irrationality in public discourse concerns widespread fears about the dangers of crime (on realism in perceptions of crime, see Young 1999). It is not my purpose to deny rising crime rates or the dangers posed by threats of violence in public places, but rather to note how dramatisations of criminality (not just criminal activities but dramas based on everyday life in control agencies) in public media seem to evoke a horrified fascination amongst mass audiences (Sparks 1992). The ways in which dramatisations in film, television and newspaper reports exaggerate the dangers of certain sorts of crimes – principally violence which may be associated with financial or sexual depredations from strangers – are well known. They fuel a climate in which the suburban household may well feel itself embattled in a hostile threatening greater society. But more specifically the moral dangers of a fragmenting cultural order are symbolised by the ease with which virtually a public panic can always be generated over dangers posed by sexual abusers of children. Here the realities of domestic sexual abuse are virtually ignored in favour of the very small number of abusive, and particularly violent, incidents by strangers. It seems that children as a symbol of otherwise impossible innocence are being idealised as a contrast to a dangerously threatened cultural order.

I have described two modes of irrationality in public discourse that are expressions of fears about perceived dangers that are undermining the order of public life. What is significant about these examples is an underlying fear of what I have called fragmentation – in effect that the boundaries to local experience are being undermined by processes of change beyond individual control. Although these fears may be irrational in certain respects they are a necessary element in any interpretation of cultural change, and they undoubtedly inform some of the shifts in forms of public identity that I will subsequently discuss in later sections of the chapter. I should also say that by picking examples I can call irrational fears, I do not mean to suggest that all fears in public discourse are irrational.[2] For example, the suspicion that international companies may conduct dangerous experiments with public health through the promotion of new technologies such as genetic modification seems entirely justified. As, indeed, do illegal acts that attempt to prevent trials supposedly legitimating these experiments. This last example reminds us that many of the fears I am thinking of stem from a discrediting of expertise that we have seen is characteristic of later modernity.

This brings me neatly to the second aspect of elaborate mechanisms of social control I mentioned above – that these mechanisms have not been able to suppress or forestall instances of popular violence against perceived threats. What I am concerned with now is the implication of centralised social discipline that citizens neither individually nor collectively should act to instil fear in, or perpetrate violence upon, others even when punishing perceived transgressions of social norms. Although this expectation, often summarised as the rule of law and the basis of modern civilisation, is very strong, there are in all complex modern societies circumstances in which citizens will feel justified in attempting to enforce their own version of summary violence upon unfortunates perceived as unacceptably deviant. These actions are invariably condemned by moral and political commentators as instances of 'mob rule', although they will also be explained by others as more or less justified responses to perceived threats or inequalities.

An example here would be the riots in Los Angeles that followed the acquittal of policemen filmed beating Rodney King. Less publicised and possibly harder to explain or justify are occasions when groups of people have acted to attack the homes or the persons of those suspected of being guilty of child abuse. The outrage this deviance attracts was also expressed by the crowds that attacked children suspected of being responsible for the death of a small boy in Liverpool (Jamie Bulger). It seems that people in these cases are attempting to violently ostracise 'unnatural' acts, as are those who attack the homes or persons of those they believe to have been identified as having contracted the HIV virus. It is appropriate to note that those who use violence to protest against structural discrimination are in a quite different situation from those who seek to punish sources of pollution or those, for example, who feel justified in using violence to attack medical personnel who facilitate terminations of pregnancies. There are, however, two things to say about these examples. First, that as soon as one starts looking there are many instances when citizens feel justified in usurping the state's responsibility for public order. Secondly, when this happens it seems that the justification across many different types of circumstance is that the state or its agencies cannot be trusted to act equitably or appropriately in enforcing a moral order.

Legitimacy in Public Discourse

The legitimacy of public order, or more precisely the institutions of public order, is given by an implied moral order – when the expectations of the latter order are violated or unfulfilled then citizens may take it upon themselves to sweep aside the conventions of public order. These are, however, relatively extreme circumstances when people have banded together probably more or less spontaneously. I have presented these outbursts as responses to fears over whether the dominant moral order can be sustained. The same interpretation can be advanced in relation to the intolerance evidenced in expressions of anger or hostility by individuals or small groups against other individuals. For example, that routinely visited upon women and members of ethnic minorities to which also we should add violence against sexual minorities. This violence is so common that it might seem to transcend my prior emphasis upon violations of a moral order. To ask if we are becoming more tolerant in mass society, or to put it another way, if in our everyday relations in public we are more relaxed about or accepting of difference and diversity, is to ask about the relationships between cultural discourse and local experience.

From all the examples I have described it is clear that the legitimacy of public order is crucial. It is unlikely ever to be absolute but instead provisional, dependent upon the perceived reasonableness of normality. By legitimacy one means an acceptance that even if particular individuals entrusted with authority behave unreasonably, the structures that underlie authority are accepted as reasonable and appropriate. Legitimacy is therefore inseparable from perceptions and understandings of appropriate relations in public and, in conjunction with a norm of tolerance for individual others, is a precondition of an effective public discourse. I have linked legitimacy and tolerance because they both seem to me to be aspects of a changing moral order in mass society that has been necessary to accommodate the shifting frameworks of everyday life.

In the following sections of the chapter I will explain what I mean by a changing moral order through a discussion of new forms for the character of public identity in late modernity. Not only does this discussion bring out more clearly what I mean by both radical democratisation and informalisation as social processes, it also shows how the thematic concerns of the forms of everyday life are being exemplified in public discourse. Since the publication of the body of work authored by Michel Foucault, there has of course been a great deal of concern in contemporary writing with power as constitutive and the mechanisms of power in social order. It is widely recognised that power and its exemplification in the disciplines of everyday life should not merely be seen as repressive but equally as facilitative. It is, to pick up again examples from the previous chapter, through modes of regulation of the body as well as the constitution of gendered identities and codes of pleasure, desire and happiness that frameworks of normality are delineated. It is, therefore, arguable that relations in public are dependent upon what is visible or more precisely what is made seeable in a particular culture. If we are in a process of transition through a fragmentation of conventional cultural norms then we have to ask about the possibilities for perception when lacking cultural frames.

Changing Forms of Authority

I have suggested that in the constitution of everyday life there is an intimate interdependence between expectations of order and the perceived legitimacy of institutional norms. These codes of conduct provide literal spaces within which individuals can situate themselves while in interaction with others. And if we learn from Elias's study (1978, 1982) of the historical interconnections between norms concerning the control of emotions, particularly aggression, and notions of individuality, we can see how these codes also provide metaphorical spaces (see also Bendelow and Williams 1998). This is because these codes articulate disciplines concerned with the interaction of bodies and how the social body is shielded from intrusive contacts and undesirable address. I have further suggested that the complex of norms and expectations that I have summarised as relations in public (spaces) is constituted as a resource for practical actions in everyday life. It is the changing character of public discourse as we enter what I suggest we will call an era of fragmented culture that will be the central concern of these chapters.

I have not so far considered the meaning of legitimacy very carefully. Normally we think of legitimacy as being equivalent to justified, so that it is conventional to speak of a legitimate expectation (for example that the trains will run on time, although sadly noting that such an expectation is frequently unfulfilled in contemporary Britain). In the context of order as in this discussion, the legitimacy of rules or norms implies that they are seen as justified (or justifiable) and that those who seek to draw our attention to or enforce them have thereby acquired an authority. It seems to me therefore that the terms 'legitimacy' and 'authority' are closely interwoven and that much of the character of public discourse stems from attempts to make it authoritative. For example in the early years of radio broadcasting in Britain, when the broadcasting company and then corporation which had been given a monopoly and was seeking to establish itself as a public service, those charged with reading the news had to dress in a costume of formal bourgeois occasions called evening dress and speak in the tones and diction of the educated bourgeoisie. Not all public discourse tries to be authoritative in this way, but public figures are inevitably expected to possess or be able to draw upon appropriate expertise such that they function as a legitimate reference point for audiences hoping to work out 'what is going on'.

The example of how these broadcasters sought to acquire authority suggests that certain positions and the institutionalised trappings that accompany these positions command respect almost independent of the actor filling the position. In hierarchical organisations with clear structures of authority such as conventional military or religious bodies, the organisation of power should not need to be disputable. In traditional societies political power has been concentrated in the hands of members of specific status groups usually delineated by the possession of titles such as the aristocracy. It has, however, become increasingly difficult to sustain the legitimacy of such organisational structures in mass societies. While it is true that the development of large bureaucracies has meant that power is increasingly exercised by offices and governed by administrative protocols, authority in public discourse legitimated by the institutions of citizenship and mass politics has needed to be acquired.

I hope it may be helpful to describe some of these changes in the nature of authority as analogous to a process of secularisation. This term is conventionally understood to mean a loss of religious commitment in modern society, but I think is more accurately used to refer to a loss of religious authority. Although participation in the rituals of the major faiths is low in most post-industrial societies, it seems likely that the proportion seeking meaning through some form of spirituality is increasing (a trend that is consistent with a more widespread willingness to look outside conventional traditions of cultural meaning). Even so, the authority of religious leaders to act as guides for personal or collective action seems thoroughly undermined. The exceptions to this generalisation are individuals who are able to harness their religious status to charismatic example, as in the case of Archbishop Tutu in South Africa, and thereby gain a degree of fame as well as political authority. I have emphasised a discrediting or distrust of expertise in the modernisation of modernisation, and what I am adding to that suggestion now is that all traditional bases of authority, not just religious, are being undermined. The consequence is that all varieties of forms of authoritative utterance in public discourse have increasingly to seek supplementary grounds for legitimacy.

What I mean by supplementary grounds can be initially clarified by reference to the British royal family. Their status is based on traditions and rituals (however much we know these traditions to have been invented over the past 100 years) so that they should be able to transcend the transience of fame in mass culture. In practice the legitimacy of the royal family has been engineered by a shift in style from the dignity of feudal authority to a model of family normality that has made their fame and prestige somehow analogous to the everyday life of their subjects (Chaney 2001a). While I will return to this example of the ambiguities of fame, the particular point I want to emphasise now is that as holders of institutionalised authority the members of the royal family had to be humanised (made into characters recognisably familiar from the dramas of mass entertainment) in order to retain their legitimacy. On a much smaller scale one can see the same process operating with other types of authority such as senior police officers, scientists and generals. The holders of these roles still employ the traditional trappings of expertise such as uniforms and appropriate props in their settings, but they are increasingly trained by public relations consultants in how to present their messages. Authority is no longer sufficient in itself but has to be adapted to the conventions of the everyday life of mass publics.

Authority in Mass Culture

I assume it is uncontroversial to maintain that there will necessarily be a multitude of voices in the public discourse of complex mass societies.

Some will be present transiently because they have been caught up in exceptional circumstances and can provide an authoritative eyewitness account. Others will be present more recurrently because they represent interest groups or social movements and thus have the legitimacy of public support. Others again will be present in public discourse because of their institutional status as, for example, religious leaders claiming a moral authority or scientists enjoying the legitimacy that derives from their expertise in particular forms of knowledge. In all these and other cases the authority with which they speak will not be unquestioned, and thus their status as legitimate contributors will need to be constantly asserted, framed and interpreted for their audiences. This process will have two consequences. One I have already briefly mentioned and that is that public figures will be driven to seek an authority through an empathetic appeal to their audiences. The second is that what we can call the core voices of public discourse will be surrounded by a multitude of commentators and interpreters. I will say a little more about this second consequence before returning to a fuller justification of the first.

The process of public discourse requires that events, occasions, themes, topics and controversies, etc. have to be recognised and made into themselves. For example, a crime wave has to be recognised as a problem before it can then generate a panic, with again appropriate expertise being introduced to explain and offer palliative measures. An important part of the job of presenters and interpreters is then to authorise the self-evidentness or taken-for-grantedness of the topics of public discourse. Through the ways in which events and issues are framed, they are both made into recognisable topics and made more or less relevant to audience interests. There is therefore an essential role for a class of supplementary public figures, both media employees and independent commentators and experts, to act as intermediaries between audiences and public life. It further follows that in order to gain the trust of those they represent, public intermediaries will be likely to speak with the accents of popular speech and to mimic the perceived stance of ordinary people or popular opinion, as indeed has happened in the public discourse of mass societies: 'The typical greetings and partings uttered by Richard and Judy [British daytime television presenters] – "morning to you", "hiya" "bye" and "see you tomorrow" – reflect a far wider process of change in late-modern culture that Norman Fairclough (1994) calls a *conversationalization of public discourse*' (Moores 1997, p. 234).

Two further points need to be made about the framing of expertise or authority. The first is that it is an infinite regress – it is neither confined to the 'serious' matters of public life nor is it a single layer of mediation. It has become apparent that every aspect of life, including leisure pursuits such as holidays and food and drink, and family relationships and a search for meaning through spiritual guidance, will generate supplementary expertise to explain, comment and generally guide audiences.

Distinctions between experts and commentators have inevitably blurred, so that public discourse has come to consist of representations of topics and issues that are almost entirely made up of dialogues and commentaries between commentators and presenters. And this leads to my second point here which is that although acting as intermediaries, those who offer what I have called supplementary expertise will and have become public figures. They will help to constitute a new class of celebrities, that is people who have a public identity through their role in public discourse rather than because of the expertise or authority they bring to that discourse.[3] As public figures they will command interest or contradictory emotions but very often a great deal of affection, as evidenced by the response to the recent (at the time of writing) murder of television presenter Jill Dando.

This particular example provides a good bridge back to the more general argument concerning the consequences of the mediation of authority. The second of these consequences I described as a process whereby public figures will be driven to seek a more empathetic rapport with their audiences. The most effective way of establishing empathy or rapport between public figures and audiences is for the former to minimise differences in character and outlook between themselves and their audiences. Thus it is not only minor figures of the celebrity class such as Jill Dando who will be famous for their ordinariness but it will be a more widespread characteristic of public figures. It is perhaps unsurprising that successful politicians who have more than most constantly to seek to maximise their public appeal have led the way in derogating their authority. In British terms the two most successful political leaders of the second half of the century, Margaret Thatcher and Tony Blair, have both concentrated on the 'common sense' of their political vision, not least through choosing to emphasise it in interviews in non-political settings rather than in more conventionally serious news commentary programmes. To say this is not to accept their self-presentation as de-ideologising politicians, both are/ were thoroughly ideological, but rather to point to how moral visions in the radical democracy of fragmented culture are articulated through the rhetoric of everyday life.

Perhaps the most obvious example of a public figure who was able to transcend the fame and appeal of previous cultural formations was Diana Spencer who became Princess of Wales. I have referred above to how the British royal family adapted to the demands of mass culture by attempting to marry some of the ceremonials of quasi-traditional forms with a representation of normality in family life (Cannadine 1983). When the heir to the throne married a pretty but otherwise unremarkable member of the aristocracy this combination was given a fresh burst of life. Subsequently the unhappiness of the marriage and a relaxation of traditional constraints on reporting (itself due to an undermining of authority in a more populist environment) meant that extraordinary revelations of the private lives of elite figures became commonplace.

As is well known, the publicising of Diana Spencer as a beautiful woman in conjunction with sympathy for her widely reported 'failings', adultery, food abuse and craving for publicity, meant that she was able to pursue a new career as a self-styled 'Queen of Hearts'. Her death in a road accident while still a young woman gave her the aura of martyrdom and generated the most extraordinary display of public grieving – to the extent that her death threatened to undermine the continued existence of the monarchy as an institution (on the ambiguities of public mourning see Kear and Steinberg 1999). It is not my intention to comment on the rights and wrongs of this story, but point to how it was possible for someone to transcend the limitations of one sort of status and through a dramatisation of a highly imaginative ordinariness achieve a global stardom that has turned her into one of the most powerful icons of contemporary popular culture (some aspects of this process are explored in Richards et al. 1999).

I began this part of the chapter by suggesting that there is an intimate interdependence between that sphere of everyday life that I have sum-marised as relations in public and the character of public discourse. In order to bring out this association, I have pursued the theme of represen-tations of authority and legitimacy that I took from an earlier discussion of the presuppositions of public order. In particular I have pointed to some trends in how the identities of public figures have been presented. My main point is that in the public discourse of changing culture, author-ity can be seen to be adapting to the presuppositions of everyday life (more generally on changing codes of public life, see Chaney 1995). Rather than public figures presenting themselves as awesome, distant or threat-ening, they increasingly strive to be as one of the neighbours. This may well be welcomed as both a consequence and celebration of radical democ-racy. In subsequent parts of the chapter I will further explore these trends, concluding with some notes on their implications for the status of intellec-tuals and the character of political life. More immediately I will look in greater detail at the changing character of fame.

Heroes and Stars

The example of the extraordinary public interest in the life and death of Diana Spencer and our more general concern with the interrelations of celebrity and authority raise the issue of whether the character of fame is changing with a new cultural era. The possibility of authoritative fame is usually discussed in social and cultural history through a concept of charisma, but rather than get caught up in whether charismatic leadership is possible in mass politics, I would rather make some distinctions between types of fame – between types of institutionalised identity.[4] The most traditional category here is the notion of heroes and heroism. These are figures in the myths and folk tales of traditional culture who are able to overcome ordeals and resolve impossible contradictory demands through exemplary accomplishments such that they become models for social values. A figure such as Robin Hood in British mythology illustrates both how the general tale and the character of leading figures can be adapted to changing cultural contexts, and how an overarching morality (promoting social justice through robbing the rich on behalf of the poor) is able to legitimate the heroism of one who might otherwise be seen as an antisocial villain. Heroes typically embody the attributes of a group such as a class, tribe, region or nation in an exemplary manner so that they transcend the mundane, and their heroism often demands a form of martyrdom in the sacrifice of their lives for the common good.

Heroes are therefore models but it is important to recognise that the nature of the model may work in at least three slightly different ways. The hero may be an ordinary person who is meant to inspire others to emulate their deeds as in the now discredited pantheon of heroes of socialist labour in Russia and China. In contrast the hero may be a leader, such as a warrior king or Comrade Stalin, who inspires others to join in a collective movement. Other heroes, such as English robber Dick Turpin, may be only inspirational in their bravery and chivalry rather than their overall moral stance. I have used examples of heroes from political movements to indicate why I am not sure that Featherstone (1992) is right to suggest that heroes are no longer tenable in contemporary society, but clearly heroism requires an uncomplicated narrative frame. The heroic tale can be recounted either orally or in the multiple reproductions of the mass media, but the delineations of stirring deeds and powerful rhetoric have to be uncompromising. There is a clear relationship between means and ends so that even heroes of capitalism are rarely faced with moral ambiguities.

In a well-known argument that is now some years old Lowenthal drew a contrast between the heroes of modernising America and later heroes of mass entertainment (1961). I shall describe this contrast as being between the heroes of an urban popular culture and the heroes of mass culture. The latter category are more effectively categorised as stars. I have already indicated that heroic narratives can be told through mass media so the difference of stardom is not in that respect, but rather in that stars are famous in every aspect of their being rather than specific accomplishments. Indeed stars may not have accomplishments, merely attributes such as a voluptuous body, although still inspiring endless amounts of attention. This suggests two further characteristics of stardom. The first is that as it is their being rather than their doing which makes them famous they can transcend their original cultural context. Thus most famously the stars of the cinema were the first figures in mass entertainment who transcended national boundaries and ideological divides. Stars are at least potentially global figures. The second characteristic of stars is that they are constituted not just in the narratives that primarily frame them but also simultaneously in a multiplicity of commentaries and interpretations; supplementary tellings that Bennett and Woollacott referred to in relation to a fictional star, James Bond, as intertextual realisations (1987).

The ways in which stars differ from heroes brings out two further intriguing and related themes that illuminate developments in mass culture. I have emphasised that heroes are extraordinary in that their accomplishments lift them above the limitations of everyday life. They are therefore realised in a narrative context – heroes are told through tales and it does not matter very much whether these tales, or indeed the heroic actors, correspond to a lived reality. In contrast, stars are very much real people (except of course for explicitly fictional constructs such as the James Bond figure already cited) and are constantly being depicted in all sorts of real-life settings. And yet the reality of star and setting is not just made mythical by the particular fictional context (film for example) in which they are set, as it is clear that film stars can become generic figures who constitute narrative themes in themselves, so that rather it is their stardom that is an elaborate fictional performance. This (potential) distinction between the person and the star's persona underlies one of the recurrent themes of both scholarly and popular writing about stars – the extent to which they are or can be authentic figures.

Stars therefore articulate for their audiences a dramatisation of identity which is quite different from a heroic dramatisation of a moral ideal. There is no requirement for stars to be exemplary, and indeed much of their fascination may lie in the inter-mixing of flaws with distinction. Stars do though act as symbols of an attitude that can be identified with as characterising an unarticulated but nevertheless recognisable outlook or stance towards the world. I think this is why stars have flourished in an era of mass photography. Clearly stars need cheap, easily reproducible means of publicity, but more substantially photographs have the capacity to express a mood or attitude through stance, props, lighting – personality. It does not matter of course if the star really believes or embodies the projected outlook, what does matter is that a significant fraction of the potential audience can instantly recognise that the image has become a voice for what otherwise could not be so effectively expressed. The power of the image of James Dean walking in the rain by a Manhattan subway that came to adorn innumerable adolescent bedrooms was the immediacy with which a generational consciousness could be both recognised and stimulated.

This analysis of the dramatisation of identity in stardom also connects to the second theme that I think stars point to as a characteristic of mass culture. This is the ways in which stars mediate the arbitrariness of ordinariness and fame. It is because stars are real people that they neces-sarily have biographies – they are the children of everyday lives and have emerged from the anonymity of the circumstances of their audience's lives. Dyer points out how frequently references to stars remind us of the arbitrariness of their discovery (1987). While in retrospect it may appear inevitable, at the time of their anonymity they show us that the excep-tional is always embedded in the here and now. Although it is obviously absurd to see Diana Spencer as an ordinary person, in order for her to transcend the status of family and hereditary privilege there had to be an empathetic revelation of her ordinariness. She could leave the institution of the monarchy behind because she engaged with the representation of authenticity in ways that their (her family of marriage's) more limited training as public figures precluded.

Diana is a provocative figure as a star because she was not a profes-sional entertainer nor earnt her living from media appearance fees, although she clearly was a source of entertainment and interest for mass audiences (in this sense she provides a bridge to the further category of celebrities). I have recognised that stars were an essential resource in the marketing of mass entertainment genres but now the category seems to transcend this role. Although Diana is an exceptional case, there are other types of stardom where the fiction/reality duality that I have described is not couched in terms of representation of fictional identities. I am thinking in particular of popular music and sports stars. In both cases they attract attention as performers for mass audiences, but their public persona, say as Keith Richard or Courtney Love, is not a fictional character but a more or less deceptive mask. Sports stars have until recently had less exagger-ated personae (although that is changing and will certainly change even more) and have traditionally been seen as heroes because their fame was based on exceptional accomplishment. My reason for seeing them as increasingly being constructed as stars is that their accomplishments are less likely to be presented as moral narratives (that is as conforming to cer-tain moral codes about playing the game, etc.). Now while their skills are clearly exceptional they purchase lifestyles that are indistinguishable from those of other entertainers and thus they join in the tension common to all stars of reconciling authentic person with distinctive persona.

My argument is, then, that stars are spectacular figures who arouse a complex of emotions including lust, envy and admiration in their audi-ences as well as concretising narrative genres (and providing a further layer of narrative complexity by occasionally playing or being used against character). Although by definition extraordinary in the ambigui-ties of accomplishment, they dramatise the construction of identities in everyday lives and actually open the door to the creation of subordin-ate galaxies of minor public figures. For example, although I have said sports figures can become stars in mass culture this has been exceptional (and usually required some heroic failings as in the case of George Best although the status of David Beckham offers an innovative bridge between stardom and celebrityhood). But in the dramatisations of ordinariness that sports figures exemplify, the stars will blaze a trail that can be followed by a host of people who acquire a temporary fame. These lesser sporting personalities are more accurately described as celebrities and bring us on to a third category of fame – one that I will suggest is particularly characteristic of later developments in mass culture.

Celebrities

Writing about celebrities earlier I described them as people who acquire an authority merely by their presence in public discourse. I want now to broaden this account by arguing that celebrities are not only people who mediate public discourse such as announcers, experts and commentators. The class will also include people who become interesting through their appearance, that is by appearing in public life. Sometimes their appearance will be legitimated by some ability to entertain as a performer or sports person, but the class will also include those who have a acquired a public identity by appearing in, for example, quiz shows, talk programmes or even just by being in advertisements (Monaco has suggested the existence of a class of paracelebrities who have no distinction whatsoever in themselves but are connected in some way to those who have a more legitimate celebrity (1978)). In their proliferation they constitute the cast of public discourse and very often in their escapades and adventures the topic of that discourse. As with stars, the appearance of celebrities is a constant commentary on the dramatisation of identity, but lacking the extraordinary personae of stardom celebrities work at the dramatisation of mundaneity. And perhaps therefore more clearly than stars, celebrities constantly ask to be appreciated for their authenticity – there is a continuous emphasis on how much they resemble or indeed simulate the audience.

It has frequently been remarked that actors and politicians are emblematic figures of modern consciousness. Because they are both concerned with the representation of identity they are forced into an explicit reflexivity about their own selves and simultaneously allow us, the audience – their constituents – a privileged glimpse of the dramatisation of persona as well as a resource for our own more limited performances (on how theatrical projects should learn from the dramatisations in everyday life, see Read 1997). My argument in this chapter has been that the expansion of public discourse through ever-enlarging media of mass communication and entertainment has meant that actors and politicians are no longer such exceptional roles. There is now a much larger cast of the famous or recognisable who as celebrities mediate between distinction and everyday life.

Even so there is still a lingering expectation of something exceptional about politicians. As representatives of social movements they might be expected to articulate a moral vision for social and public order. In practice we know that this is no longer an aspiration beyond a very generalised sense of the proper interdependence of individual and community. In practice politicians have retreated from an aspiration to distinctiveness towards an infinite responsiveness to the needs of presentation. In place of ideology there has developed a hyperreflexivity about the presentation or dramatisation of authenticity. This has meant that in the place of an authority of power, fear or expertise there is an all-pervasive authority of normality, a legitimacy of acceptability. An indicative example from a recent daily newspaper:

> When he swept into an Albanian refugee camp earlier this week, Tony Blair looked as if he had grabbed his regular Saturday outfit off the back of the bedroom chair before rushing out to the airport. His red open-neck polo shirt and black jeans are the sort of clothes the prime minister throws on at the weekend to kick a football around with his sons in the grounds of Chequers. With Tony Blair, however, little happens by chance and a great deal of thought went into what he should wear at the Elbasan camp where 4,000 refugees are housed in tents 40 miles from the Albanian capital Tirana. Close advisors, such as Alistair Campbell, wanted the prime minister to look casual – so that he could empathise with the refugees – but appear sufficiently smart so that his speech from the refugee camp carried authority back home on television.
>
> The preparations, even down to the red and black of the prime minister's clothes – which are the colours of the Albanian national flag – paid off. Blair's relaxed image contrasted with the formality of his officials at the camp, who wore shirts and ties, and refugees appeared at ease with the visiting leader amid the stifling heat of the camp.
>
> One family was touched when the prime minister took off his shoes as he entered one tent as a sign of respect to a Muslim household. In the tent, an elderly man gave the prime minister a searing account of his treatment at the hands of Serb paramilitaries; yesterday's front pages were dominated by pictures of an earnest-looking Blair listening to the man (*The Guardian*, 20/5/99, p. 4, G2).

The changes in the ways the personae of public figures are constituted are relevant to the forms of everyday life because these figures represent (embody) contrasts between the ordinariness of the everyday and the extra-ordinary: 'No matter what the category, celebrity permits a public voice; it shifts opinions, acts, decisions, feelings from the private stage to the public. It is a different order of existence' (Monaco 1978, p. 14). I assume in saying this that public figures are constituted in discourse, that is they are cultural artefacts, whose qualities and distinctiveness both help to define legitimate aspirations and the contours of normality. This is a surprisingly difficult idea to express in part I think because of ambiguities in the meaning of identification.

It is easy to say that the audience identifies with stars and heroic figures, and this has often been taken to mean that the audience seeks to emulate or even become these models. If they did so, it would probably be taken as a sign of pathology leading to a loss of personal autonomy or excessive fantasising. In practice there is little evidence of people actually changing their behaviour either to emulate the heroic models of socialist labour or the decadent glamour of idols of commercial entertainment. It seems more likely that to presume an equation of identification with imitation is part of a more general condescension to mass culture in which the popular audience is assumed to be at the mercy of exploitative tendencies of both political and entertainment elites. In some papers on the nature of fans several authors have tried to show how fandom has generally been constituted as pathological, and thus fans' work at the creation of meaning has usually been effectively denied (see Lewis 1992, Pt. 1).

Of course public figures are admirable; even when they are presented as villains their faults usually excite a degree of fascination and intrigued horror, but the admiration need not involve a loss of self. There is another meaning to identification in which something is recognised rather than taken as a model. In this sense public figures help to negotiate forms of presentation of the self or languages of social identity. Rather than leading to the intrigued consumer seeking to escape normality, public figures provide a way of enhancing the playful creativity of mundane contrasts between the self and how it might be seen by a variety of generalised others. If one way of writing the cultural history of modernity is through tracing the changing modes of authority and prestige – which can be crudely summarised as a number of ways of bringing the extra-ordinary more recognisably and routinely into the ambit of ordinary experience – then this provides another perspective on the institutionalisation of everyday life: how what is taken for granted gets to be taken.

I hope it is clear that in these ways celebrities enact the idioms of the everyday and work to further blur distinctions between public and private spheres – an idea brought out in Scannell's interpretation of the changing public sphere in an era of mass broadcasting (1989). Writing about what he calls the quality and character of broadcasting's communicative ethos, he identifies gossip as the dominant style of both dramatic representations and commentaries on televisual doings in other media formats: 'If it seems both ordinary and trivial, it is also relaxed and sociable, shareable and accessible, non-exclusive' (1989, p. 338). This communicative ethos provides the interface between public life and 'ordinary daily life' and is a function in his view of the democratisation of everyday life that has been made possible and been pursued by the organisation of broadcasting as a public service. It is not just that broadcasting, particularly in genres such as soap operas, mimics in a condescending way the triviality of audience concerns, but rather that there is a communicative ethos which has changed the character of public life: 'both as a series of structuring temporal arrangements and as a communicative style, an orientation towards relaxed, natural and spontaneous modes of address and forms of talk' (op. cit., p. 334), broadcasting has acquired what he calls a 'dailiness' so that it is embedded in everyday life (1996, Ch. 7).

Scandal Politics

I hope to have outlined a perspective on changing relations in public that is consistent both with the account of informalisation that I have developed in the previous chapter, and the stress on the ordinariness of expertise and distinction in this chapter. These moves towards privileging the idioms of the everyday in public discourse help to elucidate the shift towards what has been called 'scandal politics'. This term refers to what is seen as increasing stress in news media on revelations that are shaming for public figures (on the range of revelations, see Lull and Hinerman 1997b). Previously, the presumption of respectability for public figures would not have been breached so that a documentary made about Kennedy in the 1950s could not mention his philandering – now it would have been the point of the film. Public figures of course frequently complain that the boundaries between public doings and private backstage matters are breached in ways that are intrusive and hurtful. The defence mounted by those who seek out scandal is that it is of public interest (sells newspapers) and serves the public interest through revelations of duplicity, incompetence and hypocrisy. What is clearly being addressed in scandal politics is a conviction that for all public figures their persona is an image that has been constructed and that behind it lies a flawed human being.

A shift towards a greater emphasis on scandals in news media has been criticised on a number of grounds. First, it is clearly a form of muckraking that reveals aspects of private lives that are of no real interest or significance but are probably present in everybody's circumstances. Secondly, the revelations are often not revealed by chance but instigated through forms of pretence whereby public figures are led into making damaging revelations about for example drug-taking amongst sportsmen. Use of long-lens cameras to catch beautiful women undressed in what they thought were private settings is another aspect of these criticisms. Thirdly, and above all, this style of investigation has been criticised for focusing on personalities rather than issues. Representatives of complex outlooks are treated as more important than the reasons they are giving, intensifying an emphasis upon image rather than substance in political debate: 'Whereas once publicity meant the exposure of domination through the use of reason, the public sphere is now subsumed under a stage managed political theatre' (Stevenson 1999, p. 15).

Of course, scandals are not a new development and have been a routine source of both news and 'troubles' for those who seek to construct appearances of normality (see Thompson 1997, 2000). It does, however, seem that the attitudes that underlie scandal politics may be said to part of a broader suspicion that the powerful (in government, big business, the military – power elites generally) are inherently manipulative and duplicitous and only reveal their real reasons reluctantly if at all. This attitude is not limited to news reporting but has become a staple narrative resource for dramatisations in films, television and every media (see also Carey 1998 on rituals of shaming in broadcast dramatisations). So widespread is this distrust that it can inform the complete range of new social movements from the paranoia of religious and conservative fundamentalists to the movements of sub-politics that Beck discusses as responses to the risks of science out of control (1992). More conventionally, it has become so taken for granted that 'they' have agendas behind the appearances of events that everything from the death of a princess to the conduct of a war can plausibly be explained as the consequence of a conspiracy.

Scandal politics can be said, then, to be a natural corollary of the more general process I have called radical democratisation in which a populist climate is flattered by insiders revealing to 'us' – the mass audience – the feet of clay of those who purport to be exceptional or authoritative (Lull and Hinerman 1997a). In attempting to fend off populist suspicions of elitism public figures are driven to pursue informalisation, so that as they strive ever harder to be ordinary and pursue the values of radical democracy they are more likely to renounce conventional privileges and thus become all the more vulnerable to exposure. And indeed as we are more interested in them as personalities so we are more intrigued by their sexual foibles and their undressed bodies. It seems to me to further follow that as we are more insistently reminded of the frailties of the flesh that alternatives that purport or can be presented as more authentic come to seem all the more attractive, with of course in time further disillusionment. Above all, this mix of attitudes and expectations can be seen to be reformulating the character of authority and legitimacy in public life. There is an all too familiar double movement in which there is on the one hand an increasing and more pervasive alienation from institutionalised authority, and yet on the other a simultaneous fascination with forms of public discourse dominated by the tropes (characteristic forms of speech) of everyday life.

It is in this context that the ambiguous resonances of a figure like Diana Spencer begin to make more sense. As somebody situated at the heart of structures of traditional authority, and endowed with the privileges of wealth, beauty and glamorous lifestyle, she still managed to dramatise her alienation and communicate her engagement with the ordinary concerns of relationships and personal commitment. She was able thereby to claim a legitimacy that was outside conventional authority and could only be further confirmed by a tragic death (see the papers by Johnson, Greenhalgh and Spurlin in Kear and Steinberg 1999). Before saying any more about the sort of narrative she literally embodied, it will be helpful to turn to another morally ambiguous figure of the later twentieth century – Bill Clinton. At first pursued because of suspicions of old-fashioned corruption that stemmed from his position as a state governor, and to a large extent an inheritor of enmities generated by the indictment of Richard Nixon a generation before, Clinton was gradually revealed as adulterous, radically evasive, a liar but ultimately willing to abase himself in public confessional. Here were the moral failings of everyday life (and the familiar plots of soap operas) writ large and in extraordinary forensic detail, and yet he clearly failed to lose public confidence and retained in large part the authority and legitimacy of a national leader.

Clinton's survival can be interpreted as a cynical endorsement by pragmatic materialists. In a climate of alienation from institutionalised authority that I have described, those who felt themselves to be economically advantaged by a government were possibly indifferent to the self-evident moral failings of its leader. This is undoubtedly one of the factors involved, and yet I think Clinton's survival is more significant for an interpretation of cultural change than this. For those who held to a traditional expectation of the moral authority of a national leader, Clinton's failings were self-evident grounds for disqualification. The office gave privileges of an aura of mystique but its symbolic force had to be preserved at all costs. These views were opposed by those who were prepared to respond to Clinton as a flawed individual but still endorse him because of a broader lifestyle sensibility he represented. For this group, and it proved the larger, Clinton's failings were unfortunate and tacky but sufficiently recognisable to generate a degree of empathy and a refusal to seek disqualification. The full story obviously needs much greater detail, but the main point being made here is that in an era of discredited authority the symbolic office of national leader is reformulated away from authoritative mystique to someone straddling public–private boundaries and thereby much closer to everyday life.

There is, of course, another side to the scrutiny of scandal politics. Clinton may have been able to 'get away' with his moral failings, but other public figures have been stigmatised and punished in a variety of ways for their transgressions. Stevenson has pointed out that an English football star, Paul Gascoigne, was publicly shamed by pictures showing his bruised wife after he had beaten her: 'The footballing authorities attempted to dismiss the incident as a "private" matter … but arguably the pictures themselves and the protests of feminist groups breached the "wall" between public and private' (1999, p. 44). I personally doubt the influence of feminist groups on sport authorities, but the example is a telling indication of the relevance of everyday values to public matters. For what is significant is that an alienation from institutionalised authority has not been matched by an indifference to public behaviour. In an era of instant and exhaustive television coverage of wars, brutality, starvation and many other forms of abuse, the boundaries of other people's doings are continually breached by a global audience who demand some form of public accountability.

There is undoubtedly a much greater degree of what Thompson has called 'global scrutiny' (1995, 2000) so that the mass audiences of global television are brought into intimate familiarity with other people's suffering. There is a phenomenon of compassion fatigue whereby too many appeals for charitable aid can exhaust donors' sympathy, but the general lesson from rock concerts to alleviate famines, to sympathetic treatment of new waves of refugees, to national boycotts of, for example, the Chinese government after repression in Tienanmen Square, to international military campaigns to curtail 'ethnic cleansing', is that there is a perceived pressure from international public opinion to intervene in other countries' social policies. The limitations of this sort of humanitarian imperialism are all too visible, but the institution of global sympathy speaks to a new sort of citizenship. Particularly if one adds examples such as activists' pressures for the extension of legally enforced norms of conduct in new international groupings such as the European Union, as for example governing animal welfare and the treatment of animals being reared for consumption. These post-national norms have implications for what are often seen and defended as national cultural traditions and thereby citizenship in ways I will develop in the next chapter.

7

Citizenship in Radical Democracy

Introduction

In the previous chapter I discussed some of the ways in which the public discourse of later modernity has been changing. I have been concerned to show that the sphere of public discourse has been influenced by cultural change in ways that have had major consequences for everyday life. In particular I have explored changes in the character of the authority and legitimacy of public figures in order to make two related points. The first is that although many figures in public life are warranted by their possession of formal criteria of expertise, such as scientific qualifications, their expertise is framed and filtered for us by intermediaries whose main claim to fame is their empathetic ordinariness. The second is that characteristics of the everyday, in terms of interests, social style and concerns, are less likely to be patronised in public discourse and indeed can be said to be increasingly providing the tone and focus. I have suggested that it is an exemplification of the process of what I am calling radical democratisation that the idioms of everyday life have come to dominate the form and content of public discourse.

One aspect of the process of change is that in addition to changes in the dramaturgy of public life more empathetic values – characteristic of interpersonal relationships – seem necessary as a qualification for public office. I think this is why political figures in new conservatism, such as George W. Bush in America, seek to cloak their beliefs in competitive individualism and authoritarian social controls in a rhetoric of compassionate concern. How political leaders address 'us' as citizens is an important aspect of how ordinary people are to be involved in public life. It could be argued that if the differences in speech, dress and authority between those who have privileged status in a social order and those who are just living everyday lives are lessening, then it should follow that common representations of social experience in public culture become more accurate or authentic. This would be so because the culture would be more directly part of the lived experience of ordinary people. Culture would in an important sense have become embedded in everyday life, although this would be less true if social differences are merely being minimised in terms of populist style.

Public Broadcasting

I think it important to follow through this aspect of radical democratisation, and although it might seem a digression, I shall initially do so through a consideration of public broadcasting in modern Britain. In discussing aspects of cultural change in later modernity, I have at several points rather briefly asserted both that the facilities of mass culture industries and cultural institutions more generally have been essential resources in constituting the public sphere of mass societies. To say that culture industries have been significant is of course unremarkable (Thompson 1995), but discussion of them has largely focused on whether or not they have been able to facilitate the sort of participation in public culture that is usually held to be necessary for an effective democracy (Calhoun 1992). Amongst factors that are discussed in this respect are the ways in which marketing of mass culture industries has effectively blurred distinctions between public and private spheres, and the loss of distinctive communities or localities in the anonymous publics of mass society. More generally, the critical issue has been whether the media can still subvert orthodoxy or whether as Stevenson has put it: 'Whereas once publicity meant the exposure of domination through the use of reason, the public sphere is now subsumed under a stage managed political theatre' (1999, p. 15; see also Franklin 1994).

The initial medium for constituting the public sphere was the development of a newspaper industry but in later modernity newspapers, while remaining important, have been replaced to a significant extent by radio and television. Broadcasting was not only more instantaneous than print media it was also more truly national than print, and it was not afflicted in its early years by a stratification of the audience into class-cultural levels. The organisation of broadcasting in the United Kingdom under a mantle of public service then both made a national culture a reality and contributed in a major way to the democratisation of public life. Thus broadcasting contributed to what Crouch has called 'the democratic moment' (2000, p. 4) around the middle of the last century before later more radical developments. (Although this process is particularly salient for any history of cultural change in twentieth-century Britain, the notion of a public interest in relation to the regulation of broadcasting has been deployed in a number of nation states.) What I am suggesting is that the idea of public needs or interests has been particularly powerful as a fiction of community in recent British history, particularly I suppose during the crisis of the Second World War.

Initially founded as a commercial monopoly to reconcile the interests of state authorities in controlling a new means of public communication with those of set manufacturers eager to stimulate a market for their products, the British Broadcasting Company after five years was translated into the better known British Broadcasting Corporation. The distinctiveness of the latter body was that it was a pioneer of a new form of public body, a quango,[1] resourced by a tax on reception and given a monopoly of the production and distribution of radio broadcasts within the boundaries of the British state (as well as responsibility for overseas broadcasts). Within the Corporation the rationale for this quite extraordinary mode of regulation, and largely accepted in the wider public discourse, was that the BBC had the responsibility and the opportunity to advance national culture through serving the public. What this meant had at least two significant strands: first, that broadcasting should be open to the whole national public; and, secondly, that the Corporation did not feel itself bound to cater, either exclusively or predominately, for perceived public taste but rather to serve the public good (Curran and Seaton 1998; Chaney 1987a).

The public was therefore a fiction of political community based in a presumed national culture that as part of a democratic obligation had to be defended, strengthened and improved. The broadcasting monopoly saw itself as a gatekeeper that would provide access to culture for the mass public. But in doing so the idea of serving the public had to be given a practical form. I hope it is sufficient in this context to say that the general principle of serving the public was interpreted in Britain as an enlightened elitism. Clever people were recruited from the universities to enlighten, inform and stimulate national audiences. At its most extreme the elitism took the form in the very early years of a blithe refusal to differentiate between audiences, but more generally took the form of a degree of creative licence for production staff working within a broad stratification of cultural tastes by channels for radio and television.

This system (and it is important to recognise that it evolved through several stages) generated one of the most powerful myths of the superiority of British public life – that its broadcasting was the envy of the rest of the world. The principle of enlightened elitism survived a number of changes in the structural organisation of broadcasting such as the introduction of radio channels or services. Subsequently the more significant breaking of the monopoly with the development of commercial television was also largely contained within principles of public service broadcasting taken from the BBC and in the service of national cohesion. The institution of public service broadcasting was not therefore monolithic or unchanging, but one of the more significant moments of change came in the last quarter of the last century. Thus I think there will be general agreement with Tracey (1998) that although the Corporation remains, there has been an effective fall away from ideals of public service broadcasting. The legitimacy and resourcing of public broadcasting have been under increasing strain in Britain, suggesting that this fiction of community has at least been challenged by alternative fictions if not lost its warrant altogether.

The reasons are well known: the triumph of neo-liberal economic philosophies hostile to the provision by the state of public services that could be provided by competing (and supposedly more efficient) commercial organisations; a loss of faith in the privileges of the cultural tastes of intellectual elites that, as I will argue, is central to the process of the fragmentation of culture; both articulated through an ideology of consumerism that stresses individual choice and equality of taste as self-evident goods. All these in combination constitute the development of what I am calling radical democratisation. One should also note that technological changes such as the introduction of satellite and cable distribution facilities, allied with costs of developments like digital transmission, have all undercut the ability of governments to control national networks. It has consequentially become politically untenable to defend a commitment to the idea that public culture has an educational role, so that at best the values of public service broadcasting are defended in terms of diversity of provision rather than intrinsic value. While the paternalistic elitism of Reithian tradition may have had many unfortunate connotations, it did at least articulate a belief that there are values which are independent of public taste.

In this ideological, economic and technologically changing climate the meaning of public service has shifted from values of cultural enlightenment to an uneasy combination of better quality and a more serious, less populist, approach. That is, it seems generally felt that the BBC should be preserved because it makes or broadcasts 'better' programmes which in effect often translates as better production values. In effect, then, a fiction of the public as an imagined community, however stratified, that is grounded in a national culture has been replaced by an alternative metaphor of a market of consumers catered for by a variety of suppliers, one of whom is rather more upmarket and traditional. A public culture in the era of high modernity effectively meant a national culture – indeed a lot of BBC attitudes were inspired by a desire to resist what was seen as an encroachment by American popular or mass culture (as well as to foster a national identity). The situation in later modernity is a combination of a recognition that a national culture has at best an ambiguous status, with a replacement of the idea of public service with popular demand.

An Inadequate Public Sphere?

The popular is of course an attractive slogan – being of the people, in sympathy with ordinary outlooks, is a self-evident good in radically democratic times. It is consistent with my earlier discussion of informalisation that in all sorts of ways from the more relaxed dress styles of political leaders, to the global acceptance of a previously male working-class entertainment such as football, to the involvement of political leaders in the plots of television soap operas and series, we can see that many of the formal differentiations of more structured social order seem no longer tenable. It may be that the progress towards this more classless mass culture was an inevitable consequence of the character of mass broadcasting. As we have seen, Scannell (1989) has powerfully written of the 'experiment' in public service broadcasting 'as a public good that has unobtrusively contributed to the democratisation of everyday life' (p. 318). The difficulty, of course, with the values of public service was that it was inseparable from an enlightened paternalism in which intellectual, political and cultural elites acted as a vanguard for the masses; effectively the everyday life of mass publics was being misrepresented and as such was an integral element in what I have called the restricted democracy of high modernity.

The issue that now confronts those who would seek to make judgements about cultural change is whether moves away from public service in cultural provision towards a more radical populism, in a sense locating culture in the idioms of the everyday, have to mean the agnosticism of a world without beliefs. Another way of putting this is to ask whether it is possible to have any sense of cultural values when lacking a culture in which they are grounded. It certainly seems to me necessary and appropriate to point out that in relation to cultural choices, treating them all as equal inhibits appreciation of the distinctive. The notion of public good was valuable because it presupposed that an engagement with excellence, an ability to go beyond what is conventionally acceptable, stimulated everyday life. This presupposition was based on a commitment to the belief that an involvement in culture is a journey rather than an entertainment. But is such a commitment necessarily grounded in the implied authority of an imagined community with common values? If that social authority is no longer sustainable then the question becomes: is the only alternative an uncritical populism?

I hope that by now it will be more apparent why the aspects of cultural change relating to public life discussed in this and the preceding chapter are fundamentally important for any account of later modernity. I have referred at several points to the increasing salience of everyday life in cultural discourse remaining contentious as to the meaning of its representations. This is because increasing emphases upon the values of everyday life, itself intrinsically related to consumer populism, can easily be read as entailing a fundamental trivialisation of public life. It is very tempting to interpret everything I have written, and the sources on which I have drawn, as providing an analysis of the dissolution of the public sphere. It is not so much in terms of fears expressed in Habermas's ideas of a refeudalisation of public life through new forms of 'traditional' authority (although the powers of new global industries should not be underestimated (Murdock 1993; Murdock and Golding 1989)), but rather a dissolution of critical engagement by citizens who have been deflected by overriding concerns with everyday normality. In this critical view the public discourse of late modernity will not only lack any pretension to the rationality or unimpeded communication of Habermas's ideals, it will also accentuate the individualisation of constituent publics and substitute a cynical indifference to public values and/or a credulous acceptance of irrational superstitions.

One of the themes of what used to be called mass society politics was that the intervening secondary associations which mediate between citizens and public bodies were being dissolved by the direct address of mass communications (Kornhauser 1960). More recently, Boggs (1997) has suggested there has been a retreat from or decline in the public sphere in late-modern America in that 'politics has degenerated into a combination of electoral spectacles, interest-group machinations, and bureaucratic infighting. ... [These phenomena] ... have become equated with a truncated party system, depoliticized citizenry, and trivialized political discourse' (p. 745). Some of the instances of this degradation of public life such as a virulent indifference to political parties might be said to be particularly true of the United States more than other post-industrial societies, but Boggs's emphases on the spectacles of consumerism and the trivialisation of political discourse in the mass media as underlying causes will be seen as more generally relevant.

It seems, then, that it is a failure to represent politics as mutual collective engagement that has contributed to the well-known indices of political disillusionment such as falling electoral turn-out, the inability of dominant national political parties to recruit mass memberships, and a taken-for-granted distrust of political leaders in everyday speech. But why is their representation so unfavourable? – our political class although venal and corrupt is not more so than in earlier eras. It may be that their inability to gain control of the endemic crises of a diseased exploitative production and marketing system is inadequately masked by their empathetic ordinariness; or it may be that representations in political discourse have been made deliberately discreditable in order to rob populism of any political force. It is in this respect that Boggs argues that a retreat from the public sphere has been effectively exploited by right-wing ideologists.[2] Their aim has been to denounce public programmes of support for social welfare while hoping 'to strengthen the most oppressive and authoritarian features of the state (the military, police, prison system, controls over personal life)' (op. cit., p. 753).

I think the crucial flaw in the representation of political discourse in the democracies of later modernity has been that the ways in which individuals are typically shown being able to participate in collective activities leave them trapped in illusions. I argued in Chapter 5 in relation to the representation of sport in advertising that it individualised a collective activity. Now I want to say that more generally the representation of activities, situations, identities and styles through the symbolism of their brand or corporate identity, usually encapsulated in a visual 'logo' or look, trivialises complex social processes. Making things as complex as the reasons for education or the polluting implications of the use of nuclear power or the disease-creating potential of factory-farming into simple presentations disempowers those who seem to be being consulted. Representing these processes as everyday values such as doing well for your children, or guarding the health of your family or giving them cheap nutritious food means that more complex ethical concerns with the making of social reality can be disregarded with the consequence of a trivialised public discourse.

The central issue being raised, then, by debates over the public sphere concerns the character of citizenship in radical democracy when cultural change has effectively dissolved the framework of legitimacy that sustained politics in modernity. I have called the multi-faceted populism of later modernity a process of radical democratisation for two contradictory reasons: partly because the discrediting of authority and expertise that has been one of its defining characteristics can be seen as genuinely radical in its discrediting of much of the deforming deference to established privilege that characterised the democratic accommodation of high modernity; and partly ironically to suggest populism is illusory. Can we choose between these interpretations? I will briefly expand on each of these reasons. First, if radical in this context is emancipating, it must be because the great structural categories that have organised social identity in modern society such as class, age, gender and religion are fragmenting into new forms of collectivity (Maffesoli 1996). Further, it would follow that the central themes of ideological conflict in modernity concerning equity, tradition, authority and individuality are also being replaced by new themes of public life articulated through the more privatised concerns of the everyday.

Alternatively, the ironic sense of radical in radical democracy is the possibility that it is being used to label an effective suppression of democratic potential through banality. In the ironic view, an emphasis on the 'freedoms' of unlimited choice in the malls and markets of consumer populism allied to unlimited exposure in the public discourse of endlessly proliferating mass communication, has not meant an effective emancipation. On the contrary, its emphases upon the ordinariness of the real concerns of an individualised polity have effectively disguised a whole-scale colonisation of power by ever more extensive agencies of social control. Putting it crudely, I could say that in the pursuit of personal satisfaction in culinary, sexual and self-dramatising experiences, etc., we have missed the ways in which both real personal autonomy and a co-operative concern with others have been sacrificed to the gratifications from baubles.

Some of the material discussed in Chapter 3 does, however, suggest a further and more radical option. Rather than just throwing up our hands in despair, it could be argued that as any possibility of rational discourse has been subverted by spectacular ideology, only in the 'irrationality' of everyday life can there be any form of emancipatory space ungovernable by the homogenising discourses of corporate control. Such an 'escape attempt' must involve individual tactics of detachment such as some form of 'culture jamming' or discrediting of representation through overload – particularly subverting the reassuring lies of advertising and public relations – allied with more collective forms of resistance such as protests at meetings facilitating globalisation. In relation to this form of resistance it may well be as Klein hypothesises: 'that as more people discover the brand-name secrets of the global logo web, their outrage will fuel the next big political movement, a vast wave of opposition squarely targeting transnational corporations, particularly those with very high name-brand recognition' (2000, p. xviii).

What is crucial is that in all these interpretations the everyday has come to prominence as the primary site on which social order is either being instituted or resisted. My argument is, then, that the character of citizenship in later modernity – the public life of social actors – is inextricably bound up with the dramatisation of the everyday as a 'space' for social concerns and how that space is being used. Another way of putting this is to ask how the opportunities the space of the everyday provides are being exploited by those who seek to create audiences or customers or constituencies, and those who feel themselves more or less willingly being mobilised into one of these categories. In the rest of this chapter I will explore some aspects of the public culture of democratic participation. I fear that as there are valid elements in each of the three interpretations I have just described it is pointless for me to try to give a summary judgement on which is the best account. The prominence of everyday life as the terrain on which a new architecture of social order is being constructed means, almost paradoxically, that culture – how we represent ourselves, our experience and our values – has become central to political life. In the following sections of this chapter I will explore further aspects of the culturisation of citizenship.

Providing Public Culture

Previously in this chapter I described the changing character of the provision of broadcasting in Britain. I included this element in order to open the idea that the relationship between a typical citizen and their public culture has been changing in two ways. First, by becoming more responsive and yet, secondly, also less challenging. It is in this sense, then, that one could speak of the culture becoming impoverished and the citizens themselves being made poorer because the world they inhabit is less rewarding. I believe that it is at least in part through making these sorts of connections that there has been a growth in interest very recently in the relevance to an understanding of later modernity of an idea of cultural citizenship. It seems apparent that changing relations in public will come to effectively constitute new forms of citizenship. What I mean by this is that cultural activities as everyday concerns have come to constitute a valued means of participation in public life, and for ordinary people form an increasingly significant arena for and means of political mobilisation: 'The cultural aspects of citizenship signifies a connection with the politics of "everyday life" that is continually being rewritten by the reflexive incorporation of new ideas, narratives and frameworks' (Stevenson 1999, p. 60; Walsh 1992).[3]

Before, however, I come to discuss the connections between the cultural aspects of citizenship and the politics of everyday life directly, I propose to look briefly at the broader context of the provision of culture than just broadcasting in the later years of the last century. The reason is that the character of cultural provision by state authorities has conformed to a general characterisation of increased democratisation. Even in Britain, where the idea of there being a minister for culture in any government has traditionally been thought a rather laughable Continental invention suitable for countries that have intellectuals, we now have such a minister. However, their responsibilities have usually included media and sport as well as culture as clearly separate but related activities. The rationale for such a post has comprised a number of factors. Ever since the Second World War it has been accepted that the government has a responsibility both to sustain 'the Arts' as an ongoing creative enterprise and to make them more widely accessible to the citizenry as part of a broader educational remit. The characteristic invention of a quango like the Arts Council has thus been a medium of cultural policy while working alongside other departments and institutions charged with responsibility for preserving the nation's cultural heritage – both in terms of public collections and a broader sense of the historic landscape including stately homes and historic sites such as castles and battlefields.

A growing realisation that the 'heritage industry' is not only a strand in the inculcation of a national consciousness, but also a significant source of revenue for both providers of local services and governments through tax charges from both indigenous visitors and foreign tourists, has undoubtedly spurred a feeling that this domain should be effectively managed. The process has been further stimulated by the discovery that cultural developments such as the Lowry Centre in Salford, and the Baltic Centre and associated Quayside developments as well as the Angel of the North all in Gateshead are not only economic stimulants but have a significant role in stimulating local pride. In combination, then, there is a growing realisation that culture, despite its somewhat bizarre status in being differentiated from media and sport, is a public matter in which all citizens have both rights and it seems real interests. So culture is no longer presumed to be the preserve of privileged elites but is rather a matter of general concern much as transport.

It is of course true that the management of cultural institutions has been a matter of state policy for over 200 years as part of the broader innovations in the development of the public sphere. I want to argue, though, that in the efflorescence of cultural provision in later modernity, culture has been made to conform to the imperatives of radical democratisation. As part of this process, cosmopolitan culture while being explicitly 'different' has also been accommodated to the idioms of everyday experience. As I have said, the concept of culture was developed early in the modern era as an essential resource for identifying distinctive national identities. It was also, however, bound in with a notion of civilisation – both of peoples and of social fractions within a society.

Culture was therefore a distinctive mark of, and justification for, the privileges of elites. But at the same time notions of public art – that is cultural sites, buildings, objects, memorials and practices such as parades oriented to the anonymous masses of civil society – had to be developed and articulated in the context of a fracture within a national culture between the class cultures of middle and urban popular culture. It is unsurprising, then, that some of the early initiatives in public culture were explicitly directed at civilising the urban proletariat. For example, the use of sport and leisure facilities such as parks as civilising influences continued throughout modernity as means of national integration and inculturation of the potentially disorderly mob. If we add to these sorts of initiatives associated developments in the provision of statuary of national heroes, local war memorials (particularly after 1919), parks, stadia and other public buildings dedicated to glorious moments in national history, then we can see a determined attempt to create what Horne has called a public culture for a modern nation (1986; see also 1984).

What I have described so far has been a number of attempts at creating a national culture, but we should also recognise that these were complemented by a discursive discovery of an already existing culture (neatly captured in Hobsbawm and Ranger's phrase of the invention of tradition (1983)). I am thinking here of projects as disparate as the folk song movement and the founding of the National Trust. Inspired in part by the feeling that the all too evident urbanising of Britain meant that a traditional culture was disappearing, there was also a desire to capture or formulate the distinctiveness of a national culture partly as a source of integrative inspiration and partly to resist encroaching cosmopolitanism (Colls and Dodd 1986; Samuel 1989). Clearly the invented traditions and national rhetoric of an emergent socio-political order had to concentrate on a reconciliation of regional diversity within an overarching distinctiveness. When we turn to national cultural institutions such as museums, galleries, academies and scientific societies, however, cosmopolitan cultural values become more explicit.

In large part this was because those founding the National Gallery, the British Museum, the Royal Academy and the Royal Society, etc. were concerned with the glory of the British state, the British ruling class and its attendant intellectuals (Barlow and Trodd 2000; Haskell 1993; Smith 1993). Other cultures could be pillaged as a display of both imperial power and of the sophistication of artists and scientists who could appreciate their discoveries more adequately than less civilised foreigners. If there was a message for the indigenous working class in these imperial institutions it was to congratulate themselves at the good fortune of having been born in such a culturally superior nation. The cosmopolitan could thus be identified with the metropolitan sophistication of imperial powers, and although it might occasionally degenerate into aestheticism and decadence it was generally accepted to articulate a further aura to national culture. My point is that cosmopolitanism could be incorporated in the illusions, the imagination, of a national culture as long as an indigenous urban popular culture remained localised and fractured between the politics of imperial and class consciousness. In practice, though, the accommodation between different class levels began almost immediately to be undermined by a new culture of entertainment for the masses.

The contradictions in national cultural policy were in the middle years of the twentieth century disguised by an overarching consensus around the 'success' of public service broadcasting. It was so self-evidently a good thing to combine a policy of national integration with enlightened educational provision that it became part of the political consensus that the arts or culture more generally should form an element in this edifice. Cultural policies were, however, beginning to be questioned in part for the same sorts of reasons, and undoubtedly as part of the same shifting ideological climate, that fractured the established consensus over broadcasting. It was, though, initially surprising that a turn away from using culture to do good did not leave cultural institutions marooned and dying for lack of support. Rather they were rescued by new sorts of funding – principally lottery revenues – to become a new mode of tourism and a new engine of economic, social and cultural regeneration. Thus there has been an enormous investment in new or remodelled institutions of public culture such as galleries, museums, theatres and production companies, etc., which have bolstered the status of high culture as national and international resources as never before.

Although the content of these cultural emporia is generally as puzzling and antithetical as high art has always been to popular taste, they have become accepted as part of mainstream Britain and become a source of local pride. This is particularly true of Gormley's huge casting of an androgynous Angel in Gateshead, which although lacking any obvious rationale or function or indeed anything you can do with it, regularly attracts a considerable stream of visitors. Or as another example of successful public sculpture one could point to the Grizedale Forest in the Lake District. The attractions to politicians both local and national of using culture as the fuel of economic development are fairly obvious. The transformation of established sites and creation of new buildings in primarily rundown economically stagnant areas is a classic example of the Keynesian use of public funds as a trigger of development. These public works not only create employment but help to support new leisure industries of associated cafes, bars and other aspects of the culture economy. Plus, of course, the re-evaluation of local status and prestige helps to attract other forms of inward investment and migration so that the self-fulfilling cycle of economic decline can be at least modified and possibly reversed; not least in the rebranding involved in the fairly startling accomplishment of being able to turn districts like Gateshead into a tourist attraction.

Cultural Citizenship

One way of understanding cultural citizenship, then, is as a complex of policy issues around both the provision of cultural facilities and the regulation of cultural industries, including 'electronic and print media, music culture, heritage parks, museums and public libraries, to name just a few' (Stevenson 1999, p. 74). This is an important area of social policy and will clearly become more important as the shift from work to leisure as the central focus of individual identities and community concerns continues. It is not, however, just an issue of policy concern in the more traditional sense of bringing culture to the masses. What I will go on to argue in this section is that although in practical terms the idea that citizenship carries cultural rights has been gaining ground over the past half-century, it has not been properly appreciated at the level of public discourse that the character of culture has simultaneously been shifting from an established orthodoxy towards a more heterogeneous populism. Quite what is involved in cultural citizenship has stimulated academic interest in the theme of the extent to which cultural institutions can meet the needs of citizens in a changing cultural terrain (Kaplan 1994; Karp et al. 1992; Lumley 1998; Stevenson 2001 and further references cited therein).

Stevenson points out that conventionally discussions of citizenship begin from Marshall's distinctions between civil rights, political rights and social rights (1999, pp. 76–7). These rights of citizenship developed in the eighteenth century in the context of the emerging public sphere. This abstract space (constituted as we have seen in the new impersonal media of communication – at that time newspapers and magazines – and associated cultural forms of the novel, melodramatic theatre and the concert hall) provided a forum for the imagined communities of new national

identifications with citizen populations (Anderson 1983). To these traditional rights it has become more widely accepted that there is a fourth
dimension of cultural rights (and remembering that rights are always
complemented by obligations, Turner 2001). I want to emphasise that such
an idea of cultural rights should mean more than expectations to be able
to sample other cultures either as cuisines or tourist venues, or even a
capacity to seek support, advice or inspiration from outside local cultural
traditions, although we should recognise that these have become standard
expectations of a globalised cultural environment.

The nature of changes in the cultural terrain which I have referred to can
be quickly sketched in: the globalisation of cultural markets so that fashions in for example clothing, music and computer games are quickly diffused both regionally and internationally; technological developments
which have meant that the power of national authorities to regulate
aspects of cultural policy in for example broadcasting standards has been
radically undermined; the politicisation of identity particularly but not
exclusively in metropolitan centres which has meant that orthodoxies of
cultural appropriateness are no longer blindly accepted; and following
from this there are both growing demands for space and respect for difference and otherness and an increasingly widespread recognition that public subsidies of established cultural institutions (such as those through the
Arts Council) have worked to reinforce the hegemonic tastes and privileges of social elites; in combination, then, a fatal undermining of distinctions between high and popular cultures so that culture both spreads to
include every aspect of material culture and has taken on more of the character of marketed commodities – the suppliers again often being global
culture industries.

One effect of these changes has been that the implicit equation between
nation and culture which informed so much of the national consciousness
of high modernity seems no longer sustainable. Similarly, the power of the
nation state to enact cultural policies is being effectively curtailed, with the
further consequence that the relationship between citizen and state, at least
in the cultural sphere, is shifting from the state encompassing identifiable
rights and obligations to acting more as a facilitator of diversity and a
mediator between its citizens and global trends and markets. Interestingly
in this respect, Wouters suggests that national broadcasting which in the
early years of the century had seemed to be an irresistible force for national
cultural integration, particularly in respect of diminishing regional identities, has in later modernity functioned to legitimate diversity and thus supported moves away from a standard formal public way of speaking to a
more pervasive informality (1990; see also Chaney 1993, Ch. 4). In general,
then, I am suggesting that the cultural institutions of late-modern societies
are trying to cope with a loss of cultural authority, in terms of values,
traditions and critical discourses, while faced with a pervasive consumer

populism in which it is axiomatic that cultural supply should be governed exclusively by market relationships, and a more general proliferation of diversity through every aspect of the life-world being rendered as representation and thus stylised.

One of the points of talking about the provision of culture and its unexpected popularity is to emphasise that being familiar with cultural vocabularies is becoming increasingly commonplace in ordinary experience. Being able to participate as a citizen will increasingly involve being able to appreciate what is to count as culture (see Huyssen 1995 for more on new cultural roles for museums), and how to 'read' the semiotic constructions of social reality available in different cultural forms. If the publics of the post-cultural era are to be as adept in disentangling the entertainments of cultural industries as they have needed to be in relation to the constraints and foreclosures of public authorities, then an effective citizenship will need ever more supple resources in coping with the complexities of cultural discourse. It is in this respect that Bourdieu's notion of the unequal distribution of cultural capital, analogous to inequalities in property and financial capital, is a centrally important aspect of mechanisms of social exclusion (1984).

On a further level I want to argue that skills of empowerment in cultural citizenship concern the ways in which relations in public, as understood in these chapters, are constituted – that is, how the institutions of everyday life are framed by public discourse. Cultural citizenship is in this sense an ability to use the reflexive potential (or be able to cope with the reflexive demands) of the radical democracy of fragmented culture. In the previous chapter I have been tracing some of the ways in which dramatisations of authority and legitimacy have been changing. These are quite clearly one aspect of cultural change in late modernity, but they are also concerned with membership of public life – being a citizen and how individual membership is mediated into collective opinions and attitudes. And it is in this latter sense that I want to go on to make the more controversial claim that cultural citizenship has become more important in the life politics of radical democracy than other more traditional types of citizenship.

Citizenship, as Turner has made clear (1993), is meaningful in spheres such as legal, political and social because it guarantees an identity. If cultural policies are currently extremely confused about what sorts of rights are trying to be met, it is at least in part because of uncertainty over who citizens are and what they are members of (Roche 2001). Perhaps rather than trying to decide what sort of culture should be made available and policies for access, etc., policy makers should be concentrating on *ways in which they can facilitate citizens deciding for themselves what is to count as culture and how it is to help them decide who they are*. It is quite likely that Turner is right when he sees a positive role for new media in facilitating this more creative sense of citizenship (2001). For example, information that authorities have tried to suppress and learning about opportunities for subversive gatherings are proving very difficult to control on digital pathways. Even so, the most recent British government thoughts on broadcasting policy express a considerable degree of positive encouragement for new community media in facilitating sustainability.[4] The responsibility of cultural citizenship faced with globalising pressures is double-edged – both sustaining cultural diversity and facilitating indigenous development.

Such a vision of citizenship would be unsustainable if the cultural terrain of later modernity is seen to be completely dominated by the globalising giants of multinational culture industries. Although I am proposing that we are in general entering an era of cultural fragmentation, I recognise that this does not mean a diminution in the importance of culture industries. Indeed, the reverse as the amount of entertainment made available through film, television, recording and tourist industries for example grows constantly. It would, however, be a mistake to see cultural industries as solely producing dramatic entertainments. In addition to mass entertainments I would want to emphasise that in the fields of clothes, magazines, music production, computer games, fads such as skateboards, new food products and alternative medical therapies and health concerns, the culture being produced consists of imagery, information and accoutrements.

The cultural terrain here, then, emphasises expressive resources as much as staged entertainments, so there are not clear distinctions between producers and audiences – particularly if we include here the myriad commentators, interpreters and various modes of expertise who intervene between innovators and followers. While of course there are major entertainment corporations catering for mass audiences, their necessary involvement in fashions and constant pursuit of innovations mean that they are desperately dependent on the vitality of small-scale modes of cottage production which surround them in every cultural form. This extremely complex and fragmented picture of cultural production suggests that we ought to consider whether there is a move under way from an era of mass popular culture. Another way of putting this is to say that the established forms of cultural expression are being destabilised towards a rather incoherent and inconsistent assembly of practices popularly known as lifestyles. These are social forms which, as I have said, from the perspective of looking at individual experience offer a means of differentiation but simultaneously work to substantiate a sensibility or means of affiliation.

The theme of sensibility, as a perceived affinity in the manipulation of style, shares a lot of features with Kevin Hetherington's emphasis on shared structures of feeling[5] in what he calls the expressive identities of new social movements (1998). Such a connection between lifestyles and social movements echoes Beck's emphasis on what he calls the sub-politics of the new modernity: 'These different partial arenas of cultural and social sub-politics – media publicity, judiciary, privacy, citizens' initiative groups and the new social movements – add up to *forms of a new culture'* (1992, p. 198, emphasis in the original). Hetherington stresses the performance of expressive identities as unstable assemblies in the situations and occasions of everyday life in ways that take us back, I think, to my prior emphasis on the blurring of distinctions between production and consumption in contemporary cultural forms, so that as he says: 'If we have to speak of class at all, then we should see it as something that ... is negotiated differentially across different areas of cultural and economic life and mobile in space and time' (1998, p. 56). In the politics of new social movements (although Hetherington suggests that these social groupings can be made too rational and purposeful by being thought of as movements and therefore proposes concepts such as neo-tribes or bunds), we can see practical alternatives to traditional fictions of political community.

Politics in a Fragmented Culture

My analysis of contemporary change is, therefore, that in contrast to the coherence of the implied culture in traditions of public service, the fictions of political community transcended are scattered, local, inconsistent and unstable. In this way the 'irrationality' of the diversity of everyday life can more explicitly work as a bulwark against the rationalisations of corporate culture. The extent to which this is happening provides one of the bases for the interpretation of a fragmentation of culture with which I conclude the book. Before reaching that stage, I need to consider more carefully whether it is wholly positive that in taking on more the character of everyday life public discourse has become more 'irrational'. As I have just said, the irrationality or incoherence of the everyday (that is the impossibility of it being adequately contained within the representations of corporate entertainments) may offer the best possibility for some form of creative independence. While I would like to see this variety of informalisation as offering new promises for a variety of modes of radicalism, I am aware that breaking up traditional ideological frameworks has meant that the expressive identities of fragmented culture become more actively contested (Hall and du Gay 1996; Kershon 1998). It also seems apparent that moves away from traditional ideological frameworks have opened up spaces for more virulent identity politics that rearticulate older forms of intolerant populism.

I have noted at several points that one constraint on the expressive politics of the new culture will be provided by the culture industries who will seek economies of scale through standardisation and repetition wherever possible. More generally, it seems there are strong attractions for political and cultural leaders in the use of a vocabulary of national identification. One of the paradoxes of a drift away from nation state autonomy in economic, political and cultural spheres has been an intensification of nationalism, including regionalism, as a theme for identification. Billig has recently pointed to how nationalist claims should not just be sought in the rhetoric of major political speeches, but are also 'reproduced daily in a banally mundane way, for the world of nations is the everyday world, the familiar terrain of contemporary times' (1995, p. 6; see also Palmer (1998) who emphasises the importance of areas such as body, food and landscape in confirming everyday identity). What Billig calls the banal flagging of national identity is relevant to my discussion of the politics of identity in the public discourse of later modernity, because he shows that it is in the taken-for-granted presuppositions of public discourse that an ideologically conservative consensus is continually reiterated.

Billig points to processes of linguistic deixis in which the smallest words such as 'the', 'this' and 'us' are employed over and over again to presume, to flag and to embody a shared normality – an unproblematic ordinariness – that unites the public voice with the reader/listener against outsiders or strangers. Thus despite the multicultural sweep of global broadcasting with its often explicit tolerance, there is a grounding of the discourse in public life in presuppositions of white, heterosexual, middle-class normality (see also Chaney 1994, Ch. 3; Pickering 2001). One interpretation is that culture industries 'naturally' regress to a norm of consensual normality, and therefore find the dispersed publics of a fragmented culture too problematic. This could be, however, too thin an account. There are obviously commercial advantages, as well as different forms of cultural respectability, to be gained for those marketing services and goods from recognising distinctive styles of identity. But this very pluralism that exemplifies consumer populism necessarily leaves a vacuum in public discourse with the consequence that established traditions of appeal can appear inappropriate or irrelevant.

In this I am reiterating an early theme of the previous chapter that conventional grounds of legitimacy and with them the rationales for tolerance that have prevailed in liberal public discourse are losing their authority. Thereby opportunities are created for voices in public discourse to blur distinctions between news and comment in order to intolerantly suppress challenges to traditional identities that feel themselves threatened by a more pluralistic discourse. One example of the process I am trying to describe has been provided by phone-in programmes on usually local radios which have become dominated by hosts articulating racist, misogynistic and homophobic views. Another example, particularly in Britain, has been the emergence of national tabloid newspapers committed to the strident expression of misogynistic and xenophobic as well as other more extreme right-wing views. Although I have deliberately set my approach in this book as countering that which sees the media as having effects on people, the disproportionate influence these newspapers seem

to have on political actors – through the lack of competition in public discourse – has meant that the overall political agenda has swung sharply
towards a very conservative nationalism. In this climate the irrationality
of radical democratisation is being effectively exploited by a combination
of corporate commercial groups and heterogeneous popular interests
using a variety of imagined dangers to justify a rhetoric of vicious hostility
to cultural tolerance.[6]

Although Billig does not develop this aspect of banal nationalism, he
does suggest another not inconsistent factor when he points to the relative
decline in communal bonds in the more mobile and anonymous worlds
of mass society creating a functional predilection for unproblematic
rhetorics of shared identity. Such a role for rhetorics of tradition would
also explain why the nationalistic impetus continually goes beyond
nation states to smaller, however arbitrary, localities. Interpreted pes-
simistically, this becomes another version of the critique of mass society
and goes back to the sorts of fears expressed by social elites in the first half
of the last century about the dangers of populist democracy. While recognising the reality of those dangers, I do not think it necessary to see the
increased significance of everydayness in public discourse in completely
pessimistic terms. In the overall analysis of these chapters I have tried to
outline how in the public discourse of fragmented culture ordinariness
has become normative. In my view it is not so much that banal nationalism, and all the other forms of the banalisation of public discourse, are
ideological denials of the anomie of mass society, as that they function as
a cultural rhetoric of standardisation recoiling from the vitality and new
communalism of life politics. It would obviously be mistaken to assume
that localism is always regressive and ignore the ways in which it can
provide a footing for new modes of radicalism.

In Chapter 2 I described why Beck's analysis of individualisation in later
modernity leads him to predict the initially paradoxical consequence of a
more intense social environment. Although it is convenient to refer to these
more intense social expectations as a standardisation – and perhaps most
easily visible in the conventional surfaces of suburban lifestyles discussed
in previous chapters – I have already indicated why I think it is mistaken
to dismiss these processes as uncritical uniformity. The undermining of
established structures of authority has led to new sorts of political concerns with personal meaning or relevance in the interpretation of public
discourse. These are very often expressed as a quest for authenticity in
entertainment as much as political leadership and are I think visible in new
normative expectations for significant issues. Anthony Giddens has
described what I take to be analogous changes as a shift from a politics of
emancipation to a life politics: 'the disputes and struggles connected with
it [life politics], are about how we should live in a world where everything
that used to be natural (or traditional) now has in some sense to be chosen,

or decided about. Life politics is a politics of identity as well as choice'
(1994, pp. 90–1; see also 1991, Ch. 7).

Life politics, then, grows out of processes of individualisation and
instead of being focused on the removal of structures of disadvantage and
exclusion – as in the politics of emancipation – is more concerned with the
ordering of social relationships and institutional forms to facilitate meaningful lifestyles (it has been suggested in this respect that the politics of
Blairite Labourism is moral or cultural rather than, well, political). This
leads to both a more intense social environment and new forms of differentiation in public life. Of course the issues that are the concern of emancipatory politics have not disappeared or lost their significance, they
are, however, now being considered in different contexts with new prior-
ities: 'As the proponents of "deep ecology" assert, a movement away from
economic accumulation might involve substituting personal growth – the
cultivation of the potentialities for self-expression and creativity – for unfettered economic growth processes' (Giddens 1991, p. 223). I think it is the
diversity of life choices, significant issues, what Giddens calls the necessarily experimental character of daily life in life politics, that public discourse
has found 'irrational' and thus difficult to encompass. Presuppositions of a
normative consensus over national identity, sexual relationships and the
meaning of leisure, for example, are attempts to close down the mobility of
life politics. To treat the fragmentation of culture as merely resulting in the
creation of a multiplicity of audiences or consumers is an attempt to fore-
close the radicalism of everyday life in public discourse.

At several points in the opening chapters of this book I said that the
main way in which the interrelated themes of contemporary cultural
change and everyday life are manifest is in the renegotiation of boundaries between public and private spheres. In this chapter I have developed
this idea through an exploration of some aspects of the use of everyday
relations in public discourse. It may be helpful to speak of this hinterland
as a variety of '"intermediate zones" straddling the public and the private' (Holliday 1998, p. 104), or a 'third place', a new type of social environment populated by the loose associations of sensibility and lifestyle.[7]
These zones or places may be physical sites as in cafes, bars or clubs or
more metaphorical sites as websites or e-mail groups, but in either case
they offer the potential for what Giddens calls 'dialogic democracy' itself
generated by 'the spread of social reflexivity as a condition of day-to-day
activities' and a presumption 'that dialogue in a public sphere provides a
means of living along with the other in a relation of mutual *tolerance*'
(1994, p. 115). A fragmented culture offers at least the potential for such a
radical democracy.

8
Enchantment in Everyday Life

Rationalisation and Enchantment

In my previous chapters, particularly the last one, I have been exploring how the status and character of representations of everyday life have been changing in the public sphere. I have argued that a spectacular populism has been developed which has undermined many structures of established privilege and associated forms of deference which survived in the 'democratic moment' of high modernity. An increased emphasis upon themes and idioms of everyday life has not, however, necessarily meant that ordinary people are being taken more seriously. Instead the motifs of everyday life can in certain respects also be seen as a means of enhancing the process of rationalisation that has been the logic of modernisation. This is because aspects of the everyday are being repackaged as slogans, brands and images that tempt and enchant consumers and audiences.

The populist character of contemporary social order has meant that rationalisation or orderly compliance cannot be easily achieved through commands or even a rhetoric of common struggle. Increasingly, therefore, audiences are being enchanted by cultural industries in order to make them pliable to both those industries and governmental agencies more generally. By the phrase governmental agencies I mean to refer to both state authorities, international, national and local, and corporate concerns, particularly, but not exclusively, international cultural industries. The process of rationalisation is driven by values of rationality and expertise in which through dismantling the constituent parts of human and mechanical processes, new forms of control are created in order to manipulate social order. But the process of rationalisation has brought undoubted benefits to ordinary people in terms of raising standards of living and increasing freedoms such as self-expression, travel and more elaborate forms of entertainment. It has also, as I have frequently noted, generated its own irrationalities, including a variety of pathologies of modern life such as an increased risk of cancers, traffic accidents and environmental pollution. While these irrationalities of rationalisation have fuelled an increasing disenchantment with an ideology of 'progress', their role as political symbols is more significant as the focus of struggles of resistance against control.

I have, therefore, been trying to bring out how the spectacular populism of later modernity can be seen as overlapping layers of illusion in which idioms of the everyday are in effect an elaborate hoax. I have also, however, tried to indicate how in the same processes of political transformation new types of social consciousness have begun to emerge. These new ways of being-in-the-world are informed by distinctive attitudes and values, and have been generated by processes of individualisation and reflexivity that I have described. In part they are expressed through, and have taken on the form of, new social movements or, more generally, life politics. Being grounded in the local, in the particular, in the body and in the immediacy of tangible experience, these new ways of being-in-the-world also use the idioms of the everyday. But here the irrationality of the everyday, its lack of order and coherence, becomes a mode of self-conscious resistance. The idioms of the everyday can thus be used as the languages of new political practices.

The important point is, then, that cultural change has meant that rationalisation has become increasingly contested, and that struggles over rationalisation are increasingly located in cultural forms. In the concluding chapters of this study I will, first, discuss one aspect of the power of representations in relation to everyday experience. I will be concerned with how the increasing significance of cultural representations relates to struggles over who controls the meaning of the everyday. In particular I will be concerned with representations of the extra-ordinary or what I will call more generally the enchanting and how they relate to meanings of the everyday. Secondly, in the concluding chapter I will address the issue of cultural change and the ways in which culture is changing – and I will argue fragmenting – in later modernity.

The issue of a role for enchanting culture, and more generally for the role of the extra-ordinary, in the quotidian concerns of radical democratisation has been aptly focused by George Ritzer's most recent (at the time of writing) development of his account of the means of consumption (1999). He argues that a recent development of his long-standing concern with the means of consumption has been the innovation of what he calls cathedrals of consumption. In the means of consumption he includes the rationalisation of the production of that which is being consumed, archetypally hamburgers, as well as the media, fast-food joints, of consumption. The idea of cathedrals is a development of more traditional settings for consumption such as department stores, in which consuming is enhanced almost to the point of being treated as sacred. The development has happened as a way of re-enchanting the world that has become disenchanted through the rationalisation of modernisation. I think the point of the metaphor of sacred is to bring out how these settings – which include activities and environments such as shopping, gambling, eating, touring, malls, athletic stadiums, educational settings, mausoleums and even cities – employ spectacle in order to simulate experiences that transcend the profane functionality of servicing needs in favour of the fun and pleasure of a leisure society.

Ritzer's view of re-enchantment is part of a more general critique of the illusions of consumer culture. It is consistent with this more general critique that, when considering the implications of the increasingly widespread 'thematisation' of consumption and leisure settings (and see in this respect Gottdiener 1997 and Salmon 2000), Ritzer points to traditional themes in mass culture critiques such as homogenisation, sanitisation and the transformation or sterilisation of relationships. In doing so he raises important issues concerning the engineering of public spaces dramatised in themes or narratives which are generally simplistic and sentimental and to which I shall return later in this chapter (on the culture of themed environments, see Craik 1997). Going back to my opening remarks of this chapter, Ritzer is arguing that by focusing on everyday activities such as eating, exercising, shopping and learning, cultural industries are taking the ways ordinary people buy into the reproduction of social order and giving them a magical gloss. Their reason is in order to make these activities seemingly more exciting and rewarding, and thus encourage people to do more consuming.

A more complex reason though stems from what Ritzer has previously called the irrationalities of rationalisation. It may well be as I have said that there is a overwhelming drive to rationality in contemporary public discourse, but as I have also noted at many points, there is simultaneously an increasing distrust of authoritative expertise because it has so often generated harmful unintended consequences (i.e. its own irrationalities). One way of overcoming public distrust in governmental competence is by switching attention from rationalisation to the enchantment of spectacular display. This in turn leads us to ask about representations of the extraordinary. No doubt this topic requires a full book-length treatment in its own right, but any consideration of the everyday has to pay some attention to how what lies beyond the everyday is acknowledged and to some extent at least accommodated within it. This is not just an issue for modern culture, as in all cultures there must be some form of reciprocity between the ordinary and what may be feared, desired or worshipped as the extra-ordinary. If, however, my premise for this account has been the difficulties of representing the everyday in modernity, then how the extraordinary is to be seen, represented and accommodated is also necessarily contentious.

So far in this section I have only discussed the idea of enchantment as a form of disguise for rationalising powerful groups. While I agree with much in Ritzer's account of the role of enchantment in the rationalisation of culture in later modernity, I have, however, stressed how images and performances can combine several meanings simultaneously. It therefore follows, and particularly in the light of the politicisation of irrationality described above, that visions of the enchanting can act for ordinary people as some form of resistance to the rationalisation of governmental interests.[1] If the irrationality of the everyday stems from the messiness of lived experience, that is a consequence of social meanings becoming individualised, partial, temporary and above all reflexive, I want now to extend that thesis by saying that representations of the enchanting or extra-ordinary can embody dysfunctional (for social order) meanings. That is, in some respects such representations may work to disguise the irrationalities of rationalisation, but they may also simultaneously provide spaces or visions of alternatives that are profoundly important for the meaning of everyday life. In the next section I will begin to consider this possibility by discussing an aspect of modernist representation that may initially seem very far from the everyday.

Ways of Seeing

I have referred at several points to one of the forms of cultural change in the modern era as growing out of the self-conscious innovations of artistic avant-gardes. I acknowledged that generally as part of the self-conscious stance of 'ordinary' attitudes the formal experiments characteristic of modernism have seemed abstruse and irrelevant. For all that, the languages of artistic innovation have filtered into and shaped the cultural templates of everyday life in ways that need closer attention. Such a project needs a study in its own right, but I intend to use one example of a claimed influence of artistic practice on ordinary perception ('ways of seeing' in Berger's influential phrase, 1972), to introduce a discussion of how the outlooks of everyday life are bounded by experiences and imaginings of the extra-ordinary.

My example is taken from Spurling's biography of Matisse (1998). Writing about the period at the very end of the nineteenth century, in particular the year he spent in Corsica 1897–98, when it is apparent that Matisse was seeking to break with the styles and traditions in which he had been trained in order to extend his formal repertoire in the representation of nature, Spurling argues that he was trying to change the way we see natural spectacles. She argues that in effect it is because Matisse saw or forced himself to see in a different way, that we as the general public have changed our perceptual orientations. We can no longer see in what was previously the dominant paradigm and thus we cannot fully appreciate the shock of Matisse's innovation. We can compare the nature of the change in mode of representation but the force of the change has been lost (1998, Ch. 6).

In order to substantiate the argument, she quotes from a diary report of the experience of a local sunset written in the 1890s by two visitors to the island, and then quotes from a novel written in the 1940s. One could dispute how far these two passages sustain the point she seeks to make, or how representative they are of ways of seeing more generally, but I use her argument solely as an illustration. I am more concerned with the fact that Matisse and the two authors quoted were trying to represent the extraordinary. That is, all these people were directing attention to a feature of the environment as something especially beautiful and thus to be savoured.

One way of understanding what Matisse was trying to do is to appreciate that he was changing the character of representation (on the more general context of such an ambition, see Nochlin 1971). The painted surface was no longer mimicking the perceived world but instead became more explicitly a self-sufficient commodity, something to be enjoyed and consumed for its own sake. In doing so, that which was being represented also changed its status from being somebody's home or livelihood, etc. to being a commodity to be consumed by others. Thus in effect they were all trying to represent what we have come to see as classic tourist experiences. What do I mean by tourist experiences? That here is a way of framing the natural world so that it can be consumed as 'a spectacle', a form of entertainment made available to anonymous mass 'audiences' of visitors (see Urry 1995 on consuming places, and Green 1990 on the construction of nature as a leisure resource in nineteenth-century Paris). In support of this interpretation it is relevant that Matisse was at that time strongly influenced by Monet's experiments in the representation of nature; as it has been argued that Monet's paintings of Brittany done in the 1880s were oriented – to put it no more strongly – towards a view of the coast as a space for leisure and tourism rather than as a working environment (Herbert 1994).

Tourism is a classic example of a modern form of secular entertainment in which audiences consume representations of other people's everyday experience (MacCannell 1976), but it is also a cultural form in which the narratives or stories being dramatised are ways of seeing places or environments that are – for their visitors – out of the ordinary (I have previously discussed some of the implications of different ways of framing spaces and places in Chaney 1994, Ch. 4, on the 'tourist gaze' see Urry 1990 and Chaney 2001b).[2] Although they almost certainly did not see themselves as catering for a touristic imagination, the producers of cultural objects (in this case painters, novelists and letter-writers) were trying to articulate or formulate bridges between everyday life and out-of-the-ordinary experiences. These representations were sold as prints and books, and in the twentieth century were popularised more extensively as postcards, travel documentaries and holiday shows on television, etc. The experiences or perceptions being represented were also becoming increasingly available to mass audiences viscerally through the facilities of modern communication networks and in particular the facilities of the nascent tourist industry.

The point of this example is, then, to show that there is not an unbridge-able divide between modernist innovation and the outlooks – ways of seeing – of everyday life. The argument is not dependent on, but undoubtedly helped by, the fact that Monet's paintings have subse-quently been absorbed into popular culture not least as an object of tourism, and that even Matisse as witnessed in popular representations from greetings cards to student posters is no longer seen as outrageous. It seems that it is a distinctive feature of modern consciousness that their paintings could be both enchanting and outrageous because they were explicitly artificial. Although material objects, it is almost as though they were designed as posters or advertisements for a new way of seeing and new consumer values.[3] The idea that there are ways of seeing characteristic of everyday life in a particular period stimulates a further thought. This is that with the development of fast-paced editing in television dramas, advertisements and music videos, etc., our ways of seeing are being changed as profoundly as by the innovations of Matisse and other avant-garde artists; but this takes us to a different type of history of cultural change that I do not have space to explore here.

More relevantly for the present book, the example of Matisse's repre-sentational practice also asks us to consider the relationships between forms of the extraordinary and everyday life. My argument is that the 'ordinariness' of everyday life is bracketed at all times by an awareness of the boundaries of the normal. That which we take for granted is implic-itly contrasted with what is extra-ordinary – outside the normal. In order to see how everyday life works we have to be sensitive to the negotiations of these boundaries and to see the different ways in which the extra-ordinary is built into the texture of the ordinary. The extraordinary, then, is necessarily institutionalised – a distinction I have tried to indicate by hyphenating extra-ordinary when referring to something which is liter-ally outside normality but dropping the hyphen when referring to the institutionalised forms of the exceptional.

Seeking the Extraordinary

Tourism is a good theme with which to begin considering the ambiguous status of enchanting representations because holidays, trips, all the busi-ness of leisured travel are often described in popular speech as escapes (for an elaboration of this idea see Rojek's discussion of a variety of 'ways of escape' (1993)). To step out of everyday life into other worlds may seem to us to be one of Cohen and Taylor's 'escape attempts', but in general tourists are not throwing off the complete fabric of social order. Rather than see tourism as fleeing from the constraints of repressive banality, it is probably more appropriate to think of the activity as alleviating pressure

on time and others' expectations. Thus the escape may be to somewhere more indulgent (or less able to resist exploitation) where hedonism is licensed and where the visitor is buying a lack of responsibility for the maintenance of social order; or the conventional mores about sexual partners as in the long-established custom of secret homosexuals going to foreign countries to find partners, or other visitors buying sex with partners who would be deemed to be unacceptable, perhaps because they are below the age of consent, in their home country.

Tourists are, however, in general conforming – and complacent in their conformity – to the expectations of their role and the programmes of their holiday organisers. The ability to purchase a 'time-out' from everyday life is indubitably a modern phenomenon (the modern holiday as something sold to anonymous consumers is usually traced from Thomas Cook's first excursion in the middle of the nineteenth century) and has become very much a mass activity only in the second half of the twentieth century. The shift from the celebrations of holy days in traditional societies to the annual secular vacation is a powerful index of the diminution of the sacred in everyday life, and the full story of the bureaucratisation of mass transport, vacation resorts and themed entertainments is a more complex allegory of mass leisure. I think in fact that it is possible to use the changes in form of working-class holidays from holiday camps, to specialised resorts, to theme parks and the more complex spectacles of engineered environments as a powerful illustration of a mode of radical democratization[4] that puts the pursuit of pleasure at the heart of citizenship.

The development of tourism is therefore central to the cultural changes of mass entertainment. I have written of tourism as escaping the ordinary, and while most tourists are conformist in their different settings there is an undoubted sense of relaxation that goes with being 'away' (on the diversity of tourism, see Cohen 1979). It is because holidays are usually both enchanting and extra-ordinary that it has become quite common recently to draw upon a notion of carnival to articulate this idea of a liminal zone outside the everyday (one of the first to formulate this idea in relation to the modern holiday was Shields 1991; see also Stallybrass and White 1986). An idea of the carnivalesque is principally taken from Bakhtin's study of Rabelais in which he argued that a periodic occasion for transgression was an essential element in the maintenance of social order in medieval European culture (1984). It was not just that the carnival licensed transgressive excess as in copious eating and drinking and relaxation of sexual controls, but that in many ways the order of conventional normality was stood on its head at this time so that that which was conventionally hidden became apparent and those who were inferior humbled their superiors.

The idea of carnival as a necessary release of tensions over the constraints of a highly structured social order is attractive, and it certainly

seems that holidays or tourists sites have commonly legitimated transgressions and indulgences comparable to medieval precedents. In this
respect the example of the reputation of Club 18–30 holidays and equivalent youth-oriented holidays is very apposite. These privileged enclaves
provide sites and occasions where normal constraints can be relaxed in
the hedonism of alcohol, drugs and sex. In this sort of case though the
world outside is not being stood on its head; quite the reverse, in that
overall there is a massive affirmation of gendered stereotypes although
conventions of modesty, etc. are very noisily abandoned. It would seem,
then, that there is an important strand within urban popular culture in
which the debauched indulgence of medieval celebrations has persisted
and indeed survives into later eras of popular culture. Even so I doubt the
appropriateness of using carnival more literally than as a suggestive analogy. There are two connected reasons for this view. The first is that to presume carnival survives in contemporary culture would also assume that
late-modern social order is as structured and integrated as the intense
interdependence of medieval society. Everything we have noted about the
social changes of modernisation makes this impossible.

   This leads on to the second reason which is that spectacular occasions
or performances may well share common features of dramatization, but
that does not mean their meaning is the same. I have in a previous publication (1993, esp. Ch. 1; see also Chaney 1995) drawn a distinction
between a spectacular society and a society of spectacle in order to characterise differences in the dramatisation of social order in medieval and
late-modern cultures. I do not want to repeat the themes of that interpretation, but note the main conclusion that rather than spectacle being the
means by which the community literally encloses personal experience as
it does in medieval culture, spectacle in later modernity has become a
means of enchantment in which ever more persuasive illusions simulate
the experience of community as a stage for personal experience.

   It is therefore not difficult to view the general phenomenon of mass
tourism as elaborately choreographed mass spectacles. These are a textually mediated discourse of spectacular entertainment that makes any
meaningful representation very difficult. This because the otherness of
the visited place is experienced as a form of spectacle: 'Mass reproduction,
the imitation and "extension" of nature and history and the procession of
dramatized mass spectacle organized by the mass communication industry,
produce a social environment in which calculated myth and simulation
structure the contours of daily life' (Rojek 1993, p. 209). The logic of this
analysis is that far from being a means of escape the foreign place should
be more appropriately seen as an opportunity for recuperation, that is,
reasserting rather than undermining social order. This approach is reinforced when we appreciate that the place being visited does not have to
be very 'foreign' in order to make it a curiosity, as it is the way of seeing or

visiting that makes a touristic attitude and thus we can be as tourists in our own environment (see also Gold and Gold 2000).

The ambiguity remains though because, as I have tried to stress throughout, there is at least a duality of meaning in relation to any institutionalised activity or setting. Rudner puts it well when she writes in relation to fashion that it 'clearly regulates the female body, its appearance, and its behaviour; and yet it is also tied to the pursuit of pleasure, of "frivolity", within feminine culture' (1999, p. 88). Both aspects of regulation and opportunity for creative indulgence have to be borne in mind in relation to fashion; and equally while recognising the artificiality of virtually everything that is marketed as extraordinary within tourism, it is necessary to simultaneously acknowledge the opportunities tourism provides. In particular, stepping outside the conventions of the everyday does provide some sort of shock through estrangement. The idea that difference and variety become normal is, it seems to me, an essential part of the everyday reflexive engagement with cultural values and presuppositions that I have stressed as a characteristic feature of the changes of later modernity.

The Lure of the Forbidden

The more general point of this chapter is to argue that although the everyday has become more salient as topic and idiom in contemporary culture, this has not meant an exclusive emphasis on the 'ordinariness' of social life. Not only is the pursuit of what I am generally calling enchantment very pervasive but it is at least as two-sided in its meanings as representations of the everyday. I think it is important to pursue the ways in which representations of the extra-ordinary can be both a means of rationalisation and a practice of resistance to that rationalisation slightly further. Although Ritzer's perspective on cathedrals of consumption can be criticised, he does draw our attention to the other-worldly character of the extraordinary, how it is often staged in settings which aim to produce an alternative reality. I think this is often true of tourist settings in which visitors somewhat uneasily combine the roles of performers and audience, but it is not exclusive to tourism.

Before considering some of the other ways of staging extraordinary realities in greater detail, I should note in passing that this form of dramatic experience is not peculiar to later modernity (some nineteenth-century examples are discussed in Chaney 1993, Ch. 2). What is characteristic of contemporary culture is that considerable engineering skills and capital resources have been invested in creating extremely powerful and engrossing spectacular experiences. One obvious example of the use of capital investment in order to sustain the viability of a cultural form has been the deployment of spectacular effects in Hollywood films when faced with the cumulative competition of first television in itself, then video recordings of cinema films and other means of marketing films to domestic audiences. It has seemed to producers that the cinema as a public form of dramatic presentation has had to emphasise the distinctive force that large screens and special sound effects make possible (King 2000). The point of this sort of spectacular show has always been that it can engender a disorientation of the audience such that they feel themselves caught up in a staged alternative form of reality.

It is common to refer to these situations as dreamlike, as participants feel themselves swept along by the force of presentation or narrative in ways they cannot control (although everyday life as we have noted typically has an equivalent feeling of inevitability). The disorientation of audiences, partly induced by the suspension of conventional frames of time and space, and partly induced by the simulation of experiences which would not conventionally be accessible or necessarily desirable – such as plunging in a vehicle seemingly out of control or being pursued by a man-eating shark – is by definition extra-ordinary and literally escapes the constraints of dominant reality (although we should be aware of Crane's thesis (1994) that the genre of the horror film plays with the now widespread suspicion that contemporary everyday life is itself pregnant with the most awful terrors). The enchantment available in virtual realities, themed rides, imagineered environments and other forms of spectacular entertainment is engendered by forms of play that are more visceral than the imaginative play of children's activities. This means more generally that the pleasure of enchantment will probably be more complex than just the thrill of emancipation that disorientation can bring, and will also involve imaginative exploration of sensations that are threatening and frightening.

While the alternative realities generated by the complex engineering of entertainment industries tend to be the most spectacular generally available, there are many other modes of transcendence possible. In fact to do the topic justice would involve exhaustive description and probably lead to a discussion of the phenomenology of disorientation or the aesthetics of spectacular dramaturgy. One significant dimension, though, is a recognition that precisely because these experiences are at the edges of conventional 'normality', they are likely to be troubling for the taken-for-grantedness of the dominant social order. While the premise of this chapter has been that enchanting illusions are particularly likely to be exploited in consumer culture, a significant theme in traditional morality has always been that the boundaries of representation need to be policed. There are always fears that uncontrolled imagination may well lead to disorderly conduct (and thus of course the conventions of those cultures in which women are required to be covered except from the eyes of family members in case they excite licentiousness). Troubles may be felt to arise for those responsible for policing normality and those who claim the authority to interpret and prescribe the appropriate character of normality (for example priests or other moral arbiters), either because disorientation may be induced or because the experiences simulated may be felt to be too indulgent. I will discuss some aspects of both types of 'trouble' as they relate to changing forms of everyday life and begin with some notes on means of disorientation.

I emphasised at the beginning of the chapter that the extra-ordinary is generally rendered extraordinary through institutionalised practices and expectations governing access and use. This is very clearly true in relation to each culture's norms on use of substances that facilitate temporary states of disorientation – the sorts of things we conventionally group together as drugs or stimulants. Although drugs are hedged around with all sorts of controls on the occasions when use is legitimate and how much use is acceptable, some form of drug use is culturally universal. Therefore although drugs are usually seen to be dangerous, either because of their effects on individual behaviour and health or because they license indulgence rather than more 'responsible' forms of conformity, they are also attractive because of the enchantment through disorientation they offer. My interest in this context is in both the general spread and acceptability of new sorts of drugs and the more particular instance of an association between one drug and a form of popular music. I will begin with the latter, the rave scene, clubbing and the use of ecstasy, as it opens up some general issues in drugs and everyday life.

A major technological development underlying cultural change in the last decades of the twentieth century has been the spread of personal computers using digital coding. Not only have these computers facilitated enormous strides in office and home production; the use of digital technology in electronic communication, broadcasting, photography and visual imagery more generally and in sound recording has also led to significant changes in the production and reception of popular entertainment (Robins 1996; Wells 1997, Ch. 6; Negus 1992). More specifically, digitalisation has meant that elements of previous recordings can be combined and recombined to in effect create new recordings that have never actually been played. One way in which this possibility has been utilised has been the development of new forms of 'urban dance music' made available by DJs who put together programmes containing styles such as techno, house or jungle (Bennett 2000). Going along with the new music styles has been the development of occasions for dancing that have been particularly intense in the loudness of the music, the lack of inhibition amongst performers/dancers, the length of the occasion and generally the overall commitment to a form of participation that is well captured by Turner's notion of communitas (1969). Bridging the music and the form of participation and in a sense legitimating the occasion by exaggerating the dreamlike disorientation of participants has been the widespread use of a drug commonly called ecstasy.

In its early years the urban dance music scene was particularly associated with quasi-spontaneous mass gatherings, when although lacking formal publicity large groups of young people could be brought together to dance intensively. These raves quickly became the basis of a moral panic both because of widespread drug use and because they seemed anarchic forms of entertainment which were outside conventional structures of social order (Thornton 1994, 1995). Legislation was rushed through the British parliament to outlaw these gatherings and the drug ecstasy has remained a constant source of moral concern – particularly in the popular press. However, despite the common efforts of preachers and policemen, drug use, particularly ecstasy, has remained very widespread, with popular opinion particularly amongst the young differentiating between 'hard' addictive drugs and 'soft' recreational non-addictive drugs. The legitimacy of this distinction is not my concern here, but rather to note how extraordinary occasions largely built around a form of drug use emphasising an alternative communal reality have been institutionalised into clubs and other informal gatherings throughout British cities. These alternative forms of leisure are not only seen as threatening by authorities and conventional leisure providers, but are also seen as subversive by participants in part because the communal ethos generated is felt to override conventional gendered relationships.

The lure of the forbidden here, the enchantment of dance occasions, is therefore a combination of the intensity of communal participation and a feeling that these extraordinary settings are the focus for new forms of collective identity that are outside conventional categories of gender, ethnicity and sexuality, etc. Bennett writes of these modes of identity, following Maffesoli, as neo-tribes in a way that is explicitly critical of more traditional notions of subculture because the latter were too rigid and too tied to theories of structural conflict. Although neo-tribal affiliations are more fluid and transient, in ways that are directly linked to Hetherington's accounts of new social movements mentioned earlier, they also articulate 'a means of engaging with and negotiating forms of everyday life as they are encountered in local settings' (Bennett 2000, p. 88). What I want to take from this example of the institutionalisation of the extraordinary is therefore consistent with themes previously emphasised. Although a dramaturgy of noise and movement may find a particular drug-based means of disorientation particularly effective, both because it is forbidden by conventional authorities and because it helps to induce a powerful ethos of communalism, the resultant spectacular occasion is not so much a flight or escape from reality as a way of reconfiguring attitudes towards everyday life.

I am not so foolish as to believe that I can provide a neat little theory that will explain the increasing amount and variety of drug use in later modernity. Clearly a lot of drug use, particularly now forms of opiates are available widely and cheaply, is a response to the misery and poverty of urban deprivation. In the broken-down dilapidated housing estates of Britain's permanently poor it is hard to see drugs as a romantic subversion of the orthodoxies of competitive individualism. There are, therefore, profound personal and social pathologies implicated in the opening up of new markets for drug use in British popular culture. At the same time, however, blanket programmes of repression and suppression by social control agencies miss the ways in which a hedonism of enchantment, combined of course with the lure of the forbidden, is becoming institutionalised in the leisure culture of everyday life.

Throughout this study I have written of how the frames of normality are shifting in the course of cultural change, not to radically transform public and private spheres but rather to blur the frameworks of everyday order through more ambiguous categories. The widespread uses of drug references in popular culture from songs, to films and television dramas and literature, etc., are a mocking ironic awareness that the conventional discourses of control are at best inadequately trying to cope with the reflexivities of radical democratisation. My more general argument then is that while the extraordinary is always a powerful counterpoint to dominant reality, in a variety of ways the cultural changes of later modernity have made the extraordinary more routinely present in everyday life. One way of interpreting this process is that force of the dominant culture in defining the nature of the normal is relaxing or being undermined, an aspect of the fragmentation of culture I will discuss more fully in the final chapter.

Traditions of the Future

I have so far considered several forms of enchantment made available by mass culture industries, although these entertainments have also been used 'irrationally' in ways that challenge and maybe subvert dominant rationalisation. In these ambiguities of meaning and function non-conformity has been pretty explicit. In the concluding sections of this chapter I will consider some modes of enchantment where resistance is less apparent. They are, however, important aspects of the changing character of everyday life and illustrate interesting ways in which the enchanting visions are being accommodated in the textures of ordinary experience. Another shift in style in these sections is that they introduce a stronger focus on temporal as well as spatial ordering of everyday life. So far I have typically linked the themes of my topic, everyday life and cultural change, through spatial metaphors – so that I have written of boundaries and frameworks changing as well as ways of seeing which are essentially spatial (this is unsurprising as Lefebvre amongst others has suggested that the everyday is essentially a spatial concept (idea discussed in Bonnett 1992)).

Although in these concluding sections temporal aspects become more important, as before I will be writing within a cultural paradox. This is that in the onrushing progress of modernity there has been a simultaneous deliberate discarding of the past, while in all sorts of ways mementoes and survivals mark a widespread concern for and sentimental treasuring of the past, of personal, communal and national heritages running through so much of everyday life. I will initially explain why in certain respects in later modernity there has been a turning away from the past, so that later modernity has been characterised as 'a culture of amnesia' (Huyssen 1995). I will try to summarise the argument here by saying that representation – whether verbal or pictorial – not only gives a form or orders what is being represented, but also necessarily politicises its subject. By this I mean it introduces social relations of teller and listener as well as the point of view of presentation. In this case how the past is to be ordered as well as how it is to be understood and from whose viewpoint it is to be seen raises issues that have proved difficult to accommodate within the consensual discourses of mass culture.

Huyssen argues that representation is necessarily based in memory as this gives it a narrative structure – a proceeding from something to a conclusion. And yet memory is a form of representation that recreates its topic as it is in the narrating that it becomes memorable: 'The fissure that opens up between experiencing an event and remembering in representation is unavoidable ... {but} ... this split should be understood as a powerful stimulant for cultural and artistic creativity' (1995, p. 3). In an era when cultural activity in all its forms has reached unprecedented levels, the tension between memory and representation will be particularly powerful; and in an era of massive cultural disruption such tension will also be necessarily provocative over whose memories and whose representations are to be authoritative. Thus the difficulties that arise when we acknowledge the highly politicised memories of the last century with, as Huyssen writes, 'the memories of the Holocaust survivors only being the most salient example in the public mind' (op. cit., p. 2). In this context symbols of identity with all the ways that they depend on practices of memory and representation will become, as I have stressed throughout the book, a dominant source of concern in everyday experience (see also Samuel 1994).

It is, then, not that the past is obliterated in a culture of amnesia but rather that its representation is forced into either oblique abstractions[5] or trivialising stereotypes. Although the intertwined themes of memory and identity are staples of a culture of mass entertainment, the very proliferation of drama and representation this culture generates can be held to swamp any sense of order or significant detail. The combination of novelty and repetition in the spectacles of mass entertainment can be seen to mean that modernism's problem of critical representation becomes so hopeless that it is effectively unimaginable and thus eventuates in a 'culture of amnesia' (Bertman 2000 has recently used the same critical slogan although a different analytical strategy). I want to suggest then that although amnesia is literally a loss of memory it can also be understood as a lack of narrative order in images of past; in this sense a culture of amnesia amplifies the problem of representation that has been one of the themes of this study.

Throughout the book I have stressed that any concern with everyday life has to be in effect a concern with its representations, as it is in its forms of representation that it gets done as practical matters (as well as commented upon, interpreted, theorised, etc.). Everything I have just written about representation and memory must mean that everyday life is articulated in particularly significant ways in memories. The problematic issues of representation, therefore, might be understood as leading to an insuperable meaninglessness in everyday life, but I have tried in previous chapters to show why this interpretation would be too sweeping. If, however, there is a potential vacuum of meaning, then it becomes easier to see why it has been filled by narrative emphases on sentimentality and nostalgia. My response to what I called at the beginning of this section a paradoxical combination of a culture characterised by a forgetting of its past with simultaneously employing myriad representations of heritage and tradition, is that the past becomes particularly vulnerable to being bowdlerised. Representations of the past will be sensitive battlegrounds for contests over authenticity because group identities whether religious, nationalist, ethnic or regionally based, etc., are often both comforted and feel discredited by cultural narratives couched in sentimental and nostalgic terms, as in for example Hollywood's varying representations of native North Americans during the twentieth century.

In order to be a little more concrete I shall discuss the example of the creation of the town of Celebration by the Walt Disney Corporation. As is well known, Disney as a brand name first achieved global prominence as a film studio specialising in animated films; subsequently the company expanded through the creation of theme parks in which a number of fictional environments were elaborately devised to provide a narrative space for customers to enjoy as passengers in a variety of rides (Bryman 1995; Giroux 1999; Schickel 1968). These themed environments or worlds offer idealisations or fictional stereotypes of national and cultural themes cleverly intertwined with characters from the studio's repertory of animations that are both utopian and intensely ideological (Marin 1977; Ritzer 1999, etc.). In 1966 Walt Disney, the studio founder, evidently envisaged extending these environments into lived spaces rather than just pleasure gardens, but the actual building of a residential space based on an idealised fiction only occurred towards the end of the last century.

Of course, it could be argued that suburban developments have typically been based on a utopian strain (Chaney 1996; Silverstone 1997), and more recent developments particularly in the United States of 'gated communities' have strongly signalled a retreat from 'reality' to an idealised space (and are undoubtedly part of what Glassner 2000 has diagnosed as a pervasive but inappropriate culture of fear in contemporary America). The town of Celebration is, however, distinctive in that it is a commercial development partly sold on the strength of a brand image. Using the corporate strength of the parent company, the developers were able to remove the site from the control of public authorities so that residents effectively lack democratic controls over the government of their environment; and developers have been able to insist on a number of environmental and behavioural stipulations to ensure that the town resembles as far as possible an idealised vision of a traditional small town in an unspecified point in the American past (Frantz and Collins 1999; Ross 2000). Whether or not there ever was any reality to the model to which the community aspires, there has been no lack of people eager to become customers and inhabitants of this idealised space and subordinate themselves to an extraordinary degree of social discipline. They are therefore at least in part motivated by a nostalgia for a past that is only available in fictional rather than experiential terms, and a past that has been dramatised in terms of sentimental attachments. They also want to pitch their everyday lives in an enchanted vision that is extra-ordinary in its flight from reality.

I do not think it is particularly contentious to see Celebration as an ideological intervention. It crystallises certain fears about the dangers of disorder in modernity that have been represented as inherently associated with the cultural diversity of urban life; it does so through dramatising an interpretation of community through nostalgic and sentimental motifs. What, then, are nostalgia and sentiment as characteristics of ways of representing the past, or as ways of dramatising memory? Taking Celebration as an example, I have already noted that the idealised qualities of the community cannot have been personally experienced by its new inhabitants and it is unlikely that they are drawing upon family memories orally transmitted through generations. If they are nostalgic then in the sense of yearning for something that has been lost or passed away, their nostalgia is for something constituted in the fictions of films, television and journalism, etc. I do not mean to suggest that nostalgia as a form of memory is necessarily deceptive in that it hearkens back to something that did not exist. We do not need to know whether American small towns were ever as crime-free, well regulated and egalitarian as the mythology suggests; or indeed whether childhood or 'the homeland' were as sunny and harmonious as we like to imagine. What is important is that qualities of attachment or belongingness can be imagined as a contrast to the perceived uncertainties or insecurities of contemporary experience.

Although I have said that I am thinking more in terms of representations of time here, Celebration, and the other Disney environments, collapse time and space together in a fantasy of social control that denies any need for control. These settings then are pure spectacle, they are representations of everyday life that purport to be enchanting but in practice are the apogee of rationalisation. In this pinnacle of radical democratisation where the representation of community is through continual striving to recreate an invented or imagined tradition, there is no need for any display of governmental interests. They can be imagined to have become unnecessary because the freedoms of popular choice are always and only to choose conformity (and thus hark back to cathedrals of consumption such as shopping malls, Chaney 1990). By recognising this to be a dystopian or the reverse of utopian vision, we do not unfortunately begin to answer the question of how local identities should be presented or dramatised. In the constantly globalising pressures of the cultural changes discussed, finding spaces for local experience that have any sort of authenticity will be considered in the next section.

The Enchantment of Sentimentality

I have suggested that the intensification of culture that I have presented as the main characteristic of change in later modernity has been associated with a loss of confidence in representations of the past. Another way of putting this that is more consistent with the general theme of this chapter is that cultural industries have found it very easy to mine the past for enchanting representations that are employed in the idioms of contemporary everyday life.[6] Most commonly it is seen in all the varieties of advertising and marketing that stress the 'olde worlde', traditional character of the setting or the way the product has been made. In illustrating this process I have discussed some aspects of a particular venture in urban development. I am partly using this example because it and associated developments, such as the anodyne ideologies of communal life embodied on the royal estate at Poundbury in Dorset (see also MacCannell 1992), are the end of a recognisable continuum that begins in the conventional values of everyday life in the suburbs. More important, though, than whether these developments become models for aspirational lifestyles is the ways in which representations of tradition can be used to sentimentalise locality. It is in this respect that particular ways of representing everyday life function as a form of kitsch that has serious consequences for forms of community. I will briefly expand upon my terms here before concluding with some notes on the representation of the countryside.

Sentimentality in representation is not so much a distortion as an imputation, whereby the object, person or experience is being imbued with the associations of idealised relationships. When an older person looks at the saved birthday cards from their children they are touched by the associations of unforced affection. When those children look for a suitable card they may well think that one bearing a romantic image of countryside or idealised children or inscribed with affectionate and 'traditional' verse is appropriate to symbolise the relationship they wish to evoke. Both sides are then colluding in a romantic fiction that represents situations that, as with nostalgia, need not correspond to a particular truth. Sentiment comes in the way that symbols are used as markers of relationships, but the symbols are repetitious and stereotyped in much the way that souvenirs and mementoes of tourist trips are highly stylised and clichéd. Sentimental representations do not have to conjure the past. When newspapers print the photo of a little girl that has been abducted and probably murdered they will seek an image in which she is posed and styled as decorous and respectable. The truth of the child is irrelevant when she is being used to symbolise the emotion readers will feel at the harshness of reality being forcibly broken in upon idealised innocence.

It is, therefore, easier to see why the enchantment of sentimental and nostalgic representations is often criticised for misrepresenting actuality and for counterfeiting emotion. The very blandness and predictability of the representation of relationships are held to mean that distinctiveness is being sacrificed for trivialising stereotyping. These critical terms are themselves evocative of broader traditions of response to mass culture; and it is therefore consistent with Huyssen's suggestion of the femininity of mass culture (1986) that sentimentality and nostalgia are typically assumed to particularly appeal to feminine consumers. I think it is more appropriate, though, to see what I have called the bowdlerising tendencies in representations of the past as expressions of a predilection for kitsch in mass culture. I will not explore the topic at length, but rather take over a view of kitsch as a mode of representation that serves a distinct function in relation to the incoherence of modernity: 'Kitsch, I will argue, preserves a unique aesthetic sensibility that spurns creativity per se while it endorses a repetition of the familiar and a grounding in an affirmation of the everyday' (Brinkley 2000, p. 134). Brinkley goes on to amplify this theme by arguing that the conventions of kitsch work 'to re-embed its consumers, to replenish stocks of ontological security, and to shore up a sense of cosmic coherence in an unstable world of challenge, innovation and creativity' (op. cit., p. 135).

Kitsch has conventionally been condemned for its lack of artlike qualities (Kulka 1996), for its lack of robustness and individuality, for not aspiring to innovate in representation but to remain content to almost parody itself (see for example the work of what is claimed to be the most commercially successful living artist, Thomas Kinkade (*The Independent*, 5/5/01, p. 11), who markets limited edition reproductions of his highly stylised images of traditional settings).[7] The significance of this style of representation is not, though, in how it fails to conform to the reflexive discourse of modernism, but rather how it dramatises an enchanting representation of the past for contemporary concerns. I will illustrate this theme through some aspects of the representation of the countryside. I noted earlier that the country is inextricably located in the past as it is something we have always just lost (Williams 1973). The reason is that as an idealisation that functions as a way of talking about change, the country figures in a number of discursive contrasts: with the city; with the future; with industrialism; with class-stratified society; and with modernity. The countryside is therefore both with us and a sense of what we have lost, making it an ideal vehicle for sentimental and nostalgic representations (and interestingly in all these ways very analogous to childhood which has also become significant as a focus for idealisation in everyday life).

It was not, of course, always so, as up until the birth of the Romantic movement the countryside more usually represented brutish backwardness in drama and literature. With the Romantics and particularly in poetry and painting, the country began to be seen as the site of eternal truths, of an innocence that contrasts favourably with the corruption of urban sophistication (interestingly, Constable as one of those who first found a representational language for this ideology has remained a central source of popular motifs, see Painter 1996, 1998). The naturalness of rustic environments was, of course, as artificial as any cityscape with the development of representational traditions as in the influence of Gertrude Jekyll on English country gardens (Colls and Dodd 1986; Pugh 1990). But as with all cultural forms, the reflexive power of these traditions has meant that the country has increasingly been shaped in their terms through, for example, the influence of the National Trust; and it has thus been able to furnish images for campaigns as diverse as petrol advertising, tourist imagery and wartime propaganda.

It would be all too easy to argue that in this context representations of the countryside have become irredeemably kitsch (Chase and Shaw 1989). The sentimentality and nostalgia of the many and various ways the country as a cultural space is presented both to its own inhabitants and to visitors are too obvious to need detailing here. From property values in certain sorts of villages, to ways of dressing at country shows, to picture postcards to mass media dramas of rural life, authenticity is continually being sought and presented in a huge variety of social and cultural symbols that mean that discriminations between image and reality can never be absolute (Burchardt 2001). Not only does this situation pose immense problems for residents of the countryside as to what sort of 'place' they actually inhabit, it also generates further 'irrationalities'. Arcadian myths make it an attractive aspiration for people to imagine retiring to live in the country, but these incomers force up property prices and demand a very special type of leisure culture that is inimical with sustaining the ecology and generates massive social exclusion amongst the young and those working. More generally, we can see how in the way the discursive complex of 'the countryside' has been able to capture for itself a privileged place in a climate of a more general recapitulation of the past through invented traditions (Hobsbawm and Ranger 1983), the emerging identity of a national culture has been shaped towards preserving the privileges of a landowning class (Hewison 1987).

One example of the representational difficulties this can give rise to has been a focus of excited controversy recently. Thus hunting as a leisure activity purports to be a means of pest control. It certainly involves the use of animals for sport in ways that are clearly anathema to the majority of the population, but has been very forcefully defended as a cultural tradition that is in danger of being suppressed by a mass influenced by liberal relativism. The resulting conflict has been fought on an ideological terrain of a defence of both tradition and individual freedom under an overarching vision of community not unrelated to those discussed in the previous section. The problem here is that the rationalism of modernity is not being opposed in terms that undermine traditions of privilege and deference. Rather the reverse, so that the vision of community fails to offer a radical alternative to the exploitation of rural places by old and new forms of privilege. There is no vision of a sustainable alternative to governmental interests but rather an unchallenging accommodation as long as it allows the preservation of 'colourful traditions'. The constitution of the countryside as traditional in contrast to modernity has meant that any representation both by inhabitants and by outsiders is almost inevitably grounded in false consciousness; and it is not therefore surprising that idealising stereotypes have come to be particularly salient in dominating the space.

I have described the dominant ways of representing the countryside as colluding with both traditional and modern forms of exploitation, but it is important to recognise that these conventions are as vulnerable to the irrationalities of rationalisation as other discourses. Thus this imagery of tradition can have political and economic implications that are difficult to contain for those who would seek to exploit the economic resources of the countryside and have failed to recognise the character of later modernity. For example, the discovery that animals have been fed in such a way that diseases have jumped species and are now proving fatal to humans on a scale that may prove comparable to medieval plagues has clearly rocked any faith in the intrinsic 'naturalness' and cultural integrity of the land. Similarly, revelations that political authorities have been and are co-operating in the introduction of genetically modified crops and animals to the countryside and thus to the human food chain has provoked widespread revulsion. In both cases radical democratic needs to appear to be respecting the wishes of consumers have been flouted, further confirming both the discreditable character of elite expertise and the dangers of traditions that have made this possible. More particularly, representations of the past are either called into question or more sharply contrasted to the pollution of the everyday environment in the present.

The difficulties of representing a sustainable everyday life are not unique to the countryside, as I have emphasised throughout. Possibly because the country is enchanting for the vast majority of the contemporary population it has, however, been particularly vulnerable to the force of representational traditions that have sought to combine commercial and sentimental rationalities. Rather than cling on to the ways in which traditions have been hijacked by those who seek only to preserve the privileges of a social order, if the country is to become an enchanting alternative its inhabitants will have to embrace a more radical irrationality that emphasises the particularity of local experience. To some extent a turn to organic production has seemed a solution to commercial corruption, although it can be sentimentalised into the same sorts of nostalgic communalism that inspired the settlement at Poundbury previously mentioned. The real challenge of green politics, however, is to break apart the cultural vocabularies that have masked the lack of real distinctions between town and countryside in unending suburbia. The real challenge of green politics and the politicisation of the countryside is to find ways of representing everyday life so that we can have real food, real lives, real localities and real histories. This, however, involves politicising all the representations of everyday life in ways that would constitute massive cultural change.

9

The Fragmentation of Culture

Paradoxical Culture

In this book I have been writing about the forms of everyday life, how the sense of experienced givenness in the life-world and its multitudinous discursive representations are changing in a culture of mass leisure and entertainment. I have argued, first, that although the everyday is something we normally presume that we can take for granted, in the social and cultural changes of modernity the everyday has been felt to be disordered, possibly irrational. And, secondly, that although in later developments the everyday has become considerably more prominent, quite how it is being used and what is the order being conveyed in its representations lies at the heart of radical politics. The reason that the everyday resisted the rationalisation common to other spheres of life in modernity is that in the everyday we routinely interpret and make sense of what is going on. We make the world meaningful for ourselves. I have pointed to a variety of studies that have shown how this process is not chaotic or a complete improvisation, but although interpretation is ordered it is also necessarily a dialogue. There is an unpredictability to the process because in each and every case the reciprocity of interaction builds its own momentum.

There is therefore what we can call a banal creativity at the heart of human experience. If this is a cultural universal, and we have no reason to believe it is not, the reason it has become foregrounded in interpretations of contemporary social process is that the heightened reflexivity generated in the dislocations of modernity has necessarily forced a greater self-consciousness about the meanings of meaning. I do not want to disappear into convoluted theorisings, but it is necessary to acknowledge that what I call banal creativity does not happen in a vacuum. It is formulated and articulated in the symbolic vocabularies of institutionalised forms of representation and performance collectively available that we conventionally refer to in shorthand as a culture. The crucial characteristic of cultural change that has run through all the issues discussed in this book is that it has become increasingly paradoxical. While the vocabularies of contemporary culture are simultaneously more pervasive, elaborated and central to social life than at any previous point in history, they have also been fragmenting in the sense of losing any distinctive order or coherence. (I have avoided writing of British culture in that sentence as I do not want to suggest I am writing about a national cultural identity, but I think that the character of that paradox will differ between for example North American and European societies.)

What has been quite widely referred to as the heightened reflexivity of later modernity stems from what I have just called the loss of distinctive order, or which could be described as the dissolution of an existential grounding in the traditions of persistent social categories. Banal experience has thereby been forced into a more ironic sense of the arbitrariness of any relationship between representation and meaning. I have written about the boundaries or frameworks of everyday experience as being significantly shifted by the dominant character of textually mediated discourses. Quite how the changing texts, performances and services of cultural industries work to frame what I described in Chapter 1 as the core expectations of everyday life has been the substance of following chapters. I have tried to show that the dramatisation of symbolic boundaries between both groups and activities in cultural forms (Lamont and Fournier 1992) has not become less significant even if culture is becoming less coherent. In the profusion, however, of ways of conceiving that which is changing, and in the variety of interpretive and analytic discourses, we should be alerted to more fundamental issues for our sense of culture. In conclusion I will bring out what these issues are by explaining why I think there is a contemporary crisis in the study of culture; and why this 'crisis' as an instance of what Geertz has called (with a different reference) 'blurred genres' (1983), may be as emancipating as problematic.

A Crisis in Culture?

I will in this section elaborate a theme of possible crisis by giving four instances of current difficulties in differentiating the cultural from the social. The first of these instances goes back to the discussion at the beginning of Chapter 1 of the significance of culture in social thought. In talking about the modernity of a concept of culture I pointed to the interrelationships between an idea of a culture and the various modes of what I called 'nationness'. Although any one nation may have only a relatively brief history of sovereignty, or indeed still aspire to be invented, the idea that it has a distinctive culture is conventionally a prerequisite for authentic identity. In post-industrial Britain such an idea of a national culture has been argued to have been fatally undermined in two ways. The first is that cross-national cultural industries, allied to technological developments such as satellite broadcasting and digital transmission, have meant an inevitable degree of globalisation (some of the relevant arguments here have been discussed in Morley and Robins 1995). National authorities can no longer adequately control or police their citizens' consumption; and the production of entertainments, in music, television and film, etc., for example, for global audiences is widespread.

One example of change in national cultural styles can be taken from a recent newspaper article:

> Throughout the first half of the century opera performance tradition and singing styles were national in character. As economic, political and cultural barriers have dwindled, so the old differences between operatic traditions have weakened. Air travel, the recording industry, the communications revolution and the oligopoly of a few powerful artists' agencies have homogenised and internationalised the operatic world as they have done with music as a whole (Kettle, *The Guardian*, Saturday Review, p. 1, 26/6/99).

The export of culture is not, however, just a process of imperialistic exploitation (although see Schiller 1996), as in all sorts of ways the homogeneity of the dominant culture is being infiltrated by borrowings and imports so that Hall has emphasised the hybridity of contemporary culture (1992; see also Modood and Werbner 1997; and Lull has written persuasively of processes of transculturation, indigenisation and hybridisation in what he calls contemporary cultural give and take (2000, Ch. 5)).

The phrase 'multicultural Britain' may often be used as rhetorical aspiration, but it does indicate another way of undermining a national culture. As I have already recognised, the interaction between a variety of groups defined by cultural styles rather than class position has meant that attempts to render the essence of Britishness are inevitably heavily ideologically charged (Hebdige 1992). It should not be surprising, therefore, that a number of political leaders, particularly those on the right, have attempted recently to capture British cultural identity in a few striking traits – attempts that have usually been treated by derision by other cultural commentators. I should add, however, that although national cultural identities have been undermined, a process intensified by ever stronger international trading blocs with, in Europe now, a single currency, this has not led as I have emphasised to a diminution in nationalism as emotional identification with local identity (Jenkins and Sofos 1996; see also Featherstone 1995, esp. Chs. 5–7).

The second instance of difficulty in differentiating the cultural from the social is more directly related to issues in the field of cultural studies. It is usually acknowledged that one of the key figures in constituting this new field was the literary critic Raymond Williams, and his early books (1958, 1961) are cited as foundational texts. The status of these books is not important at this point, but they did certainly establish the discursive (and ideological) character of culture (see also Williams 1976 for an innovative glossary of discourse), pointing to basic contrasts between aesthetic and communal conceptions of culture in the modern era. Williams was also responsible for one of the key formulations of a communal conception of culture as 'a whole way of life'. This has recently been criticised as being based on a romantic, almost organic, sense of culture which sets up an impossible and inappropriate ideal (see Bennett 1998). It is well known that Williams throughout his intellectual work used his upbringing in a stable semi-rural community as a model of cultural integration (see Inglis 1995), and Bennett argues that this point of reference is both romanticising and guilty of the sort of idealisation of a cultural essence for which the elitist literary critic F. R. Leavis and his followers have been heavily criticised (disentangling Williams's critical Marxism from his Leavisite education luckily is not a task that we need attempt here).

Bennett's book (1998) is more than a critique of the theorisations of culture that have informed cultural studies so far, however, as he is more positively concerned to justify the field of cultural studies within the university curriculum. To this end he attempts to mark out a distinctive terrain for cultural studies that is also necessarily a reformulation of culture for contemporary conditions. This revised version of culture by Bennett can be summarised as the processes of inculcation that generate conformity to conventional social order: 'cultural studies is concerned with all those practices, institutions and systems of classification through which there are inculcated in a population particular values, beliefs, competencies, routines of life and habitual forms of conduct' (op. cit., p. 28). Culture is therefore the ways in which everyday life gets to be taken for granted, a view that might seem not so different from my perspective in this book except that for Bennett culture is being seen as external to, working on, its subjects. It is not being made by them in the course of everyday life as well as other spheres of social life.

While, therefore, I have problems with a view of culture as all the mechanisms of power in contemporary society, even for Bennett this does not adequately differentiate a distinctive topic. For immediately he goes on to fracture the unity of 'all those practices etc.,' because he is wary of too systematic structures of ideology. He therefore recognises that it cannot be assumed that 'all the practices, institutions and systems of classification ... are constituted in the same way or function in a common manner' (ibid.). While this is realistic it does mean that the study of culture is now being rendered as the study of different modes of power. This is a legitimate topic, but does not seem exclusively cultural nor is there self-evidently a methodology or set of methodologies by which the study of culture can gain a distinctive purchase on the operation of inculcation (particularly if one is sceptical about the value about the critical resource of 'reading' (however understood) texts). Moreover, the study of mechanisms of power is an enterprise to which a number of social sciences, particularly sociology, will feel they can contribute at least as much as cultural studies.

The third instance of 'troubles' in recognising something distinctively cultural picks up another point I made in my opening chapter about the role of intellectuals in constituting the domain of culture. In recent years in a number of fields, but particularly anthropology, work has been published that attempts to deconstruct the discovery of (particularly of other) culture. Introducing an edited collection on issues in 'writing culture' (Clifford and Marcus 1986), Clifford says the authors 'see culture as composed of seriously contested codes and representations, they assume that the poetic and the political are inseparable, that a science is in, not above, historical and linguistic processes' (Clifford 1986, p. 2). What this means is that culture is no longer to be assumed to be something to be discovered whole and autonomous, but is rather an artefact of intellectual and political processes. In effect it is a medley of competing and overlapping and thereby very probably incoherent voices that require some cultural creativity to be shaped into the intellectual edifice that traditional ethnography has prized.

If one left it there, a naive reader might assume that the burden of this perspective is that cultural analysis is more difficult than previously suspected and particularly prone to ideological bias. In fact the perspective that Clifford is introducing treats ethnography as something more than a fieldwork practice. In effect ethnography becomes a mode of reflexive consciousness that uses the cultural as an analytic resource (see also Atkinson 1990), that is helpful in developing a sensitivity to the ways in which all utterance is art – fully grounded in finely discriminated and wide-ranging contexts. In this sense ethnography can be used as a label for work in a variety of disciplines, work that will be characterised by what are sometimes seen as postmodern features. First, a concern with the poetics of social knowledge rather than its relationship to some external reality and, secondly, an interest in how the identities of author and subjects are constituted in discourse (on rethinking identities, see Hetherington 1998). Of course, it could be argued that this approach does indeed preserve the distinctiveness of the cultural, but it is in such a way that the cultural becomes a generic name for all social knowledge and, as with the study of power, the sphere of culture becomes impossible to identify.

The fourth instance of contemporary difficulty in differentiating something distinctively cultural stems from what I referred to earlier as the success of the concept at moving beyond the borders of academia. Culture has become a staple in contemporary public discourse. Some examples are the frequently cited 'culture of institutional racism' that was diagnosed in the Metropolitan Police following the inquiry into the murder of Stephen Lawrence. On other occasions commentators have pointed to the existence of institutional cultures such as legal or medical cultures to explain conservatism in recruitment practices or conceptions of good practice. And perhaps quite differently, in seeking to justify a devolution of resources and political control to ever smaller regions within the United Kingdom, activists have claimed the distinctiveness of local cultures in areas such as Cornwall (more positively on Cornish nationalism, see Vernon 1998). My point is not to suggest that these interpretations are 'wrong', but to illustrate how the use of a notion of culture has become in effect a rhetorical strategy. Culture has become a convenient way of capturing the idea that shared values develop through time as ways of making sense of local circumstances.

In one of the early books on subcultural theory (Hall and Jefferson 1976) culture was characterised as providing a 'map of meaning' (see also Jackson 1989). This is a colourful phrase but it does suggest a totalising overview, a framework or authoritative perspective, within which constituent details can be ordered and explained. The trouble with the multiplicity of ways in which culture is now being used is that particular interests are being given too great a force. Of course within particular settings such as a gay bar, a police canteen, a mothers and toddlers group, and an Orange Order Lodge in Northern Ireland there will be conventional expectations on ways of talking and shared concerns. Members will be familiar with expectations and by and large conform in those settings, but they will also participate in other settings with contrasting discourses without a damaging sense of discontinuity. In heterogeneous patterns of association we will all move between a number of 'cultures' in the course of a day. This is not particularly problematic or difficult to understand, but it does suggest that in another way culture has lost its distinctive authoritative sphere and become effectively another word for institutional settings.

Cumulatively, these arguments suggest that much of the intellectual purchase of a concept of culture, as I briefly summarised it in the introduction to the book, is no longer viable. The paradox of the cultural turn in the social sciences (Chaney 1994), has been an inability to adequately differentiate the cultural from the social – in effect that culture has been subsumed into social processes. And yet such a conclusion would seem to fly in the face of the reality that when we talk about significant changes in the lived experience of the twentieth century – and all the ways in which I have been discussing the 'culturalisation' of everyday life – they all amount to culture becoming more rather than less important. I do not intend to labour this point as it seems so self-evident, but one aspect is obviously the economic strength of the culture sector. For example, a recent government audit of 'Britain's creative sector, including music, design and advertising' found that it 'generates more than £100 bn a year and employs more than 1 m people' (*The Guardian*, p. 7, 14/3/01). If one then brackets this with the 'culturalisation' of economic and productive life that Lash and Urry have characterised as moves towards an economy of signs and spaces (1994), then the production and consumption of culture are arguably the central focus of contemporary social process. Thus if one of the characteristics of a transition to the modern era has been a differentiation of the cultural sphere, then it may be that the end of modernity is being characterised by de-differentiation – with culture replacing the social.

An argument that has been given a distinctive twist by those who argue that the use of cultural, that is signifying or semiotic, resources to constitute individual and collective identities has amounted to an aestheticisation of everyday life (Featherstone 1991; Chaney 1996, Ch. 10). This clearly touches on an important aspect of the theme of this book and has been discussed at several points in preceding chapters. For now I want only to note that even if the process is granted, its meaning remains problematic particularly in relation to the tension between rationalisation and local creativity that has been a central theme. For example, some see a greater investment in opportunities for semiotic manipulation as emancipating in that it provides a forum for mundane creativity (Featherstone 2000). On the other hand, the more pessimistic view is that a more playful instability in conventional representations indicates only that reality has become little more than an illusion. And thus, as we have seen, an increasing emphasis on spectacle, in both cultural industries' and personal narratives, is derided as an overwhelmingly insidious means of manipulation that condemns contemporary consumers to lose any control of fantasy (Debord 1981; Baudrillard 1983, 1988). Whether seen positively or negatively, this development in conjunction with the other arguments just presented once again suggests a current inability to differentiate the cultural and the social, but as I have said with the social being subsumed in the cultural.

Four Types of Popular Culture

The nature of the perceived crisis in contemporary culture is then a range of doubts about quite what is or should be seen as properly cultural. This may be dismissed as an intellectual extravagance that is irrelevant to self-evident social processes, but I have tried to indicate that cultural change is not just a matter of new technologies or new narrative genres. It is also concerned with the forms and frameworks of social experience and how we come to understand that experience. The issue of what it is that is changing in cultural change becomes fundamental to the distinctiveness of consciousness in contemporary society. In order to make this thesis clearer I shall present a very schematic overview of four types of popular culture. I am concentrating on popular culture because of the interdependence of the popular and the everyday that I initially recognised. If I want, as I do, to argue that new ways of relating self to others are being formulated in the cultural context of later modernity, then it makes more sense to look in particular at the forms of ordinary entertainment. I am therefore in this historical sketch concentrating on culture as communal entertainments rather than culture as a repertoire of resources for practical action (Swidler 1986; Wuthnow 1988), although it is inherent in the whole thrust of the book's approach that the two are interdependent.

The four types of culture that I shall briefly describe are: pre-industrial popular culture; urban popular culture; mass culture; and fragmented culture. Although they will be presented as a historical progression none of the types is entirely consistent or self-contained. What I mean by this is that the distinctions between types are idealised for the purpose of contrast.[1] In practice each stage or type overlaps with its predecessor and successor. I will constantly reiterate that elements survive from era to era and thus types interpenetrate each other. Even so the distinctions are real and do mark substantial differences in the ways of being-in-the-world for members of these cultures. In expanding upon what I mean by the fourth type, fragmented culture, I hope to elucidate the issue of a crisis in culture and its implications for everyday life.

As the name pre-industrial popular culture suggests, this type is an attempt to lump together the distinctive features of pre-industrial or early-modern popular cultures. In both rural and urban communities the way of life was governed by tradition based in the rhythm of the agricultural calendar and focused around religious festivals. I have previously described this social formation as a spectacular society (Chaney 1993) and suggested that it was a highly dramatised culture with a number of distinctive features. I also think it important to stress that in this culture performances were largely anonymous (even costly and elaborate art works for devotional purposes were not signed or authored until the emergence of the distinct social type of artist), so that producers and audience shared a common social world. And although there were distinctive features to the entertainments of the royal court and the nobility, culture was not stratified into mutually unintelligible levels and social worlds.

The emphases upon tradition, collective forms and communal participation could all suggest that pre-industrial popular culture might be better thought of as a folk culture. Names are not particularly important here but the resonance of a popular culture, that is a culture of the people, is that the cultural forms of ordinary life become marked off from more elite forms with the social consciousness of emergent class society. As the dominant traditions of a rural culture lost their authority with a combination of dislocation, through an increasing tide of urban migration, and suppression, itself involving a further combination of new abstract rhythms of work and assaults on collective bacchanalian traditions, more class-specific, commercial forms of entertainment began to emerge. An urban popular culture is then characterised by commercial forms of entertainment presented as ephemeral spectacles for the anonymous crowds of urban society.

In the history of Britain a popular theatre focused on melodrama, later joined by a music hall and variety theatre traditions and supplemented by popular sports, principally football, constituted the main initial forms of working-class culture (Cunningham 1980).

It is, however, important to bear in mind that an urban popular culture developed as part of the stratification of a class society. It was therefore inseparably bound in with the conflicts and resistance of class struggle. Much of the style of the culture, such as the collective celebrations, bawdy excess and carnivalesque imagery all associated with the working-class seaside holiday, was both grounded in the traditions of pre-industrial popular culture and a defiant alternative to the more restrained entertainments of middle-class respectability. I have emphasised that an urban popular culture was essentially commercial and produced the first stars as working-class heroes, but it was also in many respects governed by communal traditions. It encapsulated the way of life of a class culture and has frequently been the subject of nostalgic recreations, particularly amongst those on the political left who saw it as a model for an alternative social order.

An urban popular culture began to be recognisable from very early in the nineteenth century and probably remained the dominant form of popular culture until the middle of the twentieth. This dating is, however, very arguable as forms of the mass culture that was to supplant urban popular culture were significant from at least the end of the nineteenth century. A good illustration of some of the ambiguities here is provided by the history of the cultural form of the cinema. The innovation of 'moving pictures' was initially seen as a form of working-class entertainment that supplemented the existing cultural forms of the fairground and variety stage. Subsequent developments such as purpose-built cinemas, more elaborate plots and production values and aspirations towards more 'theatrical' presentations all meant that the cinema became in effect a mass medium in terms of social appeal. Above all the increasing colonisation of the British cinema by the American cultural industry as part of, in effect, constituting the first globalisation of culture, signalled the massification of popular culture. Despite this, however, British films retained a strong basis in the class culture of the audience (however bowdlerised) and only ambiguously articulated the values of a mass culture.

The social appeal of the cinema did, however, mark a significant attenuation of the traditions of an urban popular culture. More generally, the cinema can be seen to have ushered in many of the distinctive features of a mass culture. Above all mass entertainments lose a specific class character, although in a stratified society culture inevitably retains class associations (for example the differences in social identification between the audiences for ITV1 and BBC1). Not only were cultural entertainments now emphatically and overwhelmingly commercial in their organisation and rationale, they were also being made by cultural industries who produced performances that could be simultaneously available certainly throughout the nation if not globally.[2] Urban popular culture retained much of the regional character of a diverse society – well illustrated by distinctive local styles in accent as well as topic of comic entertainment (although on the variety stage regionalism could be sold to national audiences). In a mass culture regional distinctiveness survives only as sentimental association. It may well be a source of pride in relation to sport and identity as origins, but it no longer constitutes a basis for real cultural differences and certainly does not affect the diet consumed from or made available by mass culture industries.

A mass popular culture can therefore be characterised as a variety of entertainments made available as a broad social appeal, usually reinforced by strong advertising campaigns, to anonymous audiences who consume performances as commodities. In the language I am using here I think it is apparent that the connections between the emergence of mass popular culture and the dominance of consumerism are not incidental. Mass culture therefore spills out from being distinctive ways of producing and distributing performances to constitute a way of life characterised by many of the values associated with leisure and mass consumer industries. It is in this context that we can see most clearly how mass culture has often been associated with the rationalisation of 'Fordist' production processes. As well as being condemned for the irrationalities of mass marketing, this form of popular culture has also been criticised as constituting an essential element in the homogeneity of suburban lifestyles and, possibly thereby, undermining the values and traditions of high culture. In practice, I would argue that mass culture has never been as homogeneous as its name suggests, and that the status and privileges of high culture survived as an increasingly important mode of cultural capital for intellectual elites.

If mass popular culture has only come to be fully dominant in forms such as music, literature, television, tourism and fashion since the middle of the twentieth century, it may seem premature to already detect the emergence of a new type of popular culture. This is not, however, an original suggestion. There has in the discourses of social commentary since the early 1980s been a widespread concern with whether the modern era in general, and modern culture in particular, are being superseded by a postmodernism or postmodernity. In much of this writing (and other forms of representation) about the culture of late-modern societies I think there has been a fundamental confusion about whether what is being characterised as 'post-' exemplifies features of a mass popular culture or a new type of cultural formation that is paradoxically not 'a' culture. I think there are good reasons for arguing for the latter position, and in order not to get sidetracked into the persistent modernness or not of these developments I have opted for the more general name of fragmented culture for this situation.

Fragmented culture is the most eclectic of these types of culture. It is not 'post' in the sense that it comes after culture; as has already been noted and will be further developed in the next section, the era of fragmented culture is one of an extraordinary range and fertility in cultural activities. It is, however, fragmented in the sense that the cultural forms of this era lack defining characteristics in any of three aspects of production, narrative and participation. If there is a dominant style to fragmented culture it lies in those old postmodern themes of referentiality and surface. The very profusion of cultural activity both in terms of performance and commentary means that all consumers are aware of how effects have been constructed and engineered. Surfaces are deceptive, but it is in what is often called the play of self-conscious self-consciousness that pleasure is experienced in the multiplicity of association and irony of allusion. Fragmented culture, as I believe I have indicated in the preceding chapters, articulates a more fundamental instability in the social forms, and moral orders, of everyday life – although in this it is an elaboration rather than a transformation of trends inherent in the modernism of metropolitan life (Chaney 1996, Pt. 2).

Fragmented Culture

I have so far in this chapter advanced two propositions: first, that although cultural activities, institutions and industries, etc. are prominent in later modernity, the sphere of culture is becoming harder to mark off as a distinct 'space'; and, secondly, that the diffusion of culture into the general range of social activities can be characterised as a process of fragmentation. The significance of these themes is that they underlie what I called earlier the distinctiveness of consciousness in contemporary society. If cultural change matters it is because one is trying to get at how the forms of the experience of being-in-the-world are shifting. But in order to develop this account I will briefly suggest three reasons for thinking there is a process of fundamental change in the character of the culture of everyday life. In giving these reasons I will say something about how I see fragmented culture differing from mass culture.

Although I am primarily writing about change in relation to forms of dramatisation and representation I have emphasised that these have implications for the ways of seeing in the structures and order of everyday practical matters. The use of the term 'fragmented' might then be read as a suggestion that I believe there is an encroaching anomie in which more and more people will feel themselves cut off from any moral grounding, will feel alienated from any sense of community and perhaps be more susceptible to mobilisation by bizarre or extreme social movements. Although some of what I see as the positive aspects of the irrationality of the everyday has been caught up in these forms of estrangement, I hope that my stress on the persistence of moral themes in everyday life has shown why I do not believe there is a moral vacuum. It is, however, clear to me that the structures and traditions of the representations of social and cultural order are fragmenting as part of a process of transition that is not a descent into chaos but neither is it a set of minor variations (a sense of epochal change has usually been linked to notions of postmodernism – some papers critically addressing the need for new theories of culture are in Adam and Allan 1995). The following reasons for suggesting a sense of fragmentation will I hope help to pull together everything that has preceded this point in the book.

The first reason can be illustrated by an aspect of what I have emphasised throughout as the significance of rationalisation as a commercial, intellectual and administrative imperative in modernisation. I have also, however, discussed a more specific use of the rationalisation thesis – particularly associated with the 'Fordist' rationalisation of mass cultural provision. Ritzer in his book on the fast-food industry (1993) and subsequent work on what he calls 'new means of consumption' provides a powerful example of this use in a 'mass cultural' critique. While the irrationalities of McDonald's et al. are manifest and significant, I do not believe that this is an appropriate model of the development of cultural production. Manifest culture is far more frequently concerned with the production of unique objects – such as records, television programmes, films, etc. For these cultural industries the rationalisation that takes place seems to predominately relate to distribution rather than production. It is in this respect that I have emphasised the importance of brand marketing in which a distinctive commercial identity has become the focus of intensive design rather than the product.

Brands, logos and personalities as marketable identities can accommodate the individualisation of ordering and more effectively give the illusion of consumer freedom. It is in this context that the era of mass marketing is no longer growing – and here the growing opportunities of electronic commerce may prove very significant. The power of Hollywood studios and large television networks to organise the cultural diet of mass audiences has been significantly limited. New forms of reception are going to mean that advertising has to be very specifically aimed at very focused markets. In the fast-food industry as much as in other forms of cultural production there has been a proliferation of smaller 'niche' markets generating a variety of forms of provision; all of which means that producers and advertisers are going to have to be considerably more sensitive in how they characterise the social groups that characterise markets (Stern 1998; Brown 1995).

The first reason for thinking that the era of mass culture is being superseded is then part of the more general argument that the Fordist rationalisation of industrial capitalism is in a process of transition to what Lash and Urry have called an era of 'disorganised capitalism' (1994). In this era the ubiquity of the various elements of material culture symbolising prosperity and a quality of life such as cars, assorted domestic items, televisions and holidays, etc. is no longer remarkable, and lifestyles are increasingly catered for through an 'economy of signs and spaces'. Of course one recognises that there are significant sectors of the population of post-industrial societies who are effectively excluded from the fashions of lifestyle concerns, and that common entertainments are still dominated by global corporations such as Disney, but it remains true that the ways of life of more stable social formations are being supplanted by the looser associations of lifestyle tastes (Chaney 1996, Pt. 3). The relationship between culture and society is necessarily being reconsidered in the context of new social forms of lifestyles (Chaney 2000).

This leads on neatly to the second reason for detecting a new era that I am calling fragmented culture. In a number of ways it seems that cultural objects or performances are shifting from functioning as representations or depictions of social life to constituting the contexts or the terms of every-day life. Traditionally, cultural representations have been presented in a framed environment that bracketed the perspective presented and marked it off effectively as an alternative reality. This mode of performance is cap-tured well by the proscenium arch of the theatrical stage which encloses a performance space within a building which further separates the 'show' from everyday life. The same sort of analysis holds for the conventionally framed painting in an art gallery. Not only did this form of presentation articulate clear distinctions between art and life or culture and society, it also underlay an ideology of privileged authorship in which one man (and it usually was a man) was attributed with the power to have created this vision. It seems to me that the performances of fragmented culture are increasingly difficult to contain within the boundaries of theatrical space so that they bleed into the texture of everyday life.

What do I mean by performances escaping the boundaries of theatrical space? The answer is partly given by the proliferation of performance inputs which has the effect that dramas are not sectored but are continually available in every aspect of everyday life. One consequence has been that there is an insatiable demand for new products often filled by cheap dra-mas that mimic everyday life in ways that blur distinctions between fiction and reality (a process heightened by technological developments offering greater interaction between audience and performance). But perhaps more important is a second consequence that performances, particularly but not exclusively television, increasingly take on the characteristics of frag-mented attention and incoherent, overlapping narratives that characterise everyday life: 'MTV is now almost shorthand for a visual style comprising rapid alternation of clips or viewpoints with computer graphics and a "handheld" camera style that emphasises the artificiality of the medium and its incompleteness as a visual record' (Mirzoeff 1999, pp. 97–8).

In what I have said so far, I have emphasised that the blurring of genres and overlapping of performance contexts are likely to mean greater diffi-culty in differentiating types of messages and that environments lose their specificity as functional spaces. There are, however, other technological developments which go beyond ambiguities in performance to the creation of new autonomous realities (Bell and Kennedy 2000). Moves towards the creation of virtual performances through, for example, coding semiotic material in digital form so that it can be endlessly manipulated and translated through different performance settings, or the exploitation of virtual environments in cyberspace, have meant that the mode of participation in new dramatic environments is becoming increasingly engrossing. Writing of the arbitrariness of experience in these circumstances, Mirzoeff points out that: 'Once considered the clear frontier between internal subjective experience and external objective reality, the body now appears to be a fluid and hybrid borderland between the two, as subject to change as any other cultural artefact' (1999, p. 116). Clearly these developments raise fundamental questions about the meaning or even the possibility of any sort of authentic experience, particularly when the primary mode of apprehension of cultural experience is now overwhelmingly visual and seeing is no longer believing. It seems that we increasingly inhabit fictive landscapes and require new aesthetics of representation (Chaney 1994, Ch. 5).[3]

The term 'fragmented culture' is therefore justified because I want to argue both that our popular culture is moving beyond the presuppositions of conventional entertainments, and that much of the distinctiveness associated with the sphere of culture has effectively disappeared. If there is any force in this approach it must have implications for all modes of culture, not just the entertainments of popular culture. This then brings me on to my third reason for detecting a new cultural era. I have emphasised that previous eras of popular culture have always existed in the context of more elite cultural forms. Although I have argued that modernism has been a continual struggle with a crisis in the representation of modernity, and that successive avant-gardes have more specifically attacked the privileges of artistic status, art has through the greater part of the twentieth century retained its position as an essential element in the 'capital' manipulated by elites. It seems to me that an important element in the distinctiveness of contemporary culture is that the boundaries marking off and sustaining elite or high culture are increasingly being undermined and destabilised (an interesting aspect to this process is brought out in Whiting's (1998) study of the gendered ambiguities of Pop Art's embracing of the iconography of consumer culture).

Intellectual elites may well have felt themselves threatened by popular or mass culture throughout the century, but they did retain a sense of confidence in their own distinctiveness and critical importance (more generally on the significance of symbolic boundaries in maintaining cultural hierarchies see Lamont and Fournier 1992). This confidence has been substantially undermined in the modernisation of modernisation to be replaced with a series of accommodations to the populist demands of all-pervasive media of mass communication and entertainment; as Eyerman has put it: 'Professionalisation, specialisation and fragmentation rather than politicisation seem to be the fate of intellectual labour in late modern society' (1994, p. 195; see also Bauman 1987). In support of this assertion I can point to the ways in which status in the various aspects of the art world is established through the same sorts of media discourse as status in the spheres of, for example, politics or sport or cooking. If to this is added the proliferation of modes of innovation, then art is not restricted to particular social worlds or formal traditions but becomes a general name for prestige, perceived creativity and minority appeal.

The effect has been that the established distinction between classical and popular music for example is no longer clear-cut and that within each form there is a continuum between minority and more generally accessible styles. If one adds on to the initial binary distinction further forms such as jazz, folk and world music (and many other possible contenders), then innovation or seriousness is spread across the whole gamut of music-making and is not restricted to a European tradition or type of instrumentation. Another factor that one would want to introduce here has been technological innovations which have undermined the clarity of any distinction between performance and composition. This is too big an area to go into in any detail here, but the effect has been to subvert the privileged status of authorship. For some time theories of knowledge have been proclaiming the death of the author and it seems that now in a variety of cultural forms the production of environments or discourses has superseded the distinctive representation of an individual vision.[4]

My argument that the authority and legitimacy of high culture have been fatally undermined has a further major consequence. In Chapter 2 I cited Bonnett's argument (1992) that avant-garde revolt during the last century continually tried to resolve contradictory demands on the artistic role. Now it seems that more generally those working in art world settings (such as teaching institutes, critical commentators and interpreters and public foundations of various sorts, etc. (Becker 1982)) have had to consider their social role. In practice this has meant they have to continually confront why objects and performances purporting to be high culture should be made, what the relationship between these objects and their possible audiences should be, and how such objects/performances should be understood. It would not be appropriate to review all the various ways these questions have been addressed in different cultural forms. I think, however, the example of the shift to conceptual art – and thus the provision of critiques of social knowledge and values – amongst visual artists is a good example of a practical recognition of the futility of traditions of visual representation in a world lacking institutional rationale for those traditions (Zollberg 1990).

I have said at several points that one reason why the character of contemporary culture is confusing is that although one can point to a number of reasons for asserting the de-differentiation of the cultural sphere, it remains true that cultural activities, industries and practices are the focus of most people's everyday lives. Another version of this paradoxical situation arises in relation to the undermining of high culture that I have described. Although I do think that much of the authority of culture as an enclave of critical insight has been lost, as I indicated above culture as a source of prestige for corporations and national bodies seems an unquestioned (or unquestionable) good. This is indicated by an enormous investment (not least through the subvention of lottery revenues) in the institutions of public culture such as galleries, museums, theatres and production companies, etc., which have bolstered the status of high culture as a national resource as never before. The use of culture as a form of capital, for organisations, groups and individuals, has also undoubtedly underlain the development of cultural tourism and the sorts of participation that offers.

It will be apparent from the reasons I have given that an era of fragmented culture is inherently paradoxical. In fact I want to conclude this section by briefly arguing that an era of fragmented culture is riven by paradoxes or contradictions at the level of both theory and experience of everyday life. These paradoxes are a consequence of the advanced reflexivity of the modernisation of modernisation. In all sorts of ways the discourses of everyday life have been thoroughly infiltrated by the concepts and ideas of social theory, and this in turn is further part of a more general concern with the arbitraryness of collective identity. It is therefore not surprising that the lack of an effective culture is denied by the insistent performances and rhetoric of self-conscious culture and cultural expertise. I will briefly discuss the following paradoxes, all of which I think are fundamental to the character of everyday life in an era of fragmented culture: control and resistance; freedom and conformity; lifestyle and authenticity; and meaning and meaninglessness.

The first contrast sets up the terms on which the others are based. The enormous power of media of mass communication and entertainment to set agendas, prescribe ways of seeing, create desires and stigmatise dissent is widely feared in contemporary society. While the empirical substance of these fears may be hard to establish, the perception of living with unprecedented powers of control is generally accepted. It is therefore unsurprising that in all sorts of ways people seek forms of resistance or escape; everyday life has become a field or a site of struggle in which meanings are contested or reclaimed from ungraspable others. It is important in this context to look at what might be called struggles for identity. I have already noted in one of the strands of cultural change that in the blurred social structure of post-industrial society other forms of conflict, such as those focused on gender, age, ethnicity and sexuality, have come to overlay class divisions. In these struggles for identity cultural resources have been important both as means of raising consciousness and asserting rights and as the central terrain for those who have sought to reject negative stereotypes (Gilroy 1993; Pickering 2001). It is, moreover, consistent with the disorderliness of fragmented culture that increasingly these struggles for identity have shifted from battles to claim an equality with dominant groups, to struggles to defend the rights, particularly cultural rights, to difference (Owusu 1999). The same sort of process can also be seen in battles within a supranational entity such as the European Union. The desire of the administrative order to enforce common standards throughout the Union is increasingly being resisted by those who seek to retain local difference displayed in cultural styles and traditions (Jenkins and Sofos 1996). One example here could be hygiene and welfare standards for the treatment of animals in southern Europe.

If we are dominated by culture and yet seek to use cultural forms as means of resistance then it is unsurprising that contemporary culture is also seen as opportunities for freedom and self-expression while simultaneously being seen as the main means of ensuring conformity in mass society. Similarly, consumer culture may create unrivalled opportunities for the development of lifestyles that are more self-consciously artful designs and yet in the play of surfaces seem to deny any meaningfully authentic expression or action for individual actors. (Another version of this paradox is provided by the fear that the marketing of consumer culture makes authentic goods – such as the artefacts of Tibetan craftspeople – available to global audiences, and yet in so doing turns their craft into another tourist industry.) So that overall the plenitude of culture means that we are constantly aware of the play of meaning and the possibilities of enhanced meaning while simultaneously suspecting that the simulations of cultural industries render our environment fundamentally meaningless.

Each of these contradictions or paradoxes has been noted before as I have indicated by citing previous discussions. The originality of my observation is not therefore in the detail as much as in the combination – a combination that generates an endless and unresolvable search for resolution amongst how people participate in contemporary cultural forms. The distinctiveness of consciousness in fragmented culture that I have tried to bring out as the central theme of cultural change is that it is both being played out in the sphere of everyday life and using the idioms and motifs of everyday life as ways of confronting, articulating and representing the modernisation of modernisation. Many of the more intellectual strands in contemporary public discourse have gropingly tried to confront this confused and confusing situation, but have been driven into an excessively abstract theoreticism. While we cannot find better perspectives by pretending the issues are not hard to address we can try to express those difficulties as clearly as possible. However fragmented it has become, the study of culture is clearly the central issue for interpretations of contemporary social order. All of us have still to find ways of representing everyday life for ourselves.

Notes

1 Introduction: Culture and Modern Life

1. Interestingly, Bryson begins his discussion by noting two characteristics of the everyday as a topic that will become familiar as this book progresses: first, that the everyday as a topic is conventionally thought to be not very serious and not worthy of the most sustained attention; and, secondly and not unrelated, that still life as a genre of the everyday has been particularly associated with feminine spaces. Bryson distinguishes between rhopography and megalography, the latter term becoming self-evident when the former is defined (from *rhopos* meaning trivial objects, etc.) as: 'the depiction of those things which lack importance, the unassuming material base of life that "importance" constantly overlooks' (1990, p. 61).
2. Rather than scepticism or even cynicism, this attitude might be styled as a wonder at the creativity humans employ in making elaborate social institutions to disguise their ignorance and uncertainties.
3. Rationalisation is to be understood in the following work as only referring to the processes characteristic of modernity in which a combination of scientific expertise, bureaucratic administration and targeted marketing work to design social and commercial policies. (At no point do I use rationalisation in the sense of justifying or explaining.) Rationality is therefore to be understood as the set of values in which these processes are accepted unproblematically as being beneficial for society. Correspondingly non- or irrationality is being used here in the specific sense of failing to conform to the expectations of rationalisation and thus being perceived as disordered or non-compliant with the rationality of governmental interests, and not (except in a few clearly marked cases) as irrational in the more popular sense of being foolish or misguided. (Wolff 2000 has suggested that the rationality of modernity has been coded as masculine, and thus a non-rational attitude or outlook might be correspondingly seen as feminine in a way that is consistent with my more general recognition that everyday life has often been seen to be particularly associated with female experience.)
4. This remark may be puzzling as I have already said the genre of still life takes the everyday as its topic and the genre clearly pre-dates modernity, but typically still lifes imbued their mundane subject matter with a moral seriousness that transcended the topic; I do not have the space to adequately argue all aspects of the issue in this book, but I will suggest that the everyday as a topic for representation in its own right – thus observed with moral indifference in art and social theory – is a characteristically modern perspective.
5. Colin Crouch has described many of the features I am concerned with as 'post-democracy' (2000).
6. Elizabeth Wilson has written recently of contemporary culture becoming incoherent (2000) for analogous reasons.

7. It should be apparent that such claims are necessarily modes of representation that have as little or as much basis in 'reality' as any other interpretive account.
8. And more self-conscious forms of representation such as 'dirty realism' in American literature or social realist cinema.
9. I have also recently discussed the difficulties of using culture unproblematically in Chaney (2000).
10. As a form of interpretation this need not be restricted to group life but can be adapted to an interpretation of individuals as in the various modes of what have come to be called 'psy-discourses'.
11. My argument will be that the assumption that there is a core of normality provides an essential vantage-point for a phenomenology of collective life.
12. Because their view is likely to be in Bonnett's words: 'Everyday space tends to be the auditorium rather than the stage, the street rather than the cinema screen or architectural model; it is the arena of noncreativity: the "passive" space around the work of art from which the latter derives its identity as art' (1992, p. 70).
13. The desire for and the ability to produce this effect is not peculiar to literature, as will be apparent in the work of documentary photographers (see Chapter 2); I have previously discussed the work of Walker Evans and the 'truth' of his observations of the everyday (Chaney 1988).
14. Another way of putting this would be to say that the everyday is a way of finding the comfort of neighbourliness in the order of personal experience.
15. It has been suggested that feminine experience has typically functioned in this way in relation to the hubris of male discourse and it may be that the feminine, private character of everyday life has underlain its neglect in social theory.
16. People working in a number of disciplines undertake the study of culture; although I write as a sociologist, I will draw upon these broader perspectives and I shall therefore refer to this larger community of scholarship as human studies or social theory.
17. In the next chapter I discuss what I mean by modernity and why a problem of representation developed in the modern era; as that 'problem' has not been resolved, it seems more appropriate to refer to the changing character of culture as distinctive of later modernity rather than 'post' modernity.

2   Everyday Life in the Modern Era

1. The processes can be thought of as social forms (although it is not a connection Beck himself makes), in that they structure particular modes of action but are simultaneously embedded in broader processes.
2. Bryson in his study of still-life painting has commented that the close observation necessary to render the everydayness of the everyday can result in 'an overfocused and obsessional vision that ends by making everyday life seem unreal and hyper-real at the same time' (1990, p. 90).
3. It is also relevant that the leisured world the Impressionists so often pictured was itself based on the development of new 'consumerist' attitudes to the constant renewal of everyday things that underlay a more general conviction of a world in constant change – see Roche (2000).
4. In particular here one would want to point to Flaubert and his agonised struggles to represent the everyday life and interests of the provincial lower middle classes.

5. I am also regrettably ignoring that tradition of histories of private life particularly associated with the French historians Ariès and Duby; see for example Prost and Vincent (1994).
6. One of the most anguished attempts to confront the awesome responsibility of representing everyday life in both prose and photography came in James Agee's and Walker Evans's report for *Fortune* magazine eventually published as *Let Us Now Praise Famous Men* (1973; see also Chaney 1988).
7. The New Deal administration is that created by President F. D. Roosevelt in 1930s America in response to the great financial depression of the inter-war years. It pioneered a number of new forms of social intervention, including the use of cultural imagery to communicate across American society (O'Connor 1973); I will discuss the Chicago School further in the next chapter.
8. If in terms of the old adage only man bites dog is news whereas dog bites man is not, then everyday life consists of predictables such as dogs biting men.

3 Social Theory and Everyday Life

1. Another reason for citing the book by Miller and McHoul is because it is an exception to the generalisation that ethnomethodologists have not shown any great interest in issues of cultural change. I do, however, recognise that people working in the conversation analysis end of the ethnomethodological spectrum have contributed studies of institutional communication (e.g. on advertising and political rhetoric – see for example Boden and Zimmerman 1991) that are very relevant to a more general account of contemporary cultural industries. I am not, though, seeking to review all relevant work but rather indicate how the topic of everyday life – particularly as it relates to cultural change – has been constituted in social thought.
2. It is worth noting that conversation analysis has become functional for corporate rationality in that it has proved effective in exploring problems in artificial intelligence and communication technologies.
3. I should acknowledge that Giddens when he is dealing with the constitution of the self is clearly more influenced by and sympathetic to ethnomethodological work than the others (see 1984).
4. I should also note here a tradition of more formal studies of 'micro' interpersonal interaction in 'everyday' situations that tended to miss the symbolic component of interactionist accounts, e.g. Swingle (1973).
5. Shields has interestingly noted how Lefebvre was influenced by the phenomenological philosopher Martin Heidegger who in turn borrowed ideas from the Marxist philosopher Lukacs who was himself a pupil of Simmel (1998, p. 67).
6. See for example Luckmann's trenchant formulation: 'For it is the case that questions about the meaning of action are first encountered, first formulated and first answered by ordinary people, on their own terms and in their own language, and to their if not to our satisfaction. In fact, the potential and actual reconstruction of the meaning of everyday actions is constitutive of these actions, not merely a post-hoc irrelevant addition' (1989, p. 19).
7. Although the inspiration for an emphasis on alienation rather than exploitation as the main 'hurt' of capitalist economic relationships is usually taken from writings of the young Marx.
8. I gratefully acknowledge the influence of Burkitt's work (1999) in making this point.

9. I am sensitive to the fact that an analytic approach to what I have called the formulations of everyday life in an analysis of discourse (see for example Billig et al. 1988; Semin and Gergen 1990; Shotter 1993; Delin 2000), will be an essential element in a more exhaustive study, but to have adequately considered this perspective now would again have significantly shifted the character of the book.

10. The nature of the accomplishment has been well summarised by Silverstone: 'In the ordering of daily life we avoid panic, we construct and maintain our identities, we manage our social relationships in time and space, sharing meanings, fulfilling our responsibilities, experiencing pleasure and pain, with greater or lesser degrees of satisfaction and control, but avoiding for the most part the blank and numbing horror of the threat of chaos' (1994, p. 1).

4   Everyday Life and Personal Setting

1. I recognise that culture, like language, is necessarily public – my reason for using the oxymoron public culture is to point in passing to the idea that cultural performances which were previously exclusively appreciated in public settings are now increasingly consumed/appreciated in the home.

2. I do not mean to imply that hermeneutics is the main or only mode of analysis in material culture, as I am well aware that there are as many epistemologies in this as in other fields of cultural analysis; I use the term because I want to signal that essentially the study of all types of objects must seek to make them meaningful in ways that are analogous to the interpretation of more self-consciously intended (and thereby meaningful) works.

3. In this of course the study of consumer or material culture exemplifies the more general issues that run through this book on problems of how to appropriately interpret everyday life; and neither should it be missed that those who seek to counter the intellectual elitism of one critical tradition are themselves still intellectuals.

4. I use speaking as a general term for all modes of address, but obviously frequently for television the form of representation will be primarily visual rather than oral.

5. Households which are productive centres probably because they are sites of business enterprise or because public work is done 'at home' are becoming more common again in a networked society. Quite how the intermingling of work and leisure is managed in such households is a key element in reformulating everyday life, but my account presumes that distinctions between different sorts of commitments will be stubbornly insisted upon.

6. In this the personal stereo has changed the experience of private identity in public space in ways that are analogous to the changes being wrought by the ubiquitous conduct of personal conversations in public settings through mobile phones.

7. On superficial and complex aesthetic experiences see Chapter 7.

5   Dramatising the Self in Everyday Life

1. Closely related ideas about the negotiation of public discourse and the character of new social movements are explored in the next chapter, particularly the later sections.

2. It was reported in *The Guardian*, 12/4/99, G2, p. 10 that in a mixed classroom of adolescents asked to comment on their faults boys will mention failures at particular skills such as maths or games, while girls will mention features of their body such as neck, arms, thighs, breasts.
3. An exercise in pure symbolism, as Goldman and Papson point out that both the brand name and the symbol have no referent other than themselves, they are meaningless apart from their semiotic function.
4. I have noticed amongst otherwise impeccably liberal people who would never be disparaging on the grounds of ethnicity, religion or sexuality, etc., that it is acceptable to sneer at those who are overweight as obviously unattractive and probably morally deficient.
5. I should note that many who pursue sport and other forms of exercise do not see it as exclusively mortification but stress the pleasurable physical stimulus as a distinctive form of 'high'.
6. Interestingly, Wouters suggests that national broadcasting which in the early years of the century had seemed to be an irresistible force for national cultural integration, particularly in respect of diminishing regional identities, has in later modernity functioned to legitimate diversity and thus supported moves away from a standard formal public way of speaking to a more pervasive informality (see also Chaney 1993, Ch. 4).
7. I come back to the same point about the significance of new types of social space at the end of the next chapter.

6 Authority and Expertise in Public Life

1. I am referring here to remarks in speeches by leaders of the British Conservative Party, but the sentiments are not exclusive to conservatism nor are they uniquely British but are widespread in European public life. It should also be noted that this climate of fear has legitimated and possibly given impetus to what I earlier called summary assaults by 'natives' on 'strangers'.
2. I hope it is also apparent that I am not using irrational here in quite the way I have previously (and will go on to do so) referred to views of everyday life as irrational. The latter sense is of a sphere of life that is disordered from the perspective of economic and social exploitation; the irrationality I have just been discussing refers to fears that are not grounded in any sort of appropriate evidence.
3. It is interesting that in a recent newspaper article it has been pointed out that deaths of journalists now garner considerably more attention than deaths of politicians – suggesting that they are now the more substantial public figures (Wheatcroft 2001).
4. The recurrence of institutional here is meant to point to an idea that types of public identity can function as cultural forms.

7 Citizenship in Radical Democracy

1. Spelt out this stands for a quasi-autonomous non-governmental organisation.
2. As Crouch has noted in relation to his characterisation of post-democracy: 'My central contentions are that, while the forms of democracy remain fully in

place – and today in some respects are actually strengthened – politics and government are increasingly slipping back into the control of privileged elites in the manner characteristic of pre-democratic times; and that one major consequence of this process is the growing impotence of egalitarian causes' (2000, p. 4).

3. Stevenson's chapter on cultural citizenship has been very helpful for my own thinking, although I find his own definition well-meaning but muddled: 'Cultural citizenship can be said to have been met to the extent to which society makes commonly available semiotic material cultures that are necessary in order to both make social life meaningful, critique practices of domination, and allow for the recognition of difference under conditions of tolerance and mutual respect' (1999, p. 61, emphasised in original).

4. See Wessels (2000) for an example of the introduction of such an innovation; and Axford and Huggins (2000) for a more wide-ranging discussion.

5. Recognising of course that this phrase is taken from Raymond Williams although being used in a way that he would not have anticipated or approved of.

6. More generally, this strain in public discourse has helped to stimulate what Glassner has called a culture of fear (2000) in which imagined threats to idealised traditions from a variety of sources such as women, gays, foreigners, the young can be mobilised as the occasion for recurrent moral panics (see also Thompson 1998).

7. I am grateful to Sue Scott for alerting me to the potential of the 'third place' idea.

8   Enchantment in Everyday Life

1. This idea could serve as an invitation to consider the more general role of transgression in the arts and other social practices as a necessary element in the ideological currents of modernism and modernity, but unfortunately I do not have the space to pursue the opportunity; but see Jervis (1999).

2. Again I do not have the space to do it here, but it would be fascinating to pursue the connections between what I have said so far and Hochschild's (1998) view of emotions as ways of seeing.

3. An interesting elaboration of how the perceptual frameworks of experience were changing and possibly disintegrating as part of spectacular dramaturgy of consumerism comes in de Cauter (1993).

4. One that can even have the effect of popularising the cosmopolitan culture of avant-garde art (Chaney forthcoming).

5. A recourse that is particularly apparent in the memorials, proposed and constructed, for Jewish communities in Vienna and Berlin and Americans killed in Vietnam.

6. The essential idea has been elaborated more powerfully and amusingly in the extended satire on the creation of 'England' as a themed environment by Julian Barnes (1998).

7. 'What makes an object kitsch is that it is a cheap mass-produced copy of some original object or model which was considered elegant' (Gronow, 1997, p. 42).

9 The Fragmentation of Culture

1. While Cullen's (1996) history of popular culture in the United States does not use these headings, the general thrust of his narrative is interestingly analogous.
2. Generally here I am in sympathy with Carroll's philosophy of mass art (1998) in which being designed for accessibility is taken to be the primary definitional feature.
3. Most recently at the time of writing new digital technology has been used to make a mass market film in which four narratives are told simultaneously (*Time Code* directed by Mike Figgis), effectively of course fragmenting the narrative frame of performance and creating new rhythms of diegesis.
4. An illustrative example is provided by a leaflet accompanying an exhibition on Nordic Postmodernism held in Helsinki 2000 which used four themes to organise contributions: high and low – the unholy couple of art; sexuality – genres; multiple historical layers – fragmentation; and death of the artist – anonymous art (Museum of Contemporary Art 2000).

References

Abercrombie, N. (1996) *Television and Society* (Cambridge: Polity Press).

Adam, B. and S. Allan (eds) (1995) *Theorizing Culture: An Interdisciplinary Critique after Postmodernism* (London: University College London Press).

Agee, J. and W. Evans (1973) *Let Us Now Praise Famous Men* (New York: Ballantine Books).

Allan, S. (1999) *News Culture* (Buckingham: Open University Press).

Anderson, B. (1983) *Imagined Communities: Reflections on the Origin and Spread of Nationalism* (London: Verso).

Ang, I. (1996) *Living Room Wars: Rethinking Media Audiences for a Postmodern World* (London: Routledge).

Atkinson, P. (1990) *The Ethnographic Imagination: Textual Constructions of Reality* (London: Routledge).

Atkinson, P. and A. Coffey (1997) 'Analysing Documentary Realities', in D. Silverman (ed.), *Qualitative Research: Theory, Method and Practice* (London: Sage).

Attfield, J. (2000) *Wild Things: The Material Culture of Everyday Life* (Oxford: Berg).

Axford, B. and R. Huggins (eds) (2000) *New Media and Politics* (London: Sage).

Bakhtin, M.M. (1984, trans. H. Iswolsky) *Rabelais and his World* (Bloomington: Indiana University Press).

Barlow, P. and C. Trodd (eds) (2000) *Governing Cultures: Art Institutions in Victorian London* (London: Ashgate).

Barnes, J. (1998) *England, England* (London: Jonathan Cape).

Barthes, R. (1985) *The Fashion System* (London: Jonathan Cape).

Bate, D. (2000) *Photography and Surrealism: Sexuality, Colonialism and Social Dissent* (Oxford: I.B. Tauris).

Baudrillard, J. (1983, trans. P. Foss et al.) *Simulations* (New York: Semiotext(e)).

——— (1988) *America* (London: Verso).

Bauman, Z. (1987) *Legislators and Interpretors: On Modernity, Post-modernity and the Intellectuals* (Cambridge: Polity Press).

——— (1990) *Thinking Sociologically* (Oxford: Basil Blackwell).

Beck, U. (1992, trans. M. Ritter) *The Risk Society: Towards a New Modernity* (London: Sage).

——— (1995) *Ecological Politics in an Age of Risk* (Cambridge: Polity Press).

Beck, U., A. Giddens and S. Lash (1994) *Reflexive Modernization: Politics, Traditions and Aesthetics in the Modern Social Order* (Cambridge: Polity Press).

Becker, H.S. (1982) *Art Worlds* (Berkeley and Los Angeles: University of California Press).

Beck-Gernsheim, E. (1998) 'On the Way to a Post-Familial Family – From a Community of Need to Elective Affinities', *Theory, Culture and Society*, Vol. 15 (3–4), pp. 53–70.

Bell, D. and B.M. Kennedy (eds) (2000) *The Cybercultures Reader* (London: Routledge).

Bendelow, G. and S.J. Williams (eds) (1998) *Emotions in Social Life* (London: Routledge).

Benjamin, W. (1999, trans. H. Eiland and K. McLaughlin) *The Arcades Project* (Boston, Mass.: Harvard University Press).

Bennett, A. (2000) *Popular Music and Youth Culture: Music, Identity and Place* (Basingstoke: Macmillan – now Palgrave).

Bennett, T. (1998) *Culture: A Reformer's Science* (London: Sage).

Bennett, T., M. Emmison and J. Frow (1999) *Accounting for Tastes: Australian Everyday Cultures* (Cambridge: Cambridge University Press).

Bennett, T. and J. Woollacott (1987) *Bond and Beyond: The Political Career of a Popular Hero* (Basingstoke: Macmillan – now Palgrave).

Benson, D. and J. Hughes (1983) *The Perspective of Ethnomethodology* (London: Longman).

Benthall, J. and T. Polhemus (1975) *The Body as a Medium of Expression* (London: Allen Lane).

Berger, A.A. (1997) *Narratives in Popular Culture, Media and Everyday Life* (London: Sage).

Berger, J. (1972) *Ways of Seeing* (Harmondsworth: Penguin).

—— (2000) 'The Infinity of Desire', *The Guardian*, (13/7/00 G2 pp. 12–13).

Berger, P.L. and T. Luckman (1967) *The Social Construction of Reality: Everything that Passes for Knowledge in Society* (London: Allen Lane).

Berking, H. and S. Neckel (1993) 'Urban Marathon: the Staging of Individuality as an Urban Event', *Theory, Culture and Society*, Vol. 10(4).

Berman, M. (1983) *All That Is Solid Melts into Air: The Experience of Modernity* (London: Verso).

Bertman, S. (2000) *Cultural Amnesia: America's Future and the Crisis of Memory* (Westport, Conn.: Praeger).

Billig, M. (1995) *Banal Nationalism* (London: Sage).

Billig, M., S. Condor, D. Edwards, M. Gane, D. Middleton and A. Radley (1988) *Ideological Dilemmas: A Social Psychology of Everyday Thinking* (London: Sage).

Birenbaum, A. and E. Sagarin (1973) *People in Places: The Sociology of the Familiar* (London: Nelson).

Blumer, H. (1969) 'Fashion: From Class Fashion to Collective Selection' *Sociological Quarterly*, Vol. 10(1), pp. 275–91.

Boden, D. and D.H. Zinnerman (eds) (1991) *Talk and Social Structure: Studies in Ethnomethodology and Conversation Analysis* (Cambridge: Polity Press).

Boggs, C. (1997) 'The Great Retreat: Decline of the Public Sphere in Late Twentieth Century America', *Theory and Society*, Vol. 26(4), pp. 741–80.

Bonnett, A. (1992) 'Art, Ideology and Everyday Space: Subversive Tendencies from Dada to Postmodernism', *Environment and Planning D: Society and Space*, Vol. 10(4), pp. 69–86.

Booth, C. (ed., 2nd edn) (1889) *Labour and Life of of the People*, Vol. 1: *East London* (London: Williams and Northgate).

Bordo, S. (1993) *Unbearable Weight: Feminism, Western Culture and the Body* (Berkeley: University of California Press).

Bourdieu, P. (1973) 'The Berber House', in M. Douglas, op. cit.

—— (1984, trans. R. Nice) *Distinction: A Social Critique of the Judgement of Taste* (London: Routledge).

Bradbury, M. and J. McFarlane (eds) (1976) *Modernism: 1890–1930* (Harmondsworth: Penguin).

Braudel, F. (1981) *Civilisation and Capitalism from the Fifteenth to the Eighteenth Century: Vol. 1: The Structures of Everyday Life: The Limits of the Possible* (London: Collins).

Brinkley, S. (2000) 'Kitsch as a Repetitive System: A Problem for the Theory of Taste Hierarchy', *Journal of Material Culture*, Vol. 5(2), pp. 131–52.

Brookes, R. (2001) *Representing Sport* (London: Arnold).

Brown, S. (1995) *Postmodern Marketing* (London: Routledge).

Bruzzi, S. (2000) *New Documentary: A Critical Introduction* (London: Routledge).

Bryman, A. (1995) *Disney and His Worlds* (London: Routledge).

Bryson, N. (1990) *Looking at the Overlooked: Four Essays on Still Life Painting* (Cambridge, Mass.: Harvard University Press).

Buchanan, I. (2000): *Michel de Certeau: Cultural Theorist* (London: Sage).

Buck-Morss, S. (1991) *The Dialectics of Seeing: Walter Benjamin and the Arcades Project* (Cambridge, Mass.: MIT Press).

Bull, M. (2000) *Sounding out the City: Personal Stereos and the Management of Everyday Life* (Oxford: Berg).

Burchardt, J. (2001) *Urban Perceptions and Rural Realities* (London: I.B. Tauris).

Burkitt, I. (1999) *Bodies of Thought: Embodiment, Identity and Modernity* (London: Sage).

Button, G. (ed.) (1991) *Ethnomethodology and the Human Sciences* (Cambridge: Cambridge University Press).

Calhoun, C. (ed.) (1992) *Habermas and the Public Sphere* (Cambridge, Mass.: MIT Press).

Campbell, C. (1987) *The Romantic Ethic and the Spirit of Modern Consumerism* (Oxford: Basil Blackwell).

—— (1997) 'Shopping, Pleasure and the Sex War', in Falk and Campbell, op. cit.

Cannadine, D. (1983) 'The Context, Performance and Meaning of Ritual: The British Monarchy and the "Invention of Tradition" c. 1820–1977', in Hobsbawm and Ranger, op. cit.

Carey, J. (1992) *The Intellectuals and the Masses: Pride and Prejudice among the Literary Intelligentsia 1880–1939* (London: Faber and Faber).

Carey, J.W. (1998) 'Public Ritual on Television: Episodes in the History of Shame, Degradation and Excommunication', in T. Liebes and J. Curran (eds), *Media, Ritual and Identity* (London: Routledge).

Carroll, N. (1998) *A Philosophy of Mass Art* (Oxford: Clarendon Press).

—— (1986) (with, M. Pickering) 'Democracy and Communication: Mass Observation', *Journal of Communication*, Vol. 36(1).

Chaney, D. (1987a) 'Audience Research and the BBC in the 1930s', in J. Curran and P. Wingate (eds), *Impacts and Influences* (London: Constable).

—— (1987b) 'Mass Observation', in E. Barnouw (ed.), *International Encyclopedia of Communications* (New York: Oxford University Press).

—— (1988) 'Photographic Truths', *Social Discourse/Discours Social*, Vol. 1(3), pp. 397–422.

—— (1990) 'Subtopia in Gateshead: the MetroCentre as Cultural Form', *Theory, Culture and Society*, Vol. 7(4), pp. 49–68.

—— (1993) *Fictions of Collective Life: Public Drama in Late Modern Culture* (London: Routledge).

—— (1994) *The Cultural Turn: Scene-setting Essays in Contemporary Cultural History* (London: Routledge).

—— (1995) 'The Spectacle of Honour: Changing Dramatisations of Status', *Theory, Culture and Society*, Vol. 12(3).

—— (1996) *Lifestyles* (London: Routledge).

—— (1997) 'Authenticity and Suburbia', in S. Westwood and J. Williams (eds), *Imagining Cities: Scripts, Signs, Memories* (London: Routledge) pp. 140–51.

—— (1998) 'The New Materialism? The Challenge of Consumption (review article)', *Work, Employment and Society*, Vol. 12(3), pp. 533–44.

—— (2000) 'From Ways of Life to Lifestyles: Rethinking Culture as Ideology and Sensibility', in J. Lull (ed.), *Culture in the Communication Age* (London: Routledge).

—— (2001a) 'The Mediated Monarchy', in D. Morley and K. Robbins (eds), *British Cultural Studies* (Oxford: Oxford University Press).

—— (2001b) 'The Power of Metaphors in Tourism Theory', in S. Coleman and M. Crang (eds), *Tourism: Between Place and Performance* (London: Berghahn).

Chaney, D. (forthcoming) 'Cosmopolitan Art and Cultural Citizenship', *Theory, Culture and Society*.

Chaney, D. and M. Pickering (1986) 'Authorship in Documentary', in J. Corner (ed.), *Documentary and the Mass Media* (London: Edward Arnold), pp. 29–46.

Chapman, T. and J. Hockey (eds) (1999) *Ideal Homes? Social Change and Domestic Life* (London: Routledge).

Chase, M. and C. Shaw (eds) (1989) *The Imagined Past: History and Nostalgia* (Manchester: Manchester University Press).

Chaudhuri, A. (2001) 'Stressed?' *The Guardian*, 3/1/01, G2, pp. 10–11.

Clark, T.J. (1985) *The Painting of Modern Life: Paris in the Art of Manet and his Followers* (London: Thames and Hudson).

—— (1999) *Farewell to an Idea: Episodes from a History of Modernism* (London: Yale University Press).

Clifford, J. (1986) 'Introduction: Partial Truths', in Clifford and Marcus, op. cit.

—— (1988) *The Predicament of Culture: Twentieth Century Ethnography, Literature and Art* (Cambridge, Mass.: Harvard University Press).

Clifford, J. and G.E. Marcus (eds) (1986) *Writing Culture: The Poetics and Politics of Ethnography* (Berkeley, Los Angeles: University of California Press).

Cohen, E. (1979) 'A Phenomenology of Tourist Experiences', *Sociology*, Vol. 13, pp. 179–201.

Cohen, R. (1994) *Frontiers of Identity: The British and Others* (London: Longman).

Cohen, S. and L. Taylor (1978, 1st edn) *Escape Attempts: The Theory and Practice of Resistance to Everyday Life* (Harmondsworth: Penguin).

—— (1993, 2nd edn) *Escape Attempts: The Theory and Practice of Resistance to Everyday Life* (London: Routledge).

Colls, R. and P. Dodd (eds) (1986) *Englishness: Politics and Culture* (London: Croom Helm).

Corner, J. (ed.) (1986) *Documentary and the Mass Media* (London: Arnold).

Craik, J. (1994) *The Face of Fashion: Cultural Studies in Fashion* (London: Routledge).

—— (1997) 'The Culture of Tourism', in Rojek and Urry, op. cit.

Crane, D. (1992) *The Production of Culture: Media Industries and Urban Arts* (Newbury Park, Calif.: Sage).

Crane, J.L. (1994) *Terror and Everyday Life: Singular Moments in the History of the Horror Film* (London: Sage).

Crook, S. (1998) 'Minotaurs and Other Monsters: "Everyday Life" in Recent Social Theory', *Sociology*, Vol. 32(3), pp. 523–40.

Cross, G. (1993) *Time and Money: The Making of Consumer Culture* (London: Routledge).

Crouch, C. (2000) *Coping with Post-Democracy* (London: Fabian Society).

Csikszentmihalyi, M. and E. Rochberg-Halton (1981) *The Meaning of Things: Domestic Symbols and the Self* (Cambridge: Cambridge University Press).

Cubitt, G. (ed.) (1998) *Imagining Nations* (Manchester: Manchester University Press).

Cullen, J. (1996) *The Art of Democracy: A Concise History of Popular Culture in the United States* (New York: Monthly Review Press).

Cunningham, H. (1980) *Leisure in the Industrial Revolution* (London: Croom Helm).

Curran, J. and J. Seaton (1998, 5th edn) *Power without Responsibility: Press and Broadcasting in Britain* (London: Routledge).

Czyzewski, M. (1994) 'Reflexivity of Actors versus Reflexivity of Accounts', *Theory, Culture and Society*, Vol. 11(4), pp. 161–8.

Dahlgren, P. (1995) *Television and the Public Sphere: Citizenship, Democracy and the Media* (London: Sage).

Dant, T. (1999) *Material Culture in the Social World: Values, Activities, Lifestyles* (Buckingham: Open University Press).

Davidoff, L. and C. Hall (1987) *Family Fortunes: Men and Women of the English Middle Class 1780–1850* (London: Hutchinson).

Davis, F. (1992) *Fashion, Culture and Identity* (London: University of Chicago Press).

De Cauter, L. (1993) 'The Panoramic Ecstasy: On World Exhibitions and the Disintegration of Experience', *Theory Culture and Society*, Vol. 10(4).

De Certeau, M. (1984, trans. S. Rendall) *The Practice of Everyday Life* (Berkeley and Los Angeles: University of California Press).

Debord, G. (1970) *Society of the Spectacle* (Detroit: Black and Red).

——(1981) 'Perspectives for Conscious Alterations in Everyday Life', in K. Knabb (ed.), *Situationist International Anthology* (Berkeley, Calif.: Bureau of Public Secrets).

Delin, J. (2000) *The Language of Everyday Life: An Introduction* (London: Sage).

De Quieroz, J.M. (1989) 'The Sociology of Everyday Life as a Perspective', *Current Sociology*, Vol. 37(1), pp. 31–40.

Donald, J. (1999) *The City of Modern Imagination* (London: Athlone Press).

Douglas, J.D. (1971a) 'Understanding Everyday Life', in J.D. Douglas, op. cit.

——(ed.) (1971b) *Understanding Everyday Life: Toward the Reconstruction of Sociological Knowledge* (London: Routledge and Kegan Paul).

Douglas, M.A. (1966) *Purity and Danger: An Analysis of Concepts of Pollution and Taboo* (London: Routledge and Kegan Paul).

——(ed.) (1973) *Rules and Meanings: The Anthropology of Everyday Knowledge* (Harmondsworth: Penguin).

Downey, J. and J. McGuigan (eds) (1999) *Technocities: The Culture and Political Economy of the Digital Revolution* (London: Sage).

Drew, P. and J. Heritage (eds) (1992) *Talk at Work: Interaction in Institutional Settings* (Cambridge: Cambridge University Press).

Du Gay, P. S. Hall, L. Janes, H. Mackay and K. Negus (1997) *Doing Cultural Studies: The Story of the Sony Walkman* (London: Sage).

Dyer, R. (1987) *Heavenly Bodies: Film Stars and Society* (London: Macmillan – now Palgrave).

Edgley, C. and D. Brissett (1990) 'Health Nazis and the Cult of the Perfect Body', *Symbolic Interaction*, Vol. 13, pp. 257–79.

Edwards, T. (1997) *Men in the Mirror: Men's Fashion, Masculinity and Consumer Society* (London: Cassell).

Eley, G. and R.G. Suny (eds) (1996) *Becoming National* (New York: Oxford University Press).

Elias, N. (1978, trans. E. Jephcott) *The Civilising Process*, Vol. 1: *The History of Manners* (Oxford: Basil Blackwell).

——(1982, trans. E. Jephcott) *The Civilising Process*, Vol. 2: *State Formation and Civilization* (Oxford: Basil Blackwell).

Eyerman, R. (1994) *Between Culture and Politics: Intellectuals in Modern Society* (Cambridge: Polity Press).

Fairclough, N. (1994) 'Conversationalisation of Public Discourse and the Authority of the Consumer', in R. Keat, N. Whiteley and N. Abercrombie (eds), *The Authority of the Consumer* (London: Routledge).

Falk, P. (1994) *The Consuming Body* (London: Sage).

Falk, P. and C. Campbell (eds) (1997) *The Shopping Experience* (London: Sage).

Featherstone, M. (1991) *Consumer Culture and Postmodernism* (London: Sage).

——(1992) 'The Heroic Life and Everyday Life', *Theory, Culture and Society*, Vol. 9, pp. 159–82.

—— (1995) *Undoing Culture: Globalisation, Postmodernism and Identity* (London: Sage).

—— (ed.) (2000) *Body Modification* (London: Sage).

Featherstone, M. and R. Burrows (eds) (1995) *Cyberspace/Cyberbodies/Cyberpunk: Cultures of Technological Embodiment* (London: Sage).

Featherstone, M. and M. Hepworth (1991) 'The Mask of Ageing and the Postmodern Life Course', in M. Featherstone, M. Hepworth and B.S. Turner (eds), *The Body* (London: Sage).

Featherstone, M. and S. Lash (eds) (1999) *Spaces of Culture: City, Nation, World* (London: Sage).

Featherstone, M. and A. Wernick (eds) (1995) *Images of Aging: Cultural Representations of Later Life* (London: Routledge).

Felson, M. (1998) *Crime and Everyday Life* (London: Sage).

Ferguson, R. (1998) *Representing 'Race': Ideology, Identity and the Media* (London: Arnold).

Feuer, L. (ed.) (1969) *Marx and Engels – Basic Writings on Philosophy and Politics.* (Glasgow: Collins Fontana Library).

Finkelstein, J. (1989) *Dining out: A Sociology of Modern Manners* (New York: New York University Press).

—— (1991) *The Fashioned Self* (Philadelphia: Temple University Press).

Finnegan, R. (1997) '"Storying the Self": Personal Narratives and Identity', in Mackay, op. cit.

—— (1998) *Tales of the City: A Study of Narrative and Urban Life* (Cambridge: Cambridge University Press).

Fiske, J. (1989a) *Understanding Popular Culture* (London: Unwin Hyman).

—— (1989b) *Reading Popular Culture* (London: Unwin Hyman).

—— (1996): *Media Matters: Everyday Culture and Political Change* (Minneapolis: University of Minnesota Press).

—— (1998): 'Surveilling the City: Whiteness, the Black Man and Democratic Totalitarianism', *Theory, Culture and Society*, Vol. 15(2), pp. 67–88.

Flichy, P. (1995) *Dynamics of Modern Communication: The Shaping and Impact of New Communication Technologies* (London: Sage).

Forty, A. (1986) *Objects of Desire: Design and Society 1750–1980* (London: Thames and Hudson).

Franklin, B. (1994) *Packaging Politics: Political Communication in British Media* (London: Arnold – Pts 1 and 2).

Frantz, D. and C. Collins (1999) *Celebration USA: Living in Disney's Brave New Town* (New York: Holt).

Frisby, D. (1985) *Fragments of Modernity: Theories of Modernity in the Work of Simmel, Kracauer and Benjamin* (Cambridge: Polity Press).

Frisby, D. and M. Featherstone (eds) (1997) *Simmel on Culture: Selected Writings* (London: Sage).

Frith, S. (1983) 'The Pleasures of the Hearth', in *Formations of Pleasure* (London: Routledge).

Garber, M. (2000) 'Spitting, Sneezing, Smearing', *London Review of Books*, Vol. 22(15), pp. 16–17.

Gardiner, M. (2000) *Critiques of Everyday Life: An Introduction* (London: Routledge).

Garfinkel, H. (1967) *Studies in Ethnomethodology* (Englewood Cliffs NJ: Prentice-Hall).

Gauntlett, D. and A. Hill (1999) *TV Living: Television, Culture and Everyday Life* (London: Routledge).

Geertz, C. (1975) *The Interpretation of Culture: Selected Essays* (London: Hutchinson).

—— (1983) *Local Knowledge: Further Essays in Interpretive Anthropology* (New York: Basic Books).

Giddens, A. (1982) *Sociology: A Brief but Critical Introduction* (London: Macmillan – now Palgrave).

—— (1984) *The Constitution of Society: Outline of a Theory of Structuration* (Cambridge: Polity Press).

—— (1990) *The Consequences of Modernity* (Cambridge: Polity Press).

—— (1991) *Modernity and Identity: Self and Society in the Late Modern Age* (Cambridge: Polity Press).

—— (1992) *The Transformation of Intimacy: Sexuality, Love and Eroticism in Modern Societies* (Cambridge: Polity Press).

—— (1994) *Beyond Left and Right: The Future of Radical Politics* (Cambridge: Polity Press).

Gilloch, G. (1996) *Myth and Metropolis: Walter Benjamin and the City* (Cambridge: Polity Press).

Gilroy, P. (1993) *The Black Atlantic: Modernity and Double Consciousness* (London: Verso).

Giroux, H.A. (1999) *The Mouse that Roared: Disney and the End of Innocence* (New York: Rowman and Littlefield).

Glassner, B. (2000) *The Culture of Fear: Why Americans are Afraid of the Wrong Things* (New York: Basic Books).

Glassner, B. and R. Hertz (eds) (1999) *Qualitative Sociology as Everyday Life* (Thousand Oaks, Calif.: Sage).

Gleeson, J. (1998) *The Arcanum: The Extraordinary True Story of the Invention of European Porcelain* (London: Bantam Press).

Goffman, E. (1959) *The Presentation of Self in Everyday Life* (Harmondsworth: Penguin).

—— (1971) *Relations in Public: Microstudies of the Public Order* (New York: Basic Books).

—— (1974) *Frame Analysis: An Essay on the Organization of Experience* (New York: Harper and Row).

Gold, J. and M. Gold (2000) *Cities of Culture: Tourism, Promotion and Consumption of Spectacle in Western Cities since 1851* (Aldershot: Ashgate).

Goldman, R. and S. Papson (1998) *Nike Culture: The Sign of the Swoosh* (London: Sage).

Gottdiener, M. (1997) *The Theming of America: Dreams, Visions and Commercial Spaces* (Boulder, Colo.: Westview Press).

Gray, C. (1974): *Leaving the Twentieth Century: The Incomplete Work of the Situationist International* (Croydon, Surrey: Free Fall Publications).

Green, N. (1990) *The Spectacle of Nature; Landscape and Bourgeois Culture in Nineteenth-century France* (Manchester: Manchester University Press).

Greenhalgh, S. (1999) 'Our Lady of Flowers: The Ambiguous Politics of Diana's Floral Revolution', in Kear and Steinberg, op. cit.

Gronow, J. (1997) *The Sociology of Taste* (London, Routledge).

Gusfield, J.R. (1992) 'Nature's Body and the Metaphors of Food', in Lamont and Fournier, op. cit.

Habermas, J. (1989) *The Structural Transformation of the Public Sphere: An Inquiry into a Category of Bourgeois Society* (Cambridge: Polity Press).

Hall, S. (1992) 'The Question of Cultural Identity', in S. Hall, D. Held and T. McGrew (eds), *Modernity and Its Futures* (Cambridge: Polity Press).

—— (1997) 'The Work of Representation', in S. Hall (ed.), *Representation: Cultural Representations and Signifying Practices* (London: Sage).

Hall, S. and P. du Gay (eds) (1996) *Questions of Cultural Identity* (London: Sage).

Hall, S. and T. Jefferson (eds) (1976) *Resistance through Rituals: Youth Subcultures in Post-war Britain* (London: Hutchinson).

Handler, R. (1988) *Nationalism and the Politics of Culture in Quebec* (Madison: University of Wisconsin Press).

Hargreaves, J. (1994) *Sporting Females: Critical Issues in the History and Sociology of Women's Sports* (London: Routledge).

Hartley, J. (1999) *Uses of Television* (London: Routledge).

Haskell, F. (1993) *History and its Images: Art and the Interpretation of the Past* (London: Yale University Press).

Hassard, J. (1998) 'Representing Reality: *Cinéma Verité*', in Hassard and Holliday, op. cit.

Hassard, J. and R. Holliday (eds) (1998) *Organization–Representation: Work and Organizations in Popular Culture* (London: Sage).

Haug, W.F. (1986, trans. R. Bock) *Critique of Commodity Aesthetics: Appearance, Sexuality and Advertising in Capitalist Society* (Cambridge: Polity Press).

Hearn, J. and S. Roseneil (eds) (1999) *Consuming Cultures: Power and Resistance* (Basingstoke: Macmillan – now Palgrave).

Hebdige, R. (1979) *Subculture: The Meaning of Style* (London: Methuen).

——(1992) 'Digging for Britain: An Excavation in Seven Parts', in D. Strinati and S. Wagg (eds), *Come On Down: Popular Media Culture in Post-war Britain* (London: Routledge).

Heelas, P., S. Lash and P. Morris (eds) (1996) *Detraditionalization: Critical Reflections on Authority and Identity* (Oxford: Blackwell).

Heller, A. (1984, trans G.L. Campbell) *Everyday Life* (London: Routledge and Kegan Paul).

Hepworth, M. (2000) *Stories of Ageing* (Buckingham: Open University Press).

Herbert, R.L. (1994) *Monet on the Normandy Coast: Tourism and Painting 1867–1886* (New Haven: Yale University Press).

Hertz, R. (ed.) (1997) *Reflexivity and Voice* (Thousand Oaks, Calif.: Sage).

Hesse-Biber, S. (1996) *Am I Thin Enough Yet? The Cult of Thin-ness and the Commercialization of Identity* (New York: Oxford University Press).

Hetherington, K. (1998) *Expressions of Identity: Space, Performance, Politics* (London: Sage).

Hewison, R. (1987) *The Heritage Industry: Britain in a Climate of Decline* (London: Methuen).

Hobsbawm, E. (1990) *Nations and Nationalism since 1780: Programme, Myth, Reality* (Cambridge: Cambridge University Press).

Hobsbawm, E. and T. Ranger (eds) (1983) *The Invention of Tradition* (Oxford: Blackwell).

Hochschild, A.R. (1998) 'The Sociology of Emotions as a Way of Seeing', in Bendelow and Williams, op. cit.

Hodder, I. (ed.) (1991) *The Meanings of Things: Material Culture and Symbolic Expression* (London: Routledge).

Hofstede, G. (2000, 2nd edn) *Culture's Consequences: Comparing Values, Behaviors, Institutions and Organizations across Nations* (London: Sage).

Holliday, R. (1998) '*Philadelphia*: AIDS, Organization, Representation', in Hassard and Holliday, op. cit.

Hollier, D. (ed., trans., Betsy Wing) (1988) *The College of Sociology (1937–39)* (Minneapolis: University of Minnesota Press).

Horne, D. (1984) *The Great Museum* (London: Pluto Press).

——(1986) *The Public Culture: The Triumph of Industrialism* (London: Pluto Press).

Hoskins, J. (1998) *Biographical Objects: How Things Tell the Stories of Peoples' Lives* (London: Routledge).

Huyssen, A. (1986) *After the Great Divide: Modernism, Mass Culture and Postmodernism* (Basingstoke: Macmillan – now Palgrave).

Huyssen, A. (1995) *Twilight Memories: Marking Time in a Culture of Amnesia* (London: Routledge).

Inglis, F. (1995) *Raymond Williams* (London: Routledge).

Jackson, P. (1989) *Maps of Meaning: An Introduction to Cultural Geography* (London: Unwin Hyman).

Jardine, L. (1996) *Worldly Goods: A New History of the Renaissance* (London: Macmillan – now Palgrave).

Jencks, C. (1984) *The Language of Post-Modern Architecture* (London: Academy Editions).

Jenkins, B. and S.A. Sofos (eds) (1996) *Nation and Identity in Contemporary Europe* (London: Routledge).

Jenks, C. (1993) *Culture* (London: Routledge).

Jennings, H. (ed.) (1937) *May 12th: Mass-Observation Day Survey*, (London: Faber & Faber).

Jervis, J. (1998) *Exploring the Modern: Patterns of Western Culture and Civilization* (Oxford: Blackwell).

——(1999) *Transgressing the Modern: Explorations in Otherness* (Oxford: Blackwell).

Johnson, R. (1999) 'Exemplary Differences: Mourning (and not Mourning) a Princess', in Kear and Steinberg, op. cit.

Kaledin, E. (2000) *Daily Life in the United States, 1940–1959* (New York: Greenwood Press).

Kaplan, F. (ed.) (1994) *Museums and the Making of 'Ourselves': The Role of Objects in National Identity* (London: Pinter).

Karp, I., C.M. Kreamer and S.D. Lavine (eds) (1992) *Museums and Communities: The Politics of Public Culture* (Washington: Smithsonian Institution Press).

Kear, A. and D.L. Steinberg (eds) (1999) *Mourning Diana: Nation, Culture and the Performance of Grief* (London, Routledge).

Kellner, D. (1995) *Media Culture: Cultural Studies, Identity and Politics between the Modern and Postmodern* (London: Routledge).

Kershon, A.J. (ed.) (1998) *A Question of Identity* (London: Sage).

King, G. (2000) *Spectacular Narratives: Hollywood in the Age of the Blockbuster* (Oxford: I.B. Tauris).

Klein, N. (2000) *No Logo* (London: Flamingo).

Kornhauser, W. (1960) *The Politics of Mass Society* (London: Routledge and Kegan Paul).

Kulka, T. (1996) *Kitsch and Art* (Penn: Pennsylvania State University Press).

Lamont, M. and M. Fournier (eds) (1992) *Cultivating Differences: Symbolic Boundaries and the Making of Inequality* (Chicago: Chicago University Press).

Lash, S. and J. Urry (1994) *Economies of Signs and Spaces* (London: Sage).

Lefebvre, H. (1971, trans. S. Rabinovitch) *Everyday Life in the Modern World* (New York: Harper Torchbooks).

Lewis, L.A. (ed.) (1992) *The Adoring Audience: Fan Culture and Popular Media* (London: Routledge).

Livingston, E. (1987) *Making Sense of Ethnomethodology* (London: Routledge and Kegan Paul).

Löfgren, O. (1989) 'The Nationalization of Culture', *Ethnologia Europea*, Vol. 19(1).

Lowenthal, L. (1961) *Literature, Popular Culture and Society* (New Jersey: Prentice-Hall).

Luckmann, T. (1989) 'On Meaning in Everyday Life and Sociology', *Current Sociology*, Vol. 37(1), pp. 17–30.

Lull, J. (1990) *Inside Family Viewing: Ethnographic Work on Television Audiences* (London: Routledge).
—— (2000, 2nd edn) *Media Communication and Culture* (Cambridge: Polity Press).
Lull, J. and S. Hinerman (1997a) 'The Search for Scandal', in Lull and Hinerman, op. cit.
—— (eds) (1997b) *Media Scandals: Morality and Desire in the Popular Culture Marketplace* (Cambridge: Polity Press).
Lumley, R. (ed.) (1988) *Putting Cultures on Display* (London: Routledge).
Lunt, P.K. and S. M. Livingstone (1992) *Mass Consumption and Personal Identity: Everyday Economic Experience* (Buckingham: Open University Press).
Lury, C. (1996) *Consumer Culture* (London: Routledge).
Lynch, M. (2000) 'Against Reflexivity as an Academic Virtue and Source of Privileged Knowledge', *Theory, Culture and Society*, Vol. 17(3), pp. 26–54.
Lyon, D. (2001) *Surveillance Society: Monitoring Everyday Life* (Buckingham: Open University Press).
MacCannell, D. (1976) *The Tourist: A New Theory of the Leisure Class* (London: Macmillan – now Palgrave).
—— (1992) *Existing Meeting Grounds: The Tourist Papers* (London: Routledge).
Macdonald, S. (ed.) (1993) *Inside European Identities: Ethnography in Western Europe* (Oxford: Berg).
Mackay, H. (ed.) (1997) *Consumption and Everyday Life* (London: Sage).
Madge, C. and T. Harrisson (1939) *Britain by Mass Observation* (Harmondsworth: Penguin).
Maffesoli, M. (1989) 'The Sociology of Everyday Life (Epistemological elements)', *Current Sociology*, Vol. 37(1), pp. 1–16.
—— (trans. D. Smith) (1996) *The Time of the Tribes: The Decline of Individualism in Mass Society* (London: Sage).
Manning, P. (1992) *Erving Goffman and Modern Sociology* (Cambridge: Polity Press).
Marcuse, H. (1969) *An Essay on Liberation* (London: Allen Lane).
Marin, L. (1977) 'Disneyland: A Degenerate Utopia', *Glyph*, 1.
Martin, B. (1981) *A Sociology of Contemporary Cultural Change* (Oxford: Basil Blackwell).
Mellor, P.A. and C. Shilling (1997) *Re-forming the Body: Religion, Community and Modernity* (London: Sage).
Melly, G. (1972) *Revolt into Style: The Pop Arts in Britain* (Harmondsworth: Penguin).
Mennell, S. (1985) *All Manners of Food: Eating and Taste in England and France from the Middle Ages to the Present* (Oxford: Basil Blackwell).
Messaris, P. (1997) *Visual Persuasion: The Role of Images in Advertising* (London: Sage).
Miller, D. (1991) *Material Culture and Mass Consumption* (Oxford: Basil Blackwell).
—— (1998) *A Theory of Shopping* (Cambridge: Polity Press).
Miller, T. and A. McHoul (1998) *Popular Culture and Everyday Life* (London: Sage).
Mirzoeff, N. (1999) *An Introduction to Visual Culture* (London: Routledge).
Modood, T. and P. Werbner (eds) (1997) *The Politics of Multiculturalism in the New Europe: Racism, Identity and Community* (London: Zed Books).
Moerman, M. (1988) *Talking Culture: Ethnography and Conversation Analysis* (Philadelphia: University of Pennsylvania Press).
Monaco, J. (1978) 'Celebration', in J. Monaco (ed.), *Celebrity: The Media as Image-makers* (New York: Dell).
Moores, S. (1997) 'Broadcasting and its Audiences', in Mackay, op. cit.

—— (2000) *Media and Everyday Life in Modern Society* (Edinburgh: Edinburgh University Press).

Morley, D. (1986) *Family Television: Cultural Power and Domestic Television* (London: Comedia).

—— (1992) *Television, Audiences and Cultural Studies* (London: Routledge).

—— (1995) 'TV: Not so much a Visual Medium more a Visible Object', in C. Jenks (ed.), *Visual Culture* (London: Routledge).

—— (2000) *Home Territories: Media, Mobility and Identity* (London: Routledge).

Morley, D. and K. Robins (1995) *Spaces of Identity: Global Media, Electronic Landscapes and Cultural Boundaries* (London: Routledge).

Moyal, A. (1989) 'The Feminine Culture of the Telephone: People, Patterns and Policy', *Prometheus*, Vol. 7(1), pp. 5–31.

Munt, I. (1994) 'The "Other" Postmodern Tourism: Culture, Travel and the New Middle Classes', *Theory, Culture and Society*, Vol. 11(3), pp. 101–24.

Murdock, G. (1993) *The Battle for Television: Private Pleasures and Public Goods* (London: Macmillan – now Palgrave).

Murdock, G. and P. Golding (1989) 'Information Poverty and Political Inequality: Citizenship in the Age of Privatised Communications', *Journal of Communication*, Vol. 39(3), pp. 180–95.

Museum of Contemporary Art (2000) *Nordic Postmodernism* (Helsinki: Finnish National Gallery).

Myers, J. (1992) 'Nonmainstream Body Modification: Genital Piercing, Branding, Burning and Cutting', *Journal of Contemporary Ethnography*, Vol. 21(3), pp. 267–306.

Nava, M. and A. O'Shea (eds) (1996) *Modern Times: Reflections on a Century of English Modernity* (London: Routledge).

Nedelmann, B. (1990) 'Georg Simmel as an Analyst of Autonomous Dynamics: The Merry-go-round of Fashion', in M. Kaern, B.S. Phillips and R.S. Cohen (eds), *Georg Simmel and Contemporary Sociology* (Dordrecht: Kluwer), pp. 243–58.

Negrin, L. (1999) 'The Self as Image: A Critical Appraisal of Postmodern Theories of Fashion', *Theory, Culture and Society*, Vol. 16(3), pp. 99–118.

Negus, K. (1992) *Producing Pop* (London: Arnold).

Nettleton, S. and J. Watson (eds) (1998) *The Body and Everyday Life* (London: Routledge).

Nichols, B. (1991) *Representing Reality: Issues and Concepts in Documentary* (Bloomington: Indiana University Press).

Nochlin, L. (1971) *Realism* (Harmondsworth: Penguin).

Normand, T. (2000) *The Modern Scot: Modernism and Nationalism in Scottish Art 1928–1955* (London: Ashgate).

O'Connor, F. V. (ed.) (1973) *Art for the Millions: Essays from the 1930s by Artists and Administrators of the WPA Federal Art Project* (Boston: New York Graphic Society).

O'Neill, M. (1998) 'Saloon Girls: Death and Desire in the American West', in Hassard and Holliday, op. cit.

Owusu, K. (ed.) (1999) *Black British Culture and Society: A Text-reader* (London: Routledge).

Painter, C. (1986) 'The Uses of Art', Ph.D. thesis submitted under the Council for National Academic Awards regulations at Newcastle Polytechnic.

—— (1996) *At Home with Constable's Cornfield* (London: National Gallery Publications).

—— (1998) *The Uses of an Artist: Constable in Constable Country Now* (Ipswich: Ipswich Borough Council Museums and Galleries).

Palmer, C. (1998) 'From Theory to Practice: Experiencing the Nation in everyday Life', *Journal of Material Culture*, Vol. 3(2), pp. 175–99.

Parr, M. and N. Barker (1992) *Signs of the Times: A Portrait of the Nation's Tastes* (Manchester: Cornerhouse Publications).

Pickering, M. (2001) *Stereotyping: The Politics of Representation* (Basingstoke: Palgrave).

Pickering, M. and D. Chaney (1986) 'Democracy and Communication: Mass Observation', *Journal of Communication*, Vol. 36(1).

Plant, S. (1992) *Most Radical Gesture: The Situationist International in a Postmodern Age* (London: Routledge).

Potter, J. (1996) *Representing Reality: Discourse, Rhetoric and Social Construction* (London: Sage).

Prost, A. and G. Vincent (1994) *A History of Private Life: Vol. 5 Riddles of Identity in Modern Times* (Boston, Mass.: Belknap Press).

Psathas, G. (ed.) (1979) *Everyday Language: Studies in Ethnomethodology* (New York: Wiley).

Pugh, S. (ed.) (1990) *Reading Landscape: Country–City–Capital* (Manchester: Manchester University Press).

Rakow, L. (1992) *Gender on the Line: Women, the Telephone and Community Life* (Urbana: University of Illinois Press).

Raven, C. (2001) 'Love across the Divide', *The Guardian*, G2, 23/1/01.

Read, A. (1997) *Theatre and Everyday Life: An Ethics of Performance* (London: Routledge).

Richards, J., S. Wilson and L. Woodhead (eds) (1999) *Diana: The Making of Media Saint* (London: Taurus).

Ritzer, G. (1993) *The McDonaldization Thesis: An Investigation into the Changing Character of Contemporary Social Life* (London, Sage).

—— (1998) *The MacDonaldization Thesis: Explorations and Extensions* (London: Sage).

—— (1999) *Enchanting a Disenchanted World: Revolutionizing the Means of Consumption* (Thousand Oaks, Calif.: Pine Forge Press).

Roberts, J. (1998) *The Art of Interruption: Realism, Photography and the Everyday* (Manchester: Manchester University Press).

Robins, K. (1996) *Into the Image: Culture and Politics in the Field of Vision* (London: Routledge).

Roche, D. (2000) *A History of Everyday Things: The Birth of Consumption in France 1600–1800* (Cambridge: Cambridge University Press).

Roche, M. (2001) 'Citizenship, Popular Culture and Europe', in Stevenson (ed.), op. cit.

Rojek, C. (1993) *Ways of Leisure: Modern Transformations in Leisure and Travel* (Basingstoke: Macmillan – now Palgrave).

Rojek, C. and J. Urry (1997) 'Transformations of Travel and Theory in C. Rojek and J. Urry (eds), *Touring Cultures: Transformations of Travel and Theory* (London: Routledge).

Rosen, C. and H. Zerner (1984) *Romanticism and Realism: The Mythology of Nineteenth Century Art* (London: Faber and Faber).

Rosenberg, B. and D. White (1957) *Mass Culture: The Popular Arts in America* (New York: Free Press of Glencoe).

—— (1971) *Mass Culture Revisited* (New York: Van Nostrand).

Rosenthal, A. (1988) *New Challenges for Documentary* (Berkeley: University of California Press).

Ross, A. (1989) *No Respect: Intellectuals and Popular Culture* (London: Routledge).

—— (2000) *The Celebration Chronicles: Life, Liberty and the Pursuit of Property Values in Disney's New Town* (London: Verso).

Rudner, H. (1999) 'Roaming the City: Proper Women in Improper Places', in Featherstone and Lash, op. cit.

Salmon, S. (2000) 'Imagineering the Inner city? Landscapes of Pleasure and the Commodification of Cultural Spectacle in the Postmodern City', in C.L. Harrington and D.D. Bielby (eds), *Popular Culture: Production and Consumption* (Oxford: Blackwell).

Samuel, R. (ed.) (1989) *Patriotism: The Making and Unmaking of British National Identity*, Vol. 3: *National Fictions* (London: Routledge).

—— (1994) *Theatres of Memory*, Vol. 1: *Past and Present in Contemporary Culture* (London: Verso).

Sandywell, B. (1996) *Logological Investigations*, Vol. 1, *Phenomenology of Reflexivity* (London: Routledge).

Scannell, P. (1989) 'Public Service Broadcasting and Modern Public Life', *Media Culture and Society*, Vol. 11(2), pp. 135–66.

—— (1996) *Radio, Television and Modern Life: A Phenomenological Approach* (Cambridge: Polity Press).

Schickel, R. (1968) *Walt Disney* (London: Weidenfeld and Nicolson).

Schieffelin, B.B. (1993) *The Give and Take of Everyday Life: Language Socialization of Kaluli Children* (Cambridge: Cambridge University Press).

Schiller, H.I. ((1996) *Information Inequality: The Deepening Social Crisis in America* (New York: Routledge).

Schlosser, E. (2001) *Fast-Food Nation* (London: Allen Lane).

Scott, S. and D. Morgan (eds) (1993) *Body Matters: Essays on the Sociology of the Body* (London: Falmer Press).

Semin, G.R. and K.J. Gergen (eds) (1990) *Everyday Understandings: Social and Scientific Implications* (London: Sage).

Sennett, R. (1976) *The Fall of Public Man* (New York: Knopf).

Shields, R. (1991) *Places on the Margin: Alternative Geographies of Modernity* (London: Routledge).

—— (1998) *Lefebvre, Love and Struggle: Spatial Dialectics* (London: Routledge).

Shilling, C. (1993) *The Body and Social Theory* (London: Sage).

Shotter, J. (1993) *Cultural Politics of Everyday Life: Social Constructionism, Rhetoric and Knowing of the Third Kind* (Buckingham: Open University Press).

Silverstone, R. (1994) *Television and Everyday Life* (London: Routledge).

—— (ed.) (1997) *Visions of Suburbia* (London: Routledge).

Silverstone, R. and E. Hirsch (eds) (1992) *Consuming Technologies: Media and Information in Domestic Spaces* (London: Routledge).

Simmel, G. (1950, trans. and ed. K. Wolff) *The Sociology of Georg Simmel* (New York: Free Press).

—— (1971, trans. and ed. D.N. Levine) *On Individuality and Social Forms: Selected Writings* (Chicago: University of Chicago Press).

Slater, D. (1997) *Consumer Culture and Modernity* (Cambridge: Polity Press).

Smith, A.D. (1998) *Nationalism and Modernism* (London: Routledge).

Smith, D.E. (1987) *The Everyday World as Problematic: A Feminist Sociology* (Milton Keynes: Open University Press).

—— (1988) 'Feminity as Discourse', in L. Roman and L. Christian-Smith (eds), *Becoming Feminine: The Politics of Popular Culture* (Philadelphia: Falmer).

Smith, D.H. (1993) *Painting for Money: The Visual Arts and the Public Sphere in Eighteenth Century England* (London: Yale University Press).

Social Trends (2000) *Social Trends 30* (London: Office for National Statistics, HMSO).

Sontag, S. (1978) *On Photography* (London: Allen Lane).

Sparks, R. (1992) *Television and the Drama of Crime: Moral Tales and the Place of Crime in Public Life* (Milton Keynes: Open University Press).

Spicer, A. (2001) *Typical Men: The Representation of Masculinity in Popular British Cinema* (Oxford: I.B. Tauris).

Spurlin, W.J. (1999) 'I'd Rather Be the Princess than the Queen! Mourning Diana as a Gay Icon', in Kear and Steinberg, op. cit.

Spurling, H. (1998) *The Unknown Matisse: A Life of Henri Matisse*, Vol. 1: *1869–1908* (London: Hamish Hamilton).

Stallybrass, P. and A. White (1986) *The Politics and Poetics of Transgression* (London: Methuen).

Stange, M. (1989) *Symbols of Ideal Life: Social Documentary Photography in America 1890–1950* (Cambridge: Cambridge University Press).

Stern, B.B. (ed.) (1998) *Representing Consumers: Voices, Views and Visions* (London: Routledge).

Stevenson, N. (1999) *The Transformation of the Media: Globalisation, Morality and Ethics* (London: Longman).

Stevenson, N. (ed.) (2001) *Culture and Citizenship* (London: Sage).

Storey, J. (1999) *Cultural Consumption and Everyday Life* (London: Arnold).

Stott, W. (1973) *Real Things Only: Documentary and Thirties America* (New York: Oxford University Press).

Strinati, D. (1995) *An Introduction to Theories of Popular Culture* (London: Routledge).

Sudnow, D. (ed.) (1972) *Studies in Social Interaction* (New York: Free Press).

Sussex, E. (1975) *The Rise and Fall of British Documentary* (Berkeley: University of California Press).

Swann, P. (1989) *The British Documentary Film Movement 1926–46* (Cambridge: Cambridge University Press).

Swidler, A. (1986) 'Culture in Action: Symbols and Strategies', *American Sociological Review*, Vol. 51, pp. 273–86.

Swingewood, A. (1998) *Cultural Theory and the Problem of Modernity* (London: Macmillan – now Palgrave).

Swingle, P.G. (ed.) (1973) *Social Psychology in Everyday Life* (Harmondsworth: Penguin).

Tagg, J. (1988) *The Burden of Representation: Essays on Photographies and Histories* (Basingstoke: Macmillan – now Palgrave).

Terkel, S. (1970) *Hard Times: An Oral History of the Great Depression* (London: Allen Lane).

Tester, K. (1994) *The Flâneur* (London: Routledge).

Thompson, E.P. (1971) 'The Moral Economy of the English Crowd in the Eighteenth Century', *Past and Present*, 50.

Thompson, J.B. (1990) *Ideology and Modern Culture: Critical Social Theory in the Era of Mass Communication* (Cambridge: Polity), Chs 2 and 5.

—— (1995) *The Media and Modernity: A Social Theory of the Media* (Cambridge: Polity Press).

—— (1997) 'Scandal and Social Theory', in Lull and Hinerman, op. cit.

—— (2000) *Political Scandal: Power and Visibility in the Media Age* (Cambridge: Polity Press).

Thompson, K. (1998) *Moral Panics* (London: Routledge).

Thornton, S. (1994) 'Moral Panic, the Media and British Rave Culture', in A. Ross and T. Rose (eds), *Microphone Fiends: Youth Music and Youth Culture* (London: Routledge).

—— (1995) *Club Cultures: Music, Media and Subcultural Capital* (Cambridge: Polity Press).

Tracey, M. (1998) *The Decline and Fall of Public Service Broadcasting* (Oxford: Oxford University Press).

Truzzi, M. (ed.) (1968) *Sociology and Everyday Life* (Englewood Cliffs NJ: Prentice-Hall).

Tudor, A. (1999) *Decoding Culture: Theory and Method in Cultural Studies* (London: Sage).

Tulloch, J. (1999) *Performing Culture: Stories of Expertise and the Everyday* (London: Sage).

Turner, B.S. (1984) *The Body and Society: Explorations in Social Theory* (Oxford: Basil Blackwell).

—— (1993) 'Contemporary Problems in the Theory of Citizenship', in B.S. Turner (ed.), *Citizenship and Social Theory* (London: Sage).

—— (2001) 'Outline of a General Theory of Citizenship', in Stevenson (ed.), op. cit.

Turner, R. (ed.) (1974) *Ethnomethodology* (Harmondsworth: Penguin).

Turner, V.W. (1969) *The Ritual Process: Structure and Anti-structure* (Harmondsworth: Penguin).

Tzara, T. (1989) 'Lecture on Dada (1922)', in R. Motherwell (ed.), *The Dada Painters and Poets: An Anthology* (Cambridge, Mass.: Belknap Press).

Urry, J. (1990) *The Tourist Gaze: Leisure and Travel in Contemporary Societies* (London: Sage).

—— (1995) *Consuming Places* (London: Routledge).

Van Dijk, J. (1999) *The Network Society* (London: Sage).

Vaneigem, R. (1979) *The Revolution of Everyday Life* (London: Rising Free Collective).

Veblen, T. (1924) *The Theory of the Leisure Class* (New York: Viking).

Vernon, J. (1998) 'Border Crossings: Cornwall and the English (Imagi)nation', in Cubitt, op. cit.

Visser, M. (1997) *The Way We Are: The Astonishing Anthropology of Everyday Life* (New York: Kodansha Globe).

Walsh, K. (1992) *The Representation of the Past: Museums and Heritage in the Post-modern World* (London: Routledge).

Warde, A. (1997) *Consumption, Food and Taste: Culinary Antinomies and Commodity Culture* (London: Sage).

Warde, A. and L. Martens (2000) *Eating Out: Social Differentiation, Consumption and Pleasure* (Cambridge: Cambridge University Press).

Weeks, J. (1998) 'The Sexual Citizen', *Theory, Culture and Society*, Vol. 15(3–4), pp. 35–52.

Weigert, A.J. (1981) *Sociology of Everyday Life* (New York: Longman).

Weitman, S. (1998) On the Elementary Forms of the Socioerotic Life, *Theory, Culture and Society*, Vol. 15(3–4), pp. 71–110.

Wells, L. (ed.) (1997) *Photography: A Critical Introduction* (London: Routledge).

Wessels, B. (2000) 'Telematics in the East End of London: New Media as a Cultural Form, *New Media and Society*, Vol. 2(4), pp. 427–44.

Wheatcroft, G. (2001) 'Who's in Charge?' *The Guardian* (media section) (10/3/01, p. 10).

Whiting, C. (1998) *A Taste for Pop: Pop Art, Gender and Consumer Culture* (Cambridge: Cambridge University Press).

Williams, R. (1958) *Culture and Society 1780–1950* (Harmondsworth: Penguin Books).

—— (1961) *The Long Revolution* (London: Chatto and Windus).

—— (1973) *The Country and the City* (London: Chatto and Windus).

—— (1976) *Keywords: A Vocabulary of Culture and Society* (London: Croom Helm).

—— (1981) *Culture* (London: Fontana).

Willener, A. (1970 *The Action-Image of Society: On Cultural Politicization* (Andover, Hants: Tavistock).

Willis, P. (1990) *Common Culture: Symbolic Work at Play in the Everyday Cultures of the Young* (Buckingham: Open University Press).

Willis, S. (1991) *A Primer for Daily Life* (London: Routledge).

Wilson, D.S. and C.M. Laennec (1997) 'Introduction', in D.S. Wilson and D.M. Laennec (eds), *Bodily Discursions: Genders, Representations, Technologies* (Albany: State University of New York Press).

Wilson, E. (1985) *Adorned in Dreams: Fashion and Modernity* (London: Virago Press).

—— (2000) *The Contradictions of Culture: Cities, Culture, Women* (London: Sage).

Winch, P. (1958) *The Idea of a Social Science and its Relation to Philosophy* (London: Routledge and Kegan Paul).

Winston, B. (1995) *Claiming the Real: The Griersonian Documentary and its Legitimations* (London: British Film Institute).

—— (1998) *Media, Technology and Society: A History from the Telegraph to the Internet* (London: Routledge).

Wolf, N. (1991) *The Beauty Myth* (London: Anchor Books).

Wolff, J. (2000) 'The Feminine in Modern Art: Benjamin, Simmel and the Gender of Modernity', *Theory, Culture and Society*, Vol. 17(4), pp. 33–53.

Wouters, C. (1986) 'Formalization and Informalization: Changing Tension Balances in Civilising Processes', *Theory, Culture and Society*, Vol. 3(2), pp. 1–18.

—— (1990) 'Social Stratification and Informalization in Global Perspective', *Theory, Culture and Society*, Vol. 7(4), pp. 69–90.

—— (1998) 'Balancing Sex and Love since the 1960s Sexual Revolution', *Theory, Culture and Society*, Vol. 15(3–4), pp. 187–214.

Wuthnow, R. (1988) *Meaning and Moral Order: Explorations in Cultural Analysis* (Berkeley and Los Angeles: University of California Press).

Young, J. (1999) *The Exclusive Society: Social Exclusion, Crime and Difference in Late Modernity* (London: Sage).

Zollberg, V. (1990) *Constructing a Sociology of the Arts* (Cambridge: Cambridge University Press).

Author Index

Subject Index